Improving Educational Gender Equality in Religious Societies

Sumaia A. Al-Kohlani

Improving Educational Gender Equality in Religious Societies

Human Rights and Modernization Pre-Arab Spring

Sumaia A. Al-Kohlani
United Arab Emirates University (UAEU)
Al Ain, United Arab Emirates

ISBN 978-3-030-09966-4   ISBN 978-3-319-70536-1 (eBook)
https://doi.org/10.1007/978-3-319-70536-1

© The Editor(s) (if applicable) and The Author(s) 2018
Softcover re-print of the Hardcover 1st edition 2018
This work is subject to copyright. All rights are solely and exclusively licensed by the Publisher, whether the whole or part of the material is concerned, specifically the rights of translation, reprinting, reuse of illustrations, recitation, broadcasting, reproduction on microfilms or in any other physical way, and transmission or information storage and retrieval, electronic adaptation, computer software, or by similar or dissimilar methodology now known or hereafter developed.
The use of general descriptive names, registered names, trademarks, service marks, etc. in this publication does not imply, even in the absence of a specific statement, that such names are exempt from the relevant protective laws and regulations and therefore free for general use.
The publisher, the authors and the editors are safe to assume that the advice and information in this book are believed to be true and accurate at the date of publication. Neither the publisher nor the authors or the editors give a warranty, express or implied, with respect to the material contained herein or for any errors or omissions that may have been made. The publisher remains neutral with regard to jurisdictional claims in published maps and institutional affiliations.

Cover illustration: © anthony asael / Alamy Stock Photo

Printed on acid-free paper

This Palgrave Macmillan imprint is published by Springer Nature
The registered company is Springer International Publishing AG
The registered company address is: Gewerbestrasse 11, 6330 Cham, Switzerland

I dedicate this book to all Yemeni women, girls, and children, who bear most of the consequences of political instability. I also dedicate it to Yemeni teachers, who did not give up their duties even though they have not received their salary for months.

Preface

The idea for this book came to me in 2010, when Turkey was considered a good example of a successful secular Muslim country. This positive perception about Turkey made me wonder if females' rights there are far better than in Iran and Saudi Arabia when it comes to the basic right to education and joining the labor force. When females' rights in Iran are compared to females' rights in Turkey, the dress code stands out as the most obvious difference. However, I tried to avoid the argument over the dress code for women and girls, because forcing them to wear a hijab, as is the case in Iran, or to remove it, as was the case in Turkey before 2010, are, in my opinion, against females' right to choose. What made this topic more interesting was the Arab Spring in 2011 and the demand for substantial change in the political system in several countries.

The demand for a different political system comes from the failure of several previous regimes to meet the economic and political demands of the new generation. Some of those political movements demanded more a religious political system, claiming that Islam is the solution, while others were looking for a more liberal political system, arguing that the success of Turkey was just an extension of its success in implementing a secular political system. However, even today, several Muslim countries are still embroiled in debates over whether a more religious or less religious political system is better for the new, young governments that are struggling to rise. Muslim countries that managed to avoid the Arab Spring, such as Saudi Arabia, Iran, and Thailand, are also debating whether they should liberalize their constitutions, laws, and regulations to avoid future political chaos. Therefore, a key element in deciding which would be the more beneficial—a more religious or a less religious political system—is the effect on gender equality, both for human rights and for economic development reasons.

This book intends to respond to the "religious theory" that associates certain religions with gender inequality, and to the "modernization theory" that downplays the role of religion in gender inequity and associates gender inequality with socioeconomic factors. This book tests both theories and determines which is more applicable, and how the results could help policy-makers. It aims to answer several questions with regard to this subject. For example, would the choice of a more religiously liberal constitution mean better gender equality in education? Also, would the dominance of a religiously conservative constitution result in weak gender equality in education? Does modernization change the impact of a religiously conservative constitution on gender equality in education?

This book contributes to the ongoing debate over what impact Islam has on gender equality in education. It studies the impact of religious constitutions and several modernization factors, such as urbanization, fertility, oil, and income, on educational gender equality in 55 Muslim and non-Muslim countries.

The book is an interdisciplinary study drawn from the fields of world politics, public policy in education, and political religion. Combining these disciplines also involves considerable engagement with the quantitative and qualitative methods of comparative politics, religion, and education. As such, this work exists in a unique space in the broader political, religious, and educational literatures.

As I write, my hope is that this book will be useful complementary reading for courses that discuss religion, politics, and education; Islam and education; the impact of secularism and religious conservativism on educational gender equality; and differences in educational gender equality between Muslim and non-Muslim countries. Also, due to the Arab Spring and other events that raise the profile and importance of this topic, the book could be of interest to the general public as well.

Al Ain, United Arab Emirates   Sumaia A. Al-Kohlani

Acknowledgments

I would like to express my gratitude to all those who supported me during the time I was writing this book. In particular, I would like to thank my family and husband for taking a special interest in following my progress and providing all the support and comfort I needed to finish the book.

Thanks to Professor Heather Campbell for her advice and encouragement, and for all the support I have received from her since the day we met. Also, I am thankful to Dr. Emily Saunders for her interest in the book and her valuable suggestions. I am also thankful to the publisher and editorial assistant, who were supportive, patient, and helpful. I ask for forgiveness from my husband, from whom I was taken away during this experience, and from those whose names I have failed to mention.

Contents

1	**Introduction**	1
	Gender Equality Before the Arab Spring	8
	Historical Background	10
	Western Feminist Theories	12
	Religious Feminist Theories	16
	Education and Gender Equality	30
	Female Education and Economy	32
	Conclusion	34
	Outline of the Book	35
	References	38
2	**Religious Theory vs. Modernization Theory**	43
	Religious Theory	43
	Modernization Theory	54
	Conclusion	60
	References	63
3	**Research Design and Methodology**	67
	Research Questions	71
	First Hypotheses	71
	Alternative Hypotheses	72
	Data	73
	Dependent Variable	73

	Key Independent Variables	75
	Control Variables	80
	Interaction Variables	82
	The Statistical Models	83
	Expectations	84
	Method	85
	Conclusion	86
	References	87
4	**Empirical Testing and Analysis of Data**	89
	Empirical Testing and Analysis for Muslim and Non-Muslim Countries	90
	Empirical Testing and Analysis for Muslim Countries	103
	Empirical Testing and Analysis for Non-Muslim Countries	111
	Analysis of the Results	114
	Conclusion	119
	References	122
5	**Case Study**	123
	Turkey's Religious History	125
	Iran's Religious History	129
	Females' Education and Labor Force Participation	134
	Females' Education in Turkey	135
	Females' Education in Iran	136
	Data Description	138
	Empirical Testing	138
	Results for Education Enrollment	138
	Results for Labor-Force Participation	144
	Analysis of the Data	148
	Conclusion	150
	References	153
6	**Conclusion and Policy Implications**	155
	Policy Recommendations	159
	Future Studies	161
	References	162

Appendix A 163

Appendix B 173

Index 179

List of Figures

Fig. 3.1	Comparison between the educational dataset in Barro and Lee's and World Bank datasets	75
Fig. 4.1	Marginal effect for the interactive terms between Muslim countries and Constitution and Urbanization	101
Fig. 4.2	The marginal effect of the different levels of religious constitutions in Muslim countries	109
Fig. 4.3	Total female-to-male school enrollment for Muslim and non-Muslim countries (2010)	118
Fig. 4.4	Marginal effect for the interactive terms between Muslim countries and Constitution, Urbanization, and Fertility rate	120
Fig. 5.1	Female-to-male total school enrollment in Iran and Turkey (1960–2010)	139
Fig. 5.2	Female-to-male educational school enrollment, 1960–2010	142
Fig. 5.3	Ratio of female-to-male labor-force participation (%), 1990–2010	145
Fig. 5.4	Labor force by level of educational attainment (distribution; by sex and country)	146
Fig. A.1	Marginal effect of the different levels of religious constitutions in non-Muslim countries	167
Fig. A.2	Marginal effect of the different levels of religious constitutions in Muslim and non-Muslim countries	168
Fig. A.3	Marginal effect of the different levels of religious constitutions in Muslim and non-Muslim countries with fertility	170
Fig. B.1	Female-to-male total school enrollment for the first 16 countries over 50 years	173
Fig. B.2	Female-to-male total school enrollment for the second 16 countries over 50 years	174

Fig. B.3   Female-to-male total school enrollment for 12 countries over 50 years   174
Fig. B.4   Female-to-male total school enrollment for the last 11 countries over 50 years   175

List of Tables

Table 3.1	The list of countries in my sample	69
Table 3.2	Constitution coding and the variables used for coding	76
Table 3.3	This study's constitutional coding, with Fox's variables	77
Table 3.4	The frequency of the constitutional religious levels per year from 1960 to 2010	79
Table 3.5	Descriptive data for the main variables	82
Table 3.6	Variables and expected results	83
Table 4.1	Muslim/non-Muslim basic regression models	91
Table 4.2	Frequency for the levels of religious conservativeness	95
Table 4.3	Muslim/non-Muslim regression models with different constitutional religious levels	98
Table 4.4	Muslim/non-Muslim regression models with interaction terms	99
Table 4.5	Only Muslim countries with the combined model and the model with different levels of religious conservativeness	105
Table 4.6	Variables used in the models, but subsequently deleted	106
Table 4.7	Only non-Muslim countries with the combined model and the model with different levels of conservativeness	113
Table 5.1	The differences between Iran and Turkey in different religious aspects related to women's rights	133
Table 5.2	Iran and Turkey regression models with religious and modernization variables	141
Table A.1	Marginal effect for Muslim × Constitution	164
Table A.2	Marginal effect for Muslim × Urbanization	165
Table A.3	Interaction terms between the different levels of Muslim conservativeness with Urbanization	165

Table A.4	The interaction terms between the different levels of non-Muslim conservativeness with urbanization	166
Table A.5	Muslim/non-Muslim basic regression models	168
Table A.6	Muslim/non-Muslim regression models with Muslim and religiously conservative countries	169
Table A.7	Iran and Turkey regression models for the three educational levels	170
Table B.1	Detailed information on inclusion and exclusion of countries	175

CHAPTER 1

Introduction

In 2011, several countries, most of them Muslim, experienced political revolutions. Citizens took to the streets to express their dissatisfaction with the performance of their political regimes and their standard of living. Female attendance at these events was surprisingly high and brought some hope to the advocates of women's political rights. Women's role in the Arab Spring was significant, especially in Yemen, Tunisia, and Egypt. Thousands of women poured onto the streets to support the demonstrations, delivering speeches, food for protests, and singing songs. They treated and nursed the injured in makeshift hospitals, ambulances, and even in their homes when people were too afraid to go to the hospital.[1] Women put themselves at great risk when Tunisian police tried to repress the revolution by using security thugs to beat protesters. Women were also detained and some disappeared in Syria, Yemen, and Bahrain. For example, in Bahrain in 2011, at least nine doctors and four nurses were seized by the authorities and received sentences of five to fifteen years in prison.[2] Harassment and even rape by police, militants, and protesters occurred many times during protests in several countries. For instance, in Tunisia, in the central town of Kasserine, some women were raped by police after demonstrations. In Egypt, CBS reporter Lara Logan was surrounded by more than 200 people in Cairo's Tahrir Square and sexually assaulted. A Libyan woman named Iman Al-Obeidi told journalists that she had been raped by Al Gaddafi's militia.[3]

© The Author(s) 2018
S. A. Al-Kohlani, *Improving Educational Gender Equality in Religious Societies*, https://doi.org/10.1007/978-3-319-70536-1_1

The women who participated in demonstrations did not have anything in common except their demand for more rights and a better life. They were hoping to have their demands met after the establishment of new regimes. Faizah Sulimani, 29, one of the protesters in Yemen, stated that women's "demands are somehow similar to men, starting with freedom, equal citizenship, and giving women a greater role in society … Women smell freedom at Change Square where they feel more welcomed than ever before. Their fellow [male] freedom fighters are showing unconventional acceptance to their participation and they are actually for the first time letting women be, and say, what they really want."[4] However, after the end of the Arab Spring, Yemen, Libya, Tunisia, and Egypt started debating what degree of rights women should gain under the new regimes. That debate did not go well in most of these countries. An Egyptian protester told Catherine Ashton, the European Union (EU) foreign policy supremo, during a visit to Tahrir Square: "The men were keen for me to be here when we were demanding that Mubarak should go. But now he has gone, they want me to go home."[5] Women in Egypt have been ignored in decision-making processes since the revolution. For example, the Constitutional Amendments Committee did not include any women, and the interim government, which was formed to administer the country during the transitional period, contained only one female minister. In 2012, at the rise of the Muslim Brotherhood government in Egypt, the percentage of women in the House of Representatives dropped from 13 percent at the 2010 election to 2 percent. The percentage changed after Mohamed Morsi's government was overthrown, and increased to 15 percent elected and appointed women representatives. In Libya, the quota for women in parliament was dropped in 2012, resulting in the exclusion of large numbers of women from public decision-making and democratic political processes. Moreover, several laws have been amended to legalize discrimination against women, such as abolishing an old amendment that required men to have their first wife's consent when marrying a second woman.[6] In Tunisia, Article 28, which defined the status of women in a more religiously conservative way, was proposed by the Al Nahda political party; however, it did not pass due to massive public rejection and demonstrations. On top of all that came the intrastate and civil wars, which made women's standard of living much worse than before the Arab Spring in Yemen, Libya, and Syria. In both Syria and Yemen, women have been displaced with their children and have left their men, most of whom are either engaged in fighting or prevented from leaving conflict zones. The women have been struggling with poverty and exposed to exploitation, trafficking, and early and forced marriage.

The debate over women's rights after the end of those wars is still ongoing. Despite the absence of many international organizations that promote and monitor gender equality in Libya, Syria, and Yemen, political activists, members of civil societies, and academic scholars continue to study females' previous and current status, and keep trying to contribute positively to shaping the future of women's social, political, and economic roles in these countries. Some of these activists argue that "Islam is the solution," while others believe that "Secularism is the solution." There is also a third group that advocates for more economic development and modernization as a solution to women's gender inequality. Each group shows some evidence that supports its claim and provides excuses for the failure of some regimes that claim to be implementing Sharia[7] or secularism. Turkey has been used as a good example for both those who argue for Islam and those who espouse secularism. These groups look at Turkey through different lenses. For example, the supporters of secularism look at Mustafa Kemal Atatürk's period and consider it a successful one that contributed positively in establishing Turkey as a secular society. However, Islamists look at Recep Tayyip Erdoğan's early period and see a good example of the ability of Islamists to run a country successfully. Yet the political instability through which Turkey has been going since 2016 has made many scholars and observers question whether it is a model for either group.

This book contributes to that debate and shows that the slogans "Islam is the solution" and "Secularism is the solution" are both overstated. "Islam is the solution" does not seem to be the success that its advocates claim, at least in the case of educational gender equality. The book shows that both Muslim and non-Muslim religiously conservative societies educate girls less than boys. It also confirms previous literature and shows that Muslim countries do indeed educate females less than males compared to non-Muslim countries. This does not prove that "Secularism is the solution," however, it only suggests that there is a negative association between religion and educational gender equity. The more religious the country, the more educational gender inequality it has. This book does not recommend abandoning religion as a solution to gender inequality, it only suggests that liberalizing constitutions could be one way to improve educational gender equality. However, the positive effect of the change in the level of religious conservativeness toward being less conservative is neither strong nor linear. Becoming a secular country by forcing people to abandon their religion is a very difficult mission. Governments can oppress and ban people from practicing their beliefs, but the success of such policies is not guaranteed. Several societies used to be religious, then became secular, then went back to being religious. An example is those countries that used to be communist or ruled by liberal rulers such as the Shah in Iran, Atatürk in Turkey, and the monarchic regime in Egypt. Abandoning some negative practices of traditional societies and moving from being a very conservative society to one that is less conservative should not come by force; it should be achieved gradually and with respect of citizens' freedom of choice.

Due to the difficulties of changing people's religious beliefs and enforcing laws that contradict those beliefs, as well as the weak reward that emerges from that, this book offers another way to reduce educational gender inequality. Modernizing society is not any easier than oppressing people's religious beliefs, but it is more effective and it happens gradually, so people do not notice it to resist it. Modernization is a combination of several socioeconomic factors that help change lifestyles. Changing the environment in which people live forces them to adopt new values that work better in the new environment. Living in a modern society allows people to freely think about what is right and wrong and what is suitable to their lives. The literature has already proved that people who live in modern societies usually abandon many of their traditional and religious beliefs that conflict with their surroundings.[8] However, the positive effect of moderation requires either some religious liberty or at least a different religious way of interpreting women's right to access education. Educational gender equality seems to be high in countries that are religiously liberal and modern, such as Jordan and Lebanon, but low in countries that are religiously conservative and not modern, such as Yemen and Mauritania. Countries that are not highly modernized but religiously liberal, such as Algeria and Bangladesh, also have a high or average rate of educational gender equality. However, countries that are modern but religiously conservative have educational gender equality that is less than average, such as in Qatar and the Kingdom of Saudi Arabia (KSA). There are, of course, exceptions to some of these cases. For example, Iran is a religious country that is not as modernized as many other countries in the region, but it has higher gender equality. Gambia is not very urbanized, but is secular[9]; however, its educational gender equality is low.

Knowing the main elements that significantly contribute to modernization is very tricky. Scholars have used several indicators to capture what we call modernization. Some have employed urbanization, education, national gross domestic product (GDP), GDP per capita, low mortality rate, and different indicators of gender equality, such as the percentage of women in the parliament or labor force. Nevertheless, the most common variable that has been used to measure modernization is urbanization. The reason urbanization is arguably the best indicator is because minor economic development could be enough to give people the incentive to move to where they might have a chance of a better life. Moving to urban areas forces people to improve their knowledge and skills. This would have a positive reflection in many aspects of the individual's standard of living and the country's economic development. Yet, although this variable seems to be a good indicator of modernization, sometimes it can be imprecise if it is used without controlling for density, or is applied to measure change in some cultural factors that are not relevant to the research. For example, sudden economic development due to the discovery of a natural resource helps a country increase its percentage of urban areas, but that change will not be followed by a sudden shift in citizens' culture and values. In this case, using urbanization as a measure of modernization to study the change in culture might be an inaccurate approach.

This book illustrates that an increase in urbanization has a significant positive effect on increasing educational gender equality in non-Muslim countries, regardless of whether they are religiously conservative or liberal. Also, in non-Muslim countries, the positive impact of urbanization is higher than the positive impact of moving from being a conservative to a less religiously conservative society. In fact, going to extremes by declaring a secular system has a negative impact on educational gender equality in non-Muslim countries. However, in Muslim countries the situation is more complex. Urbanization there seems to have a positive impact on educational gender equality, but not a significant one, unless the country is not religiously conservative. For example, unlike the situation in Saudi Araba or Yemen, an increase in the percentage of urbanization in any of the liberal Muslim countries, such as Jordan, Lebanon, or Indonesia, would have a positive effect on educational gender equality. In contrast to non-Muslim countries, having a secular political system in Muslim countries helps significantly in improving educational gender equality.

Reducing the fertility rate seems to have a stronger positive effect on increasing educational gender equality in both Muslim and non-Muslim countries than increasing urbanization or liberalizing the constitution. This can be explained by the ability of this variable to account for economic development and cultural change. Both the common perception and the statistical empirical evidence indicate that an increase in income causes an increase in education, and that educated parents have fewer children. However, in traditional religious societies, an increase in income does not necessarily lead to a significant increase in females' education,[10] for instance in most Arabian Gulf oil-producing countries, since the main role of women in traditional societies is as a wife and mother. If money, schools, and transportation are available, a girl is likely to go to school until she gets married. Nevertheless, her chance of dropping out of school and getting married at an early age is high in religious societies, regardless of whether those societies are modern or traditional. Traditional religious societies tend to have a high birth rate compared to modern societies, because women in traditional societies get married early and are encouraged by many religions, including Islam, to have a large number of children.[11] Children in traditional societies represent wealth, since they are expected to help inside and outside the home. Girls who get married early are very likely to drop out of school at an early age as well. Traditional societies do not have many nurseries, and putting children in daycare is negatively associated with neglect. So a mother is expected to raise her children by herself or with some help from family members, but not from a stranger. Also, since nurseries and kindergartens are not subsidized by the government, they are considered very expensive for many families in traditional societies. A decrease in the birth rate indicates that people's priorities have changed. Women are no longer looked at only as wives and mothers; instead, they are expected to have a social and economic role, to participate economically inside and outside the home. So education becomes an obligation rather than a luxury. Therefore, when studying gender equality, scholars should use both the decrease in the fertility rate and the increase in urbanization to provide a better measure of modernization. I use urbanization because it is a better measure of economic development than GDP and other wealth measurements, and I use the decline in the fertility rate since it is a good measure of the effect of economic development on women's role in society.

A decrease in the fertility rate could happen due to other reasons than economic development. A low fertility rate used to occur in both traditional and modern societies. Very old traditional societies used to experience a low rate of fertility due to the lack of basic health awareness, vaccines, medicines, and health facilities. However, after the discovery of vaccines and other medical therapies, this problem hardly exists nowadays, even in traditional societies. In fact, currently traditional societies are associated with high fertility rates due to the improvement in the health sector worldwide. The increase in the fertility rate in traditional societies was not only due to improvements in health, but also because traditional societies prefer having more children for several social, economic, and religious reasons. Traditional societies still link masculinity and femininity to having a high number of children. Society regards those who are incapable of having children as inferior. Also, since traditional societies usually depend on agriculture, these societies tend to encourage having many children. Large numbers of children are also valued by many religious societies, such as those that follow Islam, Catholicism, and Hinduism. For example, Islam encourages having many children and that is supported by a text from the Holy Qur'an that says "wealth and children are [but] adornment of worldly life."[12] The Catholic Church is also supportive of having children and against the use of contraceptives and abortion. In AD 195, Clement of Alexandria wrote: "because of its divine institution for the propagation of man, the seed is not to be vainly ejaculated, nor is it to be damaged, nor is it to be wasted."[13] Hinduism also believes that children are a gift from God and rewards for previous actions or karma: "through a son one conquers the worlds, through a grandson one obtains immortality; and through the son's grandson one scends to the highest heaven."[14] Yet modernization diminishes the need to have lots of children, since doing so becomes a burden rather than helpful. The age of getting married increases because of the increase in the cost of marriage. The modern lifestyle forces people to have fewer children because of the high cost of living and the high demands of society. Also, the materialistic life in urban areas changes people's religious views.[15] Therefore, a decline in the fertility rate is a good sign of modernization. This book shows that a decrease in the fertility rate has a stronger positive effect on educational gender equality than any other religious or modernization variable.

In sum, the purpose of this book is to help feminists and political activists, as well as young governments and Muslim countries that escaped the Arab Spring, to determine the best approach to increase educational gender equality. It does not intend to measure the rights of women and gender equality in general, although knowing the level of females' school enrollment provides a good idea of where gender equality is heading. It also provides a good idea of females'—direct and indirect—contribution to the economy, since the literature has already confirmed the positive association between female education and economic growth.[16] The other goal of this book is to provide a new way of studying the effect of religions on educational gender equity. It provides an index that differentiates between the levels of conservativeness within each religion. This method offers a better understanding of the influence of religion on the educational gender gap. The book aims to answer several questions with regard to gender equality in education. For example, would the dominance of a religiously conservative constitution result in weak gender equality in education? Would having a less religiously conservative constitution help increase gender equality in education in both Muslim and non-Muslim countries? Do Muslim countries have higher gender inequality in education than non-Muslim countries? Also, does modernization, as reflected by urbanization, change the impact of a religiously conservative constitution on gender equality in education?

Gender Equality Before the Arab Spring

In today's world, improving the status of women is still one of the main challenges that the international community is struggling to meet. The United Nations' (UN) report for 2010, *The World's Women: Trends and Statistics*, demonstrates slow and uneven progress in many aspects of women's contemporary life, such as health, education, work, power and decision-making, and rates of women exposed to violence. For instance, the last 20 years have shown an improvement in female life expectancy. Women now live longer than men in all regions; however, in developing countries, pregnancy and childbirth are still life-threatening and tend to equalize life expectancy between the sexes. Women also still count for the majority of HIV-positive adults in sub-Saharan Africa, North Africa, and the Middle East.[17] They are exposed to sexual, psychological, and economic violence in all regions of the world. Physical abuse by the male partner is the most common type of abuse, since many societies consider beating a woman acceptable if she does not obey her husband.[18]

When it comes to gender disparities, particularly in education, despite the 10 percent decline in the number of illiterate women since 1990, it is estimated that 66 percent of adult illiterates are still women, and most of these women are concentrated in Africa and South-Central and Western Asia. This proportion has not changed for the last 20 years and it is likely to remain high due to population growth. In addition, although measurable progress has been made toward diminishing the gender gap in primary enrollment in most regions, 54 percent of the world's 72 million children of primary school age who are not attending school are girls. The available data also indicate that 38 countries still show gender disparities at elementary level in favor of boys, with the highest rate, 61 percent, in the Arab states, mostly concentrated in Egypt, Iraq, and Yemen. Progress in secondary enrollment lags behind that in primary education. In 2007, 42 countries out of 144 had less than 50 percent of girls in the official secondary school age group attending secondary school. Unlike elementary and secondary level, enrollment in tertiary education has expanded worldwide and men's dominance in tertiary education has been reversed. Currently, gender disparities in tertiary education are in favor of women, except in sub-Saharan Africa, and Southern and Western Asia. For instance, female tertiary enrollment is still below 40 percent in several countries, such as Afghanistan, Bangladesh, Iraq, Nepal, Bhutan, and Yemen; and is less than 20 percent in Gambia and Benin, Chad, Congo, Guinea-Bissau, and Eritrea. This is a combination of Muslim and non-Muslim countries.

An improvement in women's education should precede an improvement in women's participation in the work force; however, female participation in the labor force is still significantly low, especially in Northern Africa and Western Asia. In 2010, women's labor force participation rate in Northern Africa and Western Asia remained below 30 percent, and in Southern Asia it was below 40 percent.[19] In addition, in less developed countries, such as in sub-Saharan Africa and Southern Asia, the agriculture sector still accounts for more than half of the employment of both sexes; yet the majority are women. Furthermore, women in general are still rarely employed in jobs with status, power, and authority, being significantly "underrepresented among legislators, senior officials and managers, craft and related trade workers, and plant and machine operators and assemblers; they are heavily overrepresented among clerks, service and sales workers."[20] Women also still bear most of the responsibilities for the home, and spend at least twice as much time as men on unpaid domestic jobs such as caring for children and elderly parents, preparing meals, and doing other housework. The world furthermore lacks gender balance in decision-making positions. Female representation in national parliamentary seats remains below 17 percent, they are only 7 of 150 elected heads of state in the world, and 11 of 192 heads of government are women. Generally, women's status has improved and gender inequality has declined over the past 20 years, but many things remain to be done in order for women to reach a better standard of living.

Historical Background

Women have arrived at their current status partly due to over a century of continual effort by many scholars who study and advocate for gender equality. These studies are meant to help evaluate the progress toward achieving equal human rights and understanding the reasons behind the weak progress in some societies. The majority of these studies are referred to as "feminism studies." Feminism studies share some common goals, such as trying to define, establish, and achieve political, economic, personal, and social rights for women. Some of these studies emphasize the importance of achieving equal rights with men, while other studies demand rights within a religious frame. The accomplishment of feminist movements and studies varies depending on the topic and the culture of the society. In general, we can say that to a certain extent, gender equality has been partially achieved in many Western countries, but not to the same extent in the rest of the world.

Some Western countries like Finland, Sweden, and Denmark are examples of societies where women enjoy a high level of parliamentary representation, and where the gender gap has been closed in secondary schooling, pay, and extensive parental rights and childcare facilities. Other Western countries, such as Greece, Cyprus, Malta, Spain, and Italy, have a much less impressive record on equal pay and positions of power and decision-making.[21] The poverty gap between men and women in those countries is still high as well. In general, most of post-Communist Europe has achieved educational gender equality, but is still behind other Western countries in marriage and divorce policies, paid parental leave, affordable childcare services, equal work opportunities, and political rights. For instance, countries that have joined the EU, such as Hungary, Lithuania, and Slovenia, have passed new legislation regarding equal opportunities and the general prohibition of discrimination and sexual harassment to improve gender equality and comply with EU standards, but these laws sometimes lack some important aspects, such as referring to equal work payments.[22] For example, they do not provide a clear definition of some important terms, such as discrimination, equal gender rights, or sexual harassment. The same situation applies in South America, where several countries already have high female political participation, but gender equality in education and marriage rights still need major improvement. The progress on gender equity in most Western countries is arguably considerable due to their secular political system and modernization.

Like most Western countries, the majority of Eastern countries are secular, but they are not as modernized as their Western counterparts. Therefore, the progress in gender equality is not as widespread and significant as in Western countries. For example, South Korea has made great progress in nearly all aspects of human rights, but other countries such as Afghanistan are still behind the rest of the world in several aspects, such as education, access to the labor force, and women's freedom of movement in public without a male companion. Many other countries, such as Pakistan, India, Bangladesh, and Indonesia, also lag behind in several aspects of women's rights. However, the majority of Eastern countries have already achieved some of the feminists' goals, such as increasing females' political participation. For example, in Bangladesh and Pakistan, two women managed to become heads of state, although these two countries remain behind the rest of the world in educational gender equality and other aspects of human rights. Other countries, such as Iran, have already achieved educational gender equality, but are nevertheless very far from achieving political gender equality. The failure to make a significant improvement in all major human rights aspects can also be referred to the influence of religion and a lack of modernization.

These modest achievements in improving gender equality in the last few decades were the result of a worldwide effort. The international community's attempts to spread awareness of the importance of integrating women into development started in 1967. The UN General Assembly issued the Declaration on the Elimination of Discrimination against Women (DEDAW), which outlined the UN's view on women's rights. It paved the way for the 1968 UN International Conference on Human Rights, an important precursor to a legally binding document for members of the international community. It also led to the establishment of the UN Decade for Women in 1975, and the signing of the Convention on the Elimination of All Forms of Discrimination against Women during the Second World Conference on Women in Copenhagen in 1980. The Decade for Women provided a forum for women's voices and placed women's problems in the international arena. It gave women the opportunity to share their experience of oppression, to network, and to strategize globally. Bedsides the Second World Conference, the UN Decade was followed by several international conferences, such as the Third World

Conference on Women in Nairobi in 1985 and the Vienna World Conference in 1993, which emphasized the importance of supporting and protecting women's rights. The Vienna World Conference is considered the largest gathering in human rights history, and was attended by 7000 participants, including representatives of 171 nations and 800 non-governmental organizations (NGOs). This conference was followed by another in 1994, the Cairo International Conference on Population and Development, which stressed the importance of investing in women's health and empowerment as a key to improving gender equality. In 1995, the Beijing Fourth World Conference on Women reviewed the accomplishments of the previous two decades and adopted a new platform aimed at achieving greater equality and opportunity for women. It led to the Decade for Human Rights Education from 1995 to 2004, followed by the UN Literacy Decade: Education for All, which started in 2003 and ended in 2012. In 2014, the UN reviewed the progress of the Cairo Program of Action and came up with a new Program of Action of the International Conference on Population and Development (ICPD) beyond 2014. This emphasized the importance of equality, women's health, and the human rights of all people. It warned of the negative impact on development of ignoring these issues.[23] All these events contributed significantly to improving women's status in many aspects, but the results varied from one country to another and from one aspect to another, depending on the country's political regime and sociocultural norms. Trying to do a cross-sectional time series study of gender equality in general is challenging; therefore, in this book I focus on only one of the critical elements of human rights, females' right to be educated.

Western Feminist Theories

The first time the feminist movement was publicly discussed was in 1942 by Katherine Hepburn in a film named *Woman of the Year*; however, the term feminism did not gain widespread popularity until the 1970s. It is normally used to describe the political, cultural, and economic movements that aim to establish equal gender rights and legal protection for women. The history of feminism can be divided into three waves. The first wave of feminism started in Europe and the United States and was in the nineteenth and early twentieth centuries, which was before the term feminism even started to be used. A "true woman" at that time was expected to stay at home and meet the needs of her husband and children. She was considered biologically weak, since she was seen as having a small brain and a fragile physique. Women were required to be modest and not to engage in public activities. Those who spoke in public were considered to be displaying masculine behavior. In this wave, liberal women did not challenge the concept of differences between genders; on the contrary, they accepted that they have a natural disposition toward maternity and domesticity. Yet, they demanded that women and men were, at least in legal terms, equal in all respects. The movement focused on females' right to equal contract and property rights, as well as women's right to vote. These women strongly believed that denying them their right to vote was akin to denying them full citizenship. They argued that there is no difference between men and women that disqualifies women from voting. In fact, they argued that allowing women to vote would help them perform their roles as mothers and housewives even better. They argued that because of the difference between men and women, they needed representatives in the political arena who understood their needs.[24] Besides the liberal first-wave feminism, there was socialist/Marxist feminism, which shared liberals' demand for justice and equal opportunities for women and men. However, socialist/Marxist feminism focused more on the class struggle and working-class women. Marxist feminists look at men as the "class of 'oppressors' and of women as the 'oppressed'" ... Like Marxists, these feminists "have adopted the technique of 'consciousness raising' to reveal the true nature of 'oppression' (that is, "the patriarchy"): a 'superstructure' of lies perpetuated by those in power (men)."[25] They believe in the term "women's collective," which refers to the idea that all women have at least some characteristics in common, so, despite diversity among the different forms of feminism, they must focus on group rights and campaign for women's rights and power. Marxist feminists "hope to bring in a new world order, a new age, a new paradise (often under the aegis of a great goddess)."[26]

The second wave was in the 1960s and 1970s, and was concerned with legal and social rights for women, such as their right to abortion and divorce. The second wave was a combination of radical and socialist/Marxist feminist movements. These women condemned the world's interest in women's appearance more than what they do or think. They argued against the dual workload for women inside and outside the home. They demanded equal payment for equal work, and eliminating the gendered division of the educational system and the labor market. The women participated in movements that criticized "capitalism" and "imperialism," protested against the Vietnam War, and supported "oppressed" groups, such as the working class, black people, and homosexuals. Some of the second-wave movements demonstrated that the liberation of women would occur only with the destruction of capitalism and transformation into a socialist society instead. They insisted that women would never be freed from dependency on men and the family if they were not involved in "productive" labor. However, the radical movements focused more on the criticism of "sex roles" and the "beauty myth." Despite the major ideological differences between second-wave movements, all these women called for sisterhood and solidarity. They invested in slogans that emphasized women's unity, such as "Woman's struggle is class struggle" and "The personal is political."[27]

The third wave extends from the 1990s to the present. It challenges the second wave, which mostly represented the experience of upper-middle-class white women, and criticizes earlier waves of feminism for presenting a universal solution or definition of womanhood and for associating themselves with a particular political identity. This is an internal debate between different feminists: those who believe in differences between the sexes, and those who believe that there is no inherent difference between men and women and that the difference in gender roles is only due to the societal culture. They try to avoid thinking in categories, which divide people into "us" and "them," or see themselves as inhabiting particular identities, such as women or feminists. They are attempting to redefine feminism and study traditional and stereotypically feminine issues, such as sexist language. The "New Feminism," which refers to the third wave, is also concerned with issues relevant to globalization and investigates areas such "as violence against women, trafficking, body surgery, self-mutilation, and the overall 'pornofication' of the media."[28] Third-wave feminism is a turning point in the history of feminism, since it represents a movement "away from thinking and acting in terms of systems, structures, fixed power relations, and thereby also 'suppression'—toward highlighting the complexities, contingencies, and challenges of power and the diverse means and goals of agency."[29] All the previous feminist waves have reached many countries in the world and left some impact, such as in Europe and some countries in the Middle East and North Africa and Asia. These waves also led to the emergence of feminist theories that have manifested in a variety of disciplines.

Contemporary Western feminist theories can be divided into radical, liberal, and social. All these theories study the reason behind women's subordination to men: how it happened, how and why it spread, how it could be changed, and what life would look like without it. For instance, radical feminism considers women's oppression as the oldest form of discrimination, older than exploitation because of race and class. It celebrates women's capacity for nurturing and their physiological superiority, which is associated with love and peace. However, it accuses men of creating wars and disturbing peace. This theory has been criticized for portraying women as victims of evil men. Unlike radical feminism, social feminism argues that capitalism is the cause of class, race, and female oppression; therefore, the solution is cooperation between men and women to eliminate capitalism. However, this theory is criticized by radicalism for suggesting that women ally with men to defeat capitalism not as partners, but as subordinates. Liberalism, on the other hand, tends to believe that biological sex differences, not capitalism, are the reason for cultural gender differences. Therefore, women's rights can be gained without changing the political and economic structures of capitalism.[30] Yet this theory has been accused of elitism and of an inability to abolish the structure of women's oppression. In general, all feminist theorists attribute gender inequality to different reasons, but some feminist theorists are less dramatic and study particular aspects of gender inequality in specific sectors of social life, such as politics, education, and the family.

When it comes to education, Western public debate over females' right to education goes back as far as first-wave feminism, if not further. It can be tracked to 1872, when Edward H. Clarke, professor of materia medica at Harvard College, was invited to the New England Women's Club in Boston and chose to give a lecture related to gender in education. One year later, he published a book titled *Sex in Education or a Fair Chance for Girls*, where he argued that females who study the "boy's way" and engage in vigorous mental activity risk their health.[31] Clarke argued that extensive education for women damaged their uterus and ovaries, and exposed them to masculinization, insanity, infertility, and even death.[32] His book led to impressive studies and an array of evidence that weakened his theory and showed that education has many health, social, and economic benefits for women. For example, Julia Ward Howe was one of the scholars who challenged Clarke and provided strong evidence that contradicted his theory. In 1874, she published a book containing essays from women who had attended college. She provided data on fertility and statistics concerning career and marriage that rebutted Clarke's theory. She found that coeducation promoted healthy relationships between women and men. It also has economic advantages.[33] However, unfortunately Clarke's theory persisted for a long time and affected women's role in several areas, particularly in the work force.

When it comes to the contemporary history of education, scholars have moved from asking about women's capability for studying to whether the type of education they are receiving would help increase gender equality. Radical theorists, for example, do not trust the usefulness of an education system that is dominated by men's principles. Yet they see education as a major tool for abolishing the culture that allows men's domination over women. They study the cultural oppression that denies a women her right to full knowledge, independence, building self-esteem, and freedom from fear. Social feminism, on the other hand, does not believe in education that is dominated and run by capitalism, therefore social feminist studies concentrate on how to remove the oppression caused by capitalism, considering women's position in the family and the role they play in the economy. Socialism believes that education under a capitalist system is dangerous, since it is used to reproduce sexual and social division in the family and the work force. However, liberal theorists seem to have more faith than the previous groups in the possibility of achieving gender equality under the current international system. They believe in the critical role of education in removing the barriers that prevent women from reaching their full potential. These social stereotypical barriers could be in school, the individual psyche, or discriminatory labor practices. By removing them the problem would be solved. In sum, women's physical capability to study is no longer a controversial issue, although it is still a debatable issue in other fields, such as work-force abilities; the current problem that seems to concern feminist studies is the *type* of education that women are receiving. All three feminist theories seem to agree on the importance of the education of women for many different reasons, yet they differ in the type of education that societies need to overcome gender inequality and achieve each respective theory's ideological goals.

Religious Feminist Theories

Feminism in general can be divided into secular and religious feminism. Secular feminism is mostly active in modern societies, and religious feminism is found more in the traditional world. Western feminism is usually considered secular, although some Western feminists can be religious. Redfern and Aune (2010) polled 1265 people who identify themselves as feminists and found that two-thirds of them describe their religious views as agnostic, atheist, or no particular spirituality.[34] Because of traditional societies' resistance to accept secular feminist views, several types of religious feminism have been established. All of them still struggle to define their problems and goals. They have rarely been mentioned in the feminist literature, since religion is considered an oxymoron to feminism. Religious feminists avoid being challenging and tend to accept most of society's norms. Redfern and Aune (2010) also found that religious feminists are usually subordinate to the system of norms and laws restricting them. They reject liberal views and lean more toward patriarchy.[35] Western feminism managed to separate itself from religion and exists outside a religious framework; yet religion has been integral to the feminism that has been constructed by Muslim and Buddhist women.

Buddhist Feminism

Several Buddhist feminist scholars have written about women in the past and their own experience as modern Buddhists.[36] They have talked about the patriarchal structure of Buddhism and the "misogyny" of the Buddhist tradition.[37] They have examined the sexist structure of Buddhism and the change that has occurred to Buddhism over time. Buddhism tends to be driven by two old religions: the *śramaṇa* tradition and the Brahmanical religion. The word *śramaṇa* actually means "wanderer" and it refers to men who abandon society and its responsibilities in order to pursue their own spiritual path. This path is not meant for women, not only because of the social barriers, but also because women would have to practice austerity, wear few or no clothes, and wander alone. From the *śramaṇa* tradition comes Buddhism. Buddha left his wealth and family to practice austerity and start the Buddhist Sramanic movement. However, many Brahmin monks followed him. The Brahmanical religion is the traditional religion of India and the earliest phase of Hinduism. It is actually the religion of the householder, which refers to the man of the house. In Hinduism, a woman has "no religious identity or status of her own, and takes part in religious activities only as a servant of her husband."[38] When the *Dharmaśāstras*, "divine rules," were developed, women's situation became worse, to the point that some of their bodily functions such as menstruation and childbirth were considered dangerous and ultra-polluting to men. Women had to abide by more rules than men, and they were expected to be subordinate to men in several matters, such as authority, discipline, and ordination.[39] Nevertheless, Buddhist feminist scholars argue that current Buddhist roles are different from those of Buddha's teachings. For example, Hamilton (1996) argues that there is nothing in Buddha's teachings that is "inherently inferior and/or qualitatively different about women compared with men but thinking makes it."[40] Scholars claim that since "there are resources within Buddhist texts that promote equality between men and women, there would be no need to abandon Buddhism, but instead, promote the positive elements within the doctrine and support women from within their religious practices, rather than from an outside, 'secular' position."[41] For instance, they maintain that Buddhism originally used to be in favor of women, but religious institutional development over time has led to gender discrimination. They believe that Buddha's teachings do not differentiate between men and women and apply equally to all human beings, and that Buddha taught that "all personal relationships are reciprocal, and married women should be accorded respect, courtesy, faithfulness and authority."[42] Buddha also taught that "purity and pollution qualitatively correspond to one's state of mind: it is the unwholesomeness of negative states of mind (anger, hatred, covetousness, and so on) that is impure, and this applies to all people, men and women alike."[43] In addition, other feminist Buddhist scholars, such as Gross (1993) or Kabilsingh (1991), claim that the negative portrayal of women may have been added into the texts later, and is not the word of Buddha. Most Buddhist stories are about men, and those about women either were not preserved or were ignored in favor of stories about men. Therefore, feminist Buddhist scholars must search carefully through Buddhist religious documents to find anything that could help bolster the status of women in Buddhist societies.

Buddhist Feminism and Education

When it comes to where Buddhism stands on female education, it is arguably not supportive. The origin of this perception comes from the reluctance of Buddha to allow his aunt, Mahaprajapati, and a large group of women who accompanied her to join the renunciate community. He rejected their request several times, saying "[E]nough, O Gotami, let it not please thee that women should be allowed to do so,"[44] but eventually he accepted when these women "cut off their hair, put on saffron renunciates' robes, and travelling on foot, went on to the Buddha's next stopping place."[45] Their pitiful appearance made him change his mind. Nevertheless, he declared that women who wanted to become nuns were required to accept eight special rules as a precondition for their admission to the monastic order. These nuns were considered subordinate to the monks, not equal to them. Additionally, Buddha mentioned that because women were permitted to join the order, the Buddhist teaching (*dharma*) would live for only 500 years instead of 1000 years.[46] This indicates that allowing women to join the monastic order came at an expensive cost for Buddhism.

The negative influence of Buddha's reluctance to teach women can be seen, for example, in Thailand. Thailand's constitution still refers to Buddhism as the country's official religion. In relative terms the country is considered religiously conservative, even though we cannot call it very conservative, since the constitution does not declare that legislation must be inspired by Buddhism. However, before the establishment of the first official secular school by Rama V (1853–1910), education was limited to boys and it was given in the *wat* (temple).[47] This situation has changed in the last couple of decades and Thailand already has more females than males in elementary and tertiary education, yet it has not reached equality at secondary level. The significant improvement at elementary level was due to the National Education Act, which made the first nine years of education mandatory for both genders. The significant increase in tertiary education is due to the patriarchal nature of the society, where male chauvinism is fostered and encouraged. The gender inequality in secondary education in Thailand indicates that if people were not forced to send their girls to school, they would likely not send them. This could be due to the influence of Buddhist culture, which does not see education as so essential for girls as it is for boys.

Some scholars have considered Buddhism as one of the reasons for the historical educational gender inequality.[48] Buddhist attitudes arguably play a role in reinforcing existing social attitudes toward women's education and discourage women from exercising free critical thinking.[49] Several religious schools are available and some of them are open to both genders, but Buddhist monasteries still offer educational opportunities only for boys and men for a few weeks or permanently; girls do not have this opportunity. Although Buddhist schools do not teach everything formal schools do, they are still a good option for parents who have boys and cannot afford the cost of regular schools. As a monastic education is still not accessible to girls, poor girls have a limited choice of educational (and spiritual) guidance compared to boys. The exclusion of girls from monastic education contributes to gender disparity in education and reinforces their gender role. As I mentioned earlier, feminist Buddhist scholars have been trying to provide evidence that could help change the way in which most Buddhists understand and practice Buddhism, and contribute to changing Buddhist attitudes toward women's role inside and outside the home, yet changing religious beliefs is usually slow and takes much effort.

Islamic Feminism

Even though feminists in the Muslim world were unable to challenge the religious and cultural beliefs of their societies, they were behind many of the changes that occurred in the understanding of females' rights in their countries. Like Buddhist feminists, Islamic feminists also tried to incorporate religious scripts about gender equality that have been neglected by religious scholars. This movement was welcomed by some left-wing scholars and viewed as progress that can help leftist feminists in achieving their goals. For example, in the early 1980s, Parvin Paidar (who sometimes called herself Nahid Yeganeh) suggested that Islamic feminists and secular feminists share some concerns regarding "the legal status and social positions of women and that these could lead to future alliances."[50] In 1994, Afsaneh Najmabadi "gave a talk at the School of Oriental and African Studies, University of London, in which she described Islamic feminism as a reform movement that opens up a dialogue between religious and secular feminists."[51] She saw in a 1992 article by Shahla Sherkat, the former editor of the establishment women's magazine *Zanan*, a sign of common ground that could help pave the way toward an alliance between secular and Islamic feminists. Sherkat wrote that "the key to the solution of women's problems lies in four realms: religion, culture, law, and education. If the way is paved in these four principal domains then we can be hopeful of women's development and society's advancement."[52] Najmabadi considered Sherkat's article, as well as others that have been published weekly in *Zanan*, as good progress toward changing the interpretation of women's rights in Islam. Najmabadi discussed how the insistence of Islamic feminists on regarding gender discrimination as due to culture rather than religion could open the door for *ijtehad* (independent reasoning, religious interpretation) and the right of women to reinterpret Islamic law. It could also open a space for cooperation between Islamic and secular feminists, and this cooperation could work as a bridge between secular and religious thought.[53] In addition, Mir-Hosseini also sees several positive effects of the Islamic feminist movement, such as "subtly circumventing the dictated rules (e.g., reappropriating the veil as a means to facilitate social presence rather than seclusion, or minimizing and diversifying the compulsory hijab and dress code into fashionable styles), engaging in a feministic *ijtehad*, emphasizing the egalitarian ethics of Islam, reinterpreting the Holy *Qur'an*, and deconstructing *Sharia*-related rules in a women-friendly egalitarian fashion (e.g., in terms of birth control, personal status law, and family code to the extent of legalizing a demand for 'wages for housework')."[54] Yet several feminist scholars do not see a possibility for the alliance between left-wing and Islamic feminists that some feminists call for, as it makes no sense to them. For instance, Haideh Moghissi complains that "the term *Islamic feminism* encompasses members of the female political elite who believe in *Sharia* and its prescribed gender rights and roles,"[55] so the Islamic feminist movement should not be looked at with optimism; in fact, she believes that Islamic feminism undermines feminists' efforts to achieve secularism. Moghissi explains how some of the Holy Qur'an's verses and *Hadiths* are clear, so it would be difficult to come up with an interpretation that would meet secular feminists' expectations.[56] She argues that an alliance between Islamic and secular feminists could not be useful, since the groups do not agree on the cause of gender discrimination. Moghadam (2002) also agrees with the previous two scholars and argues that an Islamic state cannot and will not enforce "universal legal norms and guarantee[] protection of civil and human rights regardless of gender, religion, ethnicity, and class ... because it defines citizenship rights on the basis of sex and religion."[57] Nevertheless, Nayereh Tohidi warns that "secular feminists should differentiate between those Islamic women who are genuinely promoting women's rights and hence inclusionary in their politics from those who insist on fanatic or totalitarian Islam."[58] She supports Kar, a feminist lawyer, in stressing that a "reformist or women-centered interpretation of religious laws should be considered not as an alternative to secular and democratic demands, but as a component of more holistic social change."[59] This debate over the role of Islamic feminists requires an explanation of how Islamic feminism approaches the issue of gender discrimination, which some liberal feminist scholars argue is embedded in the Islamic religion.

Islamic feminist scholars rely on Islam's sacred text, the Holy Qur'an, to change their patriarchal societies. They claim that there is a misunderstanding of women's rights in Islam, so that scholars need to choose and examine their resources carefully. Riffat Hassan (1999) states that most of the confusion and misunderstanding of women's status in Islam comes from the fact that there are several religious resources that can be used to justify a certain belief: "[T]he *Qur'an* (the book of revelation believed by Muslims to be God's Word), *Sunnah* (the practical traditions of the prophet Muhammad), *Hadith* (the sayings attributed to the prophet Muhammad), *Fiqh* (jurisprudence) or *Madahib* (schools of law), and the *Shari' ah* (the code of life that regulates all aspects of Muslim life)."[60] However, he considers the Holy Qur'an and *Hadiths* as those most commonly used and they have been interpreted solely by Muslim men. He argues that many *Hadiths* are flawed and are inconsistent with the Holy Qur'an. They are mostly inspired by common stereotypes about women's ontology, biology, and psychology. For example, he claims that the notion that "the Genesis 2 idea of woman being created from Adam's rib did, in fact, become incorporated in the hadith literature is evident from a number of hadith … it is difficult to believe that it entered the Islamic tradition directly."[61] He states that the Holy Qur'an does not discriminate against women and it does not support the idea that woman was created from man, nor that she was created *for* man. He asserts that the "*Qur'an* does not create a hierarchy in which men are placed above women, nor does it pit men against women in an adversary relationship. They are created as equal creatures of a universal, just, and merciful Creator whose pleasure it is that they live—in harmony and in righteousness—together."[62] He provides several other examples of common religious misbeliefs about women and explains how the Holy Qur'an shows no sign of discrimination against women. He believes that one of the main reasons behind the limited understanding of women's rights in Islam is that "those who understand Islam do not know modernity and those who understand modernity, do not know Islam."[63] He suggests that "unless, or until, the theological foundations of the misogynistic and androcentric tendencies that have become incorporated in Muslim culture are demolished, Muslim women will continue to be brutalized and discriminated against." [64]

However, although Western feminist scholars argue that the main weakness of Islamic feminism and the reason behind the delay in embracing feminism in Muslim countries is the lack of understanding of the boundary between Islam and feminism, the delay was also due to the anticolonial and nationalist movements of the first half of the twentieth century. Muslim women who demanded equal gender rights were accused of attacking Muslim traditional culture and promoting the superiority of Western culture. They were criticized for trying to spread Western culture, which is associated in many Muslims' minds with "promiscuity, break-up of family and community, latch-key kids, and drug and alcohol abuse. Many Muslims see 'emancipated' women, not as symbols of 'modernization' but as symbols of 'Westernization.'"[65] Muslim feminists who thought of the West as a good model for intellectual and social transformation from which Muslim societies can learn were accused of being used by Western powers to continue the "onslaught on the integrity of the Islamic way of life."[66] This negative stereotype toward feminism forced Muslim feminist scholars to avoid breaking boundaries and crossing lines so that they would not be excluded from society. After the end of the anticolonial and nationalist movements, the establishment of modern nation-states in the Muslim world did not make the situation much better. The new regimes selectively tried to promote women's rights, but at the same time they tried to limit women's activism. The result of such governmental strategy varied from one regime to another and from one time period to another.

The social and governmental pressure that feminist movements have faced in the Muslim world resulted in the creation of Islamic feminism in several countries. In some Muslim countries, Islamic feminists managed to create Brotherhood Muslim women's associations. These associations are usually active and politically strong. They are well known for opposing secular regimes and they usually comprise the working, upwardly mobile, and educated middle class. These associations emphasize women's ability to fortify their role in modernizing their countries by education and their faith. Brotherhood female activists are politically active and have participated in several political campaigns in Egypt, Yemen, and Kuwait. Saba Mahmood (2001, 2005) gives some examples of Brotherhood feminist scholars, such as Zaynab Al Ghazali, who started the women's mosque movement in Egypt in 1950. The purpose of this movement was to educate women on their view of Islamic virtues and ethics. Women were taught how to dress, what to watch and not watch on the media, and where to invest their money, based on the Brotherhood's view of Islamic doctrine. However, the movement was eventually banned by the Egyptian government because it conflicted with some of the government's vision of a liberal society.[67] Dr. Heba Raouf Ezzat is another Brotherhood feminist scholar who wrote a controversial Arabic book in 1995 titled *Women and Political Action: An Islamic Perspective*. Like Zaynab Al Ghazali, she was giving religious lessons in mosques until 2014, when the government banned her lessons. Kuwait and Yemen also have their own versions of the

Muslim Brotherhood, named the Islamic Constitutional Movement (ICM) and Al-Islah political party, respectively.[68] Women in these two political organizations are politically and religiously active inside and outside their homes, yet they work within a religious framework. The visions of their social and political goals are not clear or consistent, and the future implications of their political participation seem limited due to the traditional and religious boundaries they put on themselves.[69]

Shia Islamic feminists hardly exist in the Arab world, since most of its countries are officially Sunni. Even in those countries that have a majority of Shia, or where at least 30 percent of their population are Shia, such as Iraq, Bahrain, Kuwait, Lebanon, and Yemen (Zaydi Shia), several Shia feminists are politically and academically active, but they do not bring their religious views to the political and social agenda. Examples are Dr. Rola Dasht and Dr. Massouma Al-Mubarak from Kuwait, and Dr. Mohumad Al Mutakel and Dr. Lamia Sharaf El Din from Yemen. These Shia scholars are well known for defending women's rights in their own countries, but they have not associated themselves with any particular religious sect and do not seem to be driven by any particular religious ideology. The modest role of Shia feminist scholars in Arab countries could be justified by the high political and social pressure they face, and by the fact that none of the countries mentioned applies Shia rules as the official religious guidelines.

However, in general, Shia can be divided into two branches of religious schools: *Qom*, the Iranian Shia school; and *Al Najaf*, the Iraqi Shia school. These two schools are the reference for all Shias in the world. The *Qom* school is considered more lenient than the *Al Najaf* school in some women's rights issues, such as women's political rights.[70] Yet, like the Brotherhood, there are limitations on females' rights and feminists in both schools, and the majority of Shia feminist scholars and activists are working within a religious framework. An example of a Shia feminist scholar is Shirin Ebadi, a lawyer, former judge, human rights activist, and Nobel Prize winner, who has published several articles nd books criticizing the current Iranian regime. Her first book, *Iran Awakening: A Memoir of Revolution and Hope*, which discusses women's rights, was published in 2007, and was about her public service and career experience before, during, and after the Iranian revolution in 1979. She explained how the revolution failed Iranian women, who fought strongly for it. More conservative Iranian Shia feminist scholars who are worth mentioning are Faezeh Hashemi, Jamileh Kadivar, Shahla Sherkat, and Azam Taleghani.[71] These women are well known for their political and social activities, especially since the Islamic Iranian revolution. All of them have spoken and written about women's rights in Islam and how the previous and/or current regimes have behaved toward women's rights issues.

Other religious groups, such as Salafists and Wahhabis, who are known to be the strictest Islamic religious groups and who are also engaged in political debates in regard to females' political and social rights, always express their concern about the Western model of society. These two groups advocate for females' traditional role and discourage any social and political role for women outside the home. They see women's role as limited to staying at home to take care of their husbands and children. Salafists can be found in many countries, but they are most concentered in Qatar, the United Arab Emirates, and Saudi Arabia. Wahhabis, in contrast, can be found only in Saudi Arabia. These two religious sects share many religious beliefs, especially those related to women's rights, and their differences are mostly limited to some of their political views. For example, Salafists try to separate themselves from politics, while Wahhabis have been politically involved since 1744, when Muhammad Ibn Abd al-Wahhab, the founder of the Wahhabi movement, and Muhammad bin Saud, the founder of the House of Saud, signed an alliance agreement.

Islamic Feminism and Education

With regard to education, females' education has been encouraged by Islamic feminist scholars and accepted by all Muslim religious sects and groups. Scholars argue that Islam has encouraged both genders to acquire knowledge and education. Both the Holy Qur'an and *Hadiths* emphasize the importance of education for both men and women, and consider it a duty of every Muslim man and woman to pursue knowledge throughout their life.[72] This is prevalent in both the Holy Qur'an and the *Hadiths*, in verses such as "those truly fear Allah, among His Servants, who have knowledge,"[73] and "seeking knowledge is a duty of every Muslim, man or woman,"[74] as well as "seek knowledge from the cradle to the grave."[75] In addition, a popular Sufi religious scholar, Imam Abu Hamid Muhammad ibn Muhammad al-Ghazali, confirms that religious education is meant to be for both men and women and is a necessity. He emphasizes that a woman should not leave her house without her husband's permission, unless her husband refuses to educate her, in which case she can leave the house to seek knowledge without his permission. He asserts that a man who does not perform his duty to educate his wife is at fault.[76] Furthermore, Islamic feminist scholars have argued that Islam not only promotes women to be equal to men, but encourages them to seek knowledge and education wherever they find it and to use this knowledge to help fellow human beings.[77] For example, the Prophet Mohammed himself used to encourage women to attend his lectures, and by the time of the Prophet's death there were many women scholars, such as his wives Aisha bint Abu Bakr and Hafsa bint Umar, as well as his daughter Fatima and niece Zaynab bint Ali. All of them used to give religious lessons to both men and women.

Scholars such as Adnan Abd Rashid (2014) argue that education helps to strengthen a Muslim's faith and bring them closer to God, and allows them to gain knowledge and wisdom. God said: "O people, we created you from the same male and female, and rendered you distinct peoples and tribes, that you may recognize one another. The best among you in the sight of GOD is the most righteous."[78] Rashid also adds that Islam advocates women's education, "because if a women is educated, she will bring children who are educated and will transform the community into an educated one."[79] Siti Walidah, an influential religious Islamic scholar in Indonesia who established several religious schools with her husband, Ahmed Dahlan, used to give girls lessons on the importance of a woman's awareness of her responsibilities toward God, her husband, and children; she stressed that a woman should be "smart and capable of educating her children well."[80] She taught Indonesian "girls on how to become a good wife"[81] … "[A] wife, who is independent and able to be socially active, just like Aisha (Prophet's Mohamed's wife)."[82] In general, Islamic feminist scholars suggest that Islam places equal rights on both men and women—with a few differences in certain issues that can be justified—and views education and the acquisition of knowledge as duties for every Muslim, whether male or female. Therefore, according to many religious Muslim scholars education is regarded as a fundamental human right, which Islam has supported to pave the way for Muslim women to gain respect and a decent living.

However, many other scholars have argued that religions, Islam in particular, are an obstacle to women's education, free thinking, and innovation.[83] Some Islamic religious sects and scholars put several conditions on girls going to school. These conditions are linked to the traditional view of a woman's role as a mother and a wife. The traditional religious perception has excluded women from the public space and associated them with the domestic sphere. Their domestic roles involve cooking, cleaning, giving birth, and being devoted to men and their husbands. Women appearing in public has been considered taboo, not only because of their responsibility for domestic duties, but also because the public space is seen as dangerous for women due to their physical vulnerability. A *Hadith* claimed to be said by Prophet Mohammed is: "I have not left behind me any *fitnah* (temptation) more harmful to men than women."[84] Women are exposed to danger because of their physical appearance, which is considered *fitnah* since men cannot easily fight the temptation of women. This idea of *fitnah* stems from the concept of *awra*, which refers to the private parts of men and women. This was interpreted by religious scholars to refer to men's and women's bodies as a source of temptation. However, some religious scholars considered a woman's entire body *awra* (some scholars made an exception for the face and hands), while man's *awra* is only the area between his navel and his knees. Therefore, since a woman's body seems to be more tempting than a man's body and a woman's body may pose danger, veiling and sex segregation became necessities.

Still today in many Muslim societies, a woman who decides to display her *awra* (this could be her face or other parts of her body, depending on the society) would be associated with shame. Religious scholars who hold this belief refer to the Holy Qur'an and the story of Adam and Eve, when they were expelled from the garden of paradise because the display of their *awra* had made them ashamed of each other, so that they covered themselves with leaves.[85] In addition, scholars argue that God instructed the Prophet Mohammed to command Muslim women to use veils by saying: "O Prophet! Tell thy wives and thy daughters and the women of the believers to draw their cloaks close round them (when they go abroad). That will be better, so that they may be recognized and not annoyed."[86] Some religious scholars also believe that God commanded men and women to "lower their gaze and guard their modesty" to each other, and women to "not display their beauty and ornaments" to men whom they are prohibited from marrying.[87] Moreover, a *Hadith* narrated by Abu Hurairah, the Prophet Mohammed's companion and the most prolific narrator of *Hadiths*, mentions that the Prophet said: "[F]aith is some 70 odd parts and shame is one of the parts of faith." This means that a faithful Muslim is expected to feel shame if God's role is broken and/or *awra* is displayed. These Holy Qur'an verses and *Hadiths* have been interpreted in many different ways, but the common interpretations are not in favor of women who demand freedom of movement and to choose their own style of dress. These Qur'an verses and *Hadiths* have been used by many religious scholars as strong evidence of the requirement for veiling, and their interpretation has played a significant historical role in women's exclusion from public education.

Since education for a woman in traditional Muslim societies is deemed unnecessary due to her expected traditional role, which is limited to devoting herself to her family, women's educational status varied according to their social class. In the past, education in many Muslim traditional societies was limited to boys. A few aristocratic families sent their girls to elementary schools, but those schools were coeducational. They were established by Western occupiers, such as the British, French, and Dutch. For example, in Indonesia during the Dutch occupation (1600s–1945), "conservative Javanese Muslims avoided sending their children, let alone daughters, to these schools because they were managed by the Dutch colonial, which was considered infidel. They believed that the Dutch schools, education, and clothing were *haram* (prohibited in accordance to Islamic law), and going to such schools, obtaining the education, and imitating their fashion and customs were considered part of infidelity."[88] Consequently, girls from religious families were taught how to read the Holy Qur'an at home by their families. Girls from poor families did not receive any type of education. However, the main role for all girls from all social classes, both those who received some education and those who did not, remained as mothers and wives, and they were expected to stay home until they got married.[89]

The reluctance to send girls to school was not limited to the religious perception of the traditional role of women as not requiring education, but also to the concept of *awra*, which was not solved by veiling. Veiling was not considered enough to avoid temptation, therefore physical distance between the sexes became important. Religious scholars argued that God ordered that those who believed should "not enter the houses of the Prophet except when you are permitted ... and when you ask [his wives] for something, ask them from behind a partition (*hijab*). That is purer for your hearts and their hearts."[90] *Hijab* is an Arabic word that has several meanings. For instance, it can mean veiling, but it can also mean borders, such as "the visual," or to hide something from sight, "the spatial," which separates or makes a border, and "the ethical," referring to something that is forbidden."[91] The common interpretation of this verse is that women's and men's social interaction should be restricted, and since a veil does not do that segregation by sex was used. Some feminist scholars limit God's command in this verse to the way Muslim men were supposed to communicate with the Prophet Mohammed's wives; others argue that it applies to all Muslim women, since all Muslim women should strive to be like the Prophet Mohammed's wives. In any case, both spatial segregation and veiling seem to share the basic essence of treating women differently in public spaces. Veiling and sex segregation were established and became embedded in the culture of Muslim societies. By Islamic law, a Muslim woman is expected to cover her entire body or parts of it out of modesty, and should limit her interaction with men. These rules have affected females' education, because providing enough segregated schools is expensive and associated with other problems, such as the lack of women teachers.

Several Muslim countries still enforce the wearing of veils and segregation for women. For example, Rafeda Al-Hariri (1987) states that in Saudi Arabia, from the age of 9, a girl must avoid appearing in public and must cover her hair and wear a long dress. Some religious scholars require the face and hands to be covered. Segregation between girls and boys in schools is a must, and schools for girls have to be run by female teachers and administrators. A girl must use a specially chaperoned bus or go to school with a male companion who is a family member.[92] These rules are applied in many Muslim countries, such as Yemen, Indonesia, and Mauritania, but their implementation and women's respect for these instructions vary based on how strict the government and the society are in enforcing these rules.

Overall, Islamic feminists have achieved major success in highlighting religious statements that show support for females' education and refuting most of the misinterpretation of the Holy Qur'an's verses and forged *Hadiths*. They have also succeeded in achieving some of their demands in regard to providing the required educational atmosphere to increase females' school enrollment. Through international organizations' pressure and governments' cooperation, governments' commitment to enforcing some of the previously strict rules has decreased, and the number of segregated schools in some traditional Muslim societies has increased to encourage conservative families to send their girls to school. In addition, international and governmental commitment to privatization has helped loosen some of the rules, such as allowing private schools to choose whether they want to establish segregated or coeducational schools. However, more work still needs to be done in several Muslim countries and in various other aspects of gender equality.

In sum, women's right to education and other social, political, and economic aspects has been met or partially met in many Western countries, but more remains to be accomplished in the rest of the world. Western feminist movements have played a major role in speeding up progress, but religious feminist movements, such as the Buddhist and Muslim feminist movements, have failed to achieve the same result. It remains difficult to define religious feminism because it is still evolving. However, in general, religious feminism seeks gender equality and justice, but within a religious framework. Islamic feminists can be found in several Islamic sects and religious groups, but they are mostly concentrated in Brotherhood and Shia groups in Iran. Islamic feminists in most of the Arab world, such as in Egypt, have been experiencing governmental rejection, so progress has fluctuated. Feminism among Buddhist believers and in the Muslim world is not limited to Buddhist or Islamic feminism: other forms of feminism exist, such as secular feminism, which also struggles to define itself without being socially resisted. Muslim secular or liberal feminists attempt to influence women's status by collaborating with the existing social structure, and some have been willing to cooperate with religious feminists, who invoke religious principles and look to religion for support and legitimacy. They try to lead societal and religious change without threatening men or damaging their own image as Muslim women who respect their cultural and traditional roles.

Females' education is one of the areas that used to be controversial, and both feminist and religious scholars have debated whether women need to be as educated as men. While secular feminists clearly see many advantages of educating women, religious scholars have different positions. Some of them are supportive of women's education, but impose some restrictions; others believe that the harm that could result from sending girls to school outweighs the benefit. Religious feminists have been trying to convince both religious groups, using religious resources, that females' education is required by religion and that with a few adjustments, such as imposing the veil or providing segregated schools, there will be no harm from education.

EDUCATION AND GENDER EQUALITY

The reason this book focuses on females' education is because it is crucial, not just because it is a basic human right, but also because it has a positive impact on many other aspects of human rights, such as changing attitudes toward gender equality. Scholars have found that education is associated with an increase in positive attitudes toward gender equality.[93] They have established that attitudes toward gender equality have improved over time, but that progress varies depending on the society's religion and some socioeconomic factors. The improvement has been significant in modern societies, but it remains an obstacle in many traditional societies. Inglehart explains that "in traditional societies, both men and women often accept substantial gender inequalities. But societal modernization is transforming everyone's life experience, *especially* women."[94] The change includes but is not limited to women's "autonomy, expanding literacy and educational opportunities, and strengthening the social safety net, especially for maternal and child care, reproductive control, and provision for the elderly."[95] He indicates that the "support for gender equality in the political sphere, in the workplace, and in the home is also explained by many of the standard factors commonly associated with cultural shifts, including education, religiosity, marital status, and postmaterialism."[96] He finds that the change in attitude toward being more egalitarian "was strongest, as expected, among the younger generation, women, the better educated, and the less religious."[97]

Other scholars, such as Suzanne Tallichet and Fern Willits (1986), have also studied the change in people's attitudes toward gender roles. They conducted a survey in 1970 of 11,000 high school sophomores living outside Pennsylvania, asking participants questions related to their opinions on gender equality in education, the labor force, decision-making roles, and more. In 1981, they contacted some of the participants and asked them the same questions. They found that attitudes about gender roles changed over the 11-year period and that the change was positively related to employment, income, and education. Educated "[w]omen shifted their sex-role attitudes markedly away from traditional ideas" and the majority rejected the "ideas that education and job opportunities are more important for boys, and that every girl should marry, stay at home, have children and leave the major family decisions to her husband."[98] Unlike Inglehart, Tallichet, and Willits, who used many indicators to study the factors that influence the change in attitudes toward gender equality, other scholars have conducted focused studies to confirm the positive association between education and attitude change toward egalitarianism. A longitudinal study by Fan and Marini (2000), which covered the period from 1979 to 1987 with a representative sample of 8822 US youths aged 14–22, shows that females have more egalitarian gender role attitudes than males, but that the result varies based on parents' education and the continuation of education of the female. The study finds that the higher the parents' education, the more likely the children are to have egalitarian gender role attitudes, and the continuation of education changes the attitudes toward gender roles for both sexes in many areas, such as sharing responsibility for household tasks.[99] During the same year, another published article for a study that was conducted by Karin L. Brewster and Irene Padavic (2000) contained a bigger sample from the General Social Survey (GSS) for the United States from 1977 to 1996. These scholars asked a total of 13,966 people four questions, two related to women's work and family responsibilities, and two related to the consequences for children of women's employment outside the home. They also find that college-educated people hold more egalitarian attitudes and that education affects female egalitarian attitudes more than it does male egalitarian attitudes. A further study was done in the Detroit metropolitan area by Cunningham (2008) during the period from 1961 to 1993. This followed and recorded the change in gender attitudes for a probability sample of the selected sample of white mothers who gave birth in 1961. It finds that women's education is associated with a decrease in women's support for the male breadwinner and female homemaker family model. Another study was done in China, a developing country, by Xiaoling Shu (2004) in 1991, and confirms the conclusions of previous scholars. Shu (2004) finds that the more educated a person, the more likely he/she is to have egalitarian gender attitudes. Like others, he establishes that the positive effect of education largely exists more for women than for men. All of these studies prove the positive association between education and changing attitudes toward more egalitarian societies. This association appears stronger among women than men. The higher the parents' and children's education, the more positive change in the attitude toward gender equality and the traditional stereotype of female and male family roles. The change toward a more egalitarian society normally would reflect positively on economic and other aspects of human lives.

Female Education and Economy

Despite the supportive research on the positive impact of education on gender equality, the literature regarding the impact of female education on the economy is varied in its conclusions. Some scholars, such as Robert J. Barro and J.W. Lee (1993) and a report from Forbes (1997), claim that the association between female education and economic growth is negative and significant. Barro and Lee find that primary female education has positive effects on the GDP growth rate through fertility reduction. Male educational attainment is significant in terms of its direct effects on GDP growth. However, with reference to the secondary education of women, studies show that this has an insignificant or negative effect on GDP growth in developing countries. Barro and Lee justify this by saying that the negative effect of the secondary education of women on GDP growth is due to the high percentage of male labor-force participation, compared to female labor-force participation, in developing countries.[100] In contrast, Stokey (1996) suggests that Barro and Lee's finding was affected by outliers—Hong Kong, Singapore, Taiwan, and Korea—where there are high levels of economic growth, but low levels of female schooling. He believes that if these countries were deleted from the sample, it is likely that the result would be different; however, these countries cannot be removed without justification. In addition, Dollar and Gatti (1999) find a positive association when measuring economic growth by the share of female adults with some secondary education. They claim that introducing regional "dummies" explains the difference in results.

Several other scholars, such as Knowles and Lorgelly (2002), find a positive relationship between female education and the rise of labor productivity in the long run. Sharmistha Self and Richard Grabowski (2004) have also established a strong causal impact of female education at all education levels and income growth in India for the time period 1966–1996. Other scholars, such as Anne Hill and Elizabeth M. King (1995), claim an indirect positive impact of female education on the economy through the improvement of women's productivity in the home, which in turn can increase family health, child survival, and the investment in children's human capital.[101] Finally, Stephan Klasen and Francesca Lamanna (2009) "find that gender gaps in education and employment considerably reduce economic growth."[102] Klasen and Lamanna (2009) argue that a reduction in economic growth can be noticed in countries where there is a reduction in the gender gap in education, but not in the labor force. For example, economic growth was slow in the Middle East and North Africa, or in countries where there are more females in the labor force but there is still a high gender gap in education, such as in South Asia. In general, most current literature supports the positive impact of female education on economic development, whether directly or indirectly.

Conclusion

Although the argument over the importance of females' political, social, and economic rights goes back several centuries, the improvement varies from one society to another and from one human rights aspect to another. Knowing the reasons behind this variation and the best way to approach the gender inequality problem is important for both old and new political regimes. Now more than ever, nations are demanding high respect for human rights, in particular women's rights. Governments that do not try to be proactive and listen to their citizens' demands are likely to be challenged by anger and to face a revolution in one form or another. Therefore, knowing why and how to improve females' status should start by improving women's access to education. Scholars so far have attributed the variation in the internationally modest achievement in improving women's status, particularly education, to the deep influence of traditional culture and the level of modernization. Feminist studies have focused more on culture and the influence of religion. Some have considered religion the main reason behind gender inequality; others have argued that the misunderstanding of religions is the problem. In either case, all feminist movements are demanding changes in women's status and looking for more equal gender rights. Feminist theories argue that improving equality between people, especially in education, is not just a fundamental principle of human rights, it is also a critical component of economic prosperity. A nation needs its people's full capacity to modernize and succeed. Women's right to have access to education is essential to achieving that goal. Leaving half of society illiterate will have negative implications for all aspects of society's quality of life. Feminists suggest that education improves people's attitude toward gender equality, and empowers women by providing them with the skills they need to be financially independent. Feminist movements have challenged the traditional and religious roles that women are expected to fulfill in society in the hope of improving women's political, social, and economic status.

Other social science scholars have drifted away from asking why gender inequality exists to considering why gender inequality needs to be changed. They argue that gender inequality has a tremendous negative effect on countries' development. For example, they associate educational gender inequality with slow economic growth, increase in population, and decrease in health, reflected in a high mortality rate and low life expectancy. It is also associated with weak innovation and inadequate labor skills. Some of these scholars, such as Daniel Lerner (1958), saw modernization as the solution to changing attitudes toward more gender equality. Lerner (1958) provided evidence showing that modernization could weaken the negative impact of the traditional life and improve all human rights aspects, including, but not limited to, education. His argument has been challenged by scholars who see religion as the main barrier to modernization. The bottom line is that, unlike some political, economic, personal, and social rights for women, females' right to education is currently not a disputable topic, either in Western feminist studies or religious feminist studies. What is debatable is why many females are still uneducated.

Outline of the Book

The following chapters illustrate the relationship between educational gender equality, religion, and modernization. Chapter 2 introduces the two main theories that could explain educational gender inequality, religious theory and modernization theory, discussing the underlying framework of the study in detail. This is followed by Chap. 3, which introduces the method used to categorize the level of governments' religious conservativeness and the panel-corrected standard error model that is employed in order to analyze 55 Muslim and non-Muslim countries from 1960 to 2010. Following this, Chap. 4 looks at the results of the statistical models. It lists the potential policy findings and their implications. Chapter 5 provides a case study: a comparison between a religious and a secular Muslim country, Turkey and Iran. Finally, Chap. 6 ends the book with the conclusions, recommendations for policy makers, and ideas for future studies.

Notes

1. Rice, X. et al. (2011). Women have emerged as key players in the Arab spring. *The Guardian*. Accessed July 16, 2017. https://www.theguardian.com/world/2011/apr/22/women-arab-spring
2. Chulov, M. (2011). Bahrain doctors jailed for treating injured protesters. *The Guardian*. Accessed July 16, 2017. https://www.theguardian.com/world/2011/sep/29/bahrain-protester-death-sentence
3. Women's International League of Peace and Freedom. (2011). Accessed July 16, 2017. http://www.peacewomen.org/content/international-women-arab-spring-other-side-story
4. Ibid.

5. Ibid.
6. Al Arabia. (2013). Libyan men now allowed to remarry without consent of first wife: court rule. Accessed July 16, 2017. http://english.alarabiya.net/articles/2013/02/07/264927.html
7. Islamic law based on the teaching of the Holy Qur'an and the Prophet Mohammed's instructions (*Hadiths*).
8. Berger (2001: 4).
9. Liberal countries refer to countries that do not enforce any particular religious instructions and do not necessarily separate religion from state.
10. Cochrane (1979: 26).
11. Cochrane (1979: 91).
12. Qur'an Al-Kahf (18: 46).
13. The Instructor of Children (2:10:91:2).
14. Bodyayana (2. 16.6); has been declared in the Veda.
15. Inglehart and Norris (2003: 58).
16. e.g., Schultz (1994), Hill and King (1995), Murthi et al. (1995), Klasen (1999), Dollar and Gatti (1999), Forsythe and Korzeniewicz (2000), World Bank (2001), Klasen and Lamanna (2009).
17. UN report (2010: vii).
18. UN report (2010: x).
19. UN report (2010: ix).
20. Ibid.
21. Plantenga, Remery, Figueiredo, and Smith (2009: 27–29).
22. Sedelmeier (2009: 8–11).
23. United Nations. International Decades. http://www.un.org/en/sections/observances/international-decades/
24. Krolokke and Sorensen (2005: 5).
25. Sharma and Young (1999: 14).
26. Ibid.
27. Krolokke and Sorensen (2005: 10).
28. Krolokke and Sorensen (2005: 17).
29. Krolokke and Sorensen (2005: 21).
30. Eisenstein (1984: xix–xx).
31. Clarke (1884: 18).
32. Clarke (1884: 39).
33. Howe (1874: 186).
34. Redfern and Aune (2010: 160).
35. Redfern and Aune (2010: 155).
36. See Rita Gross (1980, 1993), Nancy Falk (1980), and Sandra Bell (2000).
37. Hamilton (1996: 91–104).
38. Hamilton (1996: 93).
39. Hamilton (1996: 97).

40. Hamilton (1996: 103–104).
41. Starkey and Tomalin (2013: 61).
42. Hamilton (1996: 96).
43. Hamilton (1996: 97).
44. Gross (1993: 32).
45. Ibid.
46. Ibid.
47. Starkey and Tomalin (2013: 60).
48. Kabilsingh (1991), Tomalin (2006).
49. Kabilsingh (1991: 2).
50. Moghadam (2002: 1137).
51. Moghadam (2002: 1143–1144).
52. *Zanan* (1992: 2).
53. Moghadam (2002: 1144).
54. Mir-Hosseini (1998: 283–85).
55. Moghadam (2002: 1148–1149).
56. Moghadam (2002: 1148).
57. Moghadam (2002: 1162).
58. Tohidi (1998: 287).
59. Tohidi (1998: 287).
60. Hassan (1999: 248).
61. Ibid.
62. Hassan (1999: 262).
63. Hassan (1999: 252).
64. Ibid.
65. Hassan (1999: 251).
66. Ibid.
67. Mahmood (2001: 4).
68. González (2013: 12).
69. González (2013: 13).
70. González (2013: 14).
71. It is worth noting that not all scholars I referred to as Islamic feminist scholars would consider themselves Islamic feminists; some may consider themselves liberal feminists, such as Ebadi, since her thinking is somewhere between the two extremes of secular and religious.
72. Ibid.
73. Fatir (35 Verse No 28).
74. Ibn Majah (Vol. 1, Book 1, Hadith 224).
75. Ibn Majah (Vol. 1, Book 1, Hadith 214).
76. *Ihya' 'Ulum ad-Din* (vol. 2: 32–36, 42–44); *At-Tibr al-Masbuk fi Nasiat al-Muluk* (p. 163–164). http://www.muslimheritage.com/article/al-ghazalis-theory-education#ftn61

77. Adeel (2010: 104).
78. Qur'an Al-Hujuraat (49: verse 13).
79. Rashid (2014: 136).
80. Aryanti (2013: 86).
81. Aryanti (2013: 87).
82. Ibid.
83. Discussed in next chapter.
84. Narrated by al-Bukhaari, the book of marriage, the door of what is safe from women's evil, (7/8), No. (5096), Muslim, the book of slavery, the door of the most poor people of Paradise, 2097), no. (2740).
85. Qur'an al-A`raf (chapter 7: 22; ṭā hā chapter 20: 121).
86. Qur'an sūrat l-aḥzāb (chapter 33: 59).
87. Qur'an sūrat l-nūr (24: 30–31).
88. Aryanti (2013: 86).
89. Ibid.
90. Qur'an sūrat l-aḥzāb (chapter 33: 53).
91. Aryanti (2013: 89).
92. Al-Hariri (1987: 55).
93. See Tallichet and Willits (1986), Brewster and Padavic (2000), Fan and Marini (2000), Ciabattari (2001), Moore and Vanneman (2003), Bryant (2003), and Brooks and Bolzendahl (2004).
94. Inglehart and Norris (2003: 19).
95. Ibid.
96. Inglehart and Norris (2003: 27).
97. Inglehart and Norris (2003: 43).
98. Tallichet and Willits (1986: 225).
99. Fan and Marini (2000: 279).
100. See Appendix A, Point 2.
101. See Hill and King (1995), Klasen (1999, 2000, 2002), Murthi et al. (1995), Schultz (1994), World Bank (2001).
102. Klasen and Lamanna (2009: 1).

References

Adeel, G. (2010). Status of Women in Islam: A Critical Analysis on a Matter of Equality, 104. Retrieved from https://www.alislam.org/message-thaqalayn/vol-11-no-1-spring-2010/status-women-islam-critical-analysis-matterequality/status

Al-Hariri, R. (1987). Islam's Point of View on Women's Education in Saudi Arabia. *Comparative Education, 23*(1), 51–57.

Aryanti, T. (2013). Shame and Borders: The 'Aisyiyah's Struggle for Muslim Women's Education in Indonesia. In *Gender, Religion and Education in a Chaotic Postmodern World* (pp. 83–92). Netherlands: Springer.

Barro, R. J., & Lee, J. W. (1993). International Comparisons of Educational Attainment. *Journal of Monetary Economics, 32*(3), 363–394.

Bell, S. (2000). Being Creative with Tradition: Rooting Theravada Buddhism in Britain. *Journal of Global Buddhism, 1,* 1–23.

Brewster, K. L., & Padavic, I. (2000). Change in Gender Ideology, 1977–1996: The Contributions of Intracohort Change and Population Turnover. *Journal of Marriage and Family, 62*(2), 477–487.

Brooks, C., & Bolzendahl, C. (2004). The Transformation of US Gender Role Attitudes: Cohort Replacement, Social-Structural Change, and Ideological Learning. *Social Science Research, 33*(1), 106–133.

Bryant, A. N. (2003). Changes in Attitudes Toward Women's Roles: Predicting Gender-Role Traditionalism Among College Students. *Sex Roles, 48*(3–4), 131–142.

Centre for Social Development, Humanitarian Affairs (United Nations), UNICEF, United Nations Population Fund, United Nations Development Fund for Women, United Nations. Statistical Division, et al. (2010). *The World's Women…: Trends and Statistics.* United Nations.

Ciabattari, T. (2001). Changes in Men's Conservative Gender Ideologies Cohort and Period Influences. *Gender & Society, 15*(4), 574–591.

Clarke, E. H. (1884). *Sex in Education: Or, a Fair Chance for Girls.* Houghton Mifflin.

Cochrane, S. H. (1979). *Fertility and Education: What Do We Really Know?* Baltimore: Johns Hopkins University Press for the World Bank.

Dollar, D., & Gatti, R. (1999). *Gender Inequality, Income, and Growth: Are Good Times Good for Women?* (Vol. 1). Washington, DC: Development Research Group, The World Bank.

Eisenstein, H. (1984). *Contemporary Feminist Thought.* London: Unwin.

Falk, N. A. (1980). The Case of the Vanishing Nuns: The Fruits of Ambivalence in Ancient Indian Buddhism. In N. A. Falk & R. Gross (Eds.), *Unspoken Worlds: Women's Religious Lives* (pp. 207–224). New York: Harper & Row.

Fan, P. L., & Marini, M. M. (2000). Influences on Gender-Role Attitudes During the Transition to Adulthood. *Social Science Research, 29*(2), 258–283.

Forbes, K. J. (1997). *A Reassessment of the Relationship Between Inequality and Growth* (MIT Working Paper).

Forsythe, N., Korzeniewicz, R. P., & Durrant, V. (2000). Gender Inequalities and Economic Growth: A Longitudinal Evaluation. *Economic Development and Cultural Change, 48*(3), 573–617.

González, A. (2013). *Islamic Feminism in Kuwait: The Politics and Paradoxes.* Springer.

Gross, R., & Falk, N. A. (1980). *Unspoken Worlds: Women's Religious Lives in Non-Western Cultures.* San Francisco: Harper & Row.

Gross, R. M. (1993). *Buddhism After Patriarchy: A Feminist History, Analysis, and Reconstruction of Buddhism.* Albany: State University of New York Press.

Hamilton, S. (1996). Buddhism: The Doctrinal Case for Feminism. *Feminist Theology,* 4(12), 91–104.
Hassan, R. (1999). Feminism in Islam. In A. Sharma & K. K. Young (Eds.), *Feminism and World Religions* (pp. 248–279). Albany, NY: State University of New York Press.
Hill, M. A., & King, E. (1995). Women's Education and Economic Well-Being. *Feminist Economics,* 1(2), 21–46.
Howe, J. W. (Ed.). (1874). *Sex and Education: A Reply to Dr. EH Clarke's "Sex in Education."* Roberts Brothers.
Inglehart, R., & Norris, P. (2003). *Rising Tide: Gender Equality and Cultural Change Around the World.* Cambridge University Press.
Kabilsingh, C. (1991). *Thai Women in Buddhism.* Berkeley: Parallax.
Klasen, S. (1999). Social Exclusion, Children and Education: Conceptual and Measurement Issues. Retrieved from https://pdfs.semanticscholar.org/d864/4b283d234c66369c317b3005864ae71e0669.pdf
Klasen, S. (2000). Does Gender Inequality Reduce Growth and Development? Evidence from Cross-Country Regressions. Retrieved from https://epub.ub.uni-muenchen.de/1602/1/paper_212.pdf
Klasen, S. (2002). Low Schooling for Girls, Slower Growth for All? Cross-Country Evidence on the Effect of Gender Inequality in Education on Economic Development. *The World Bank Economic Review,* 16(3), 345–373. Retrieved from http://documents.banquemondiale.org/curated/fr/382741468330879895/pdf/773960JRN0200200Schooling0for0Girls.pdf
Klasen, S., & Lamanna, F. (2009). The Impact of Gender Inequality in Education and Employment on Economic Growth: New Evidence for a Panel of Countries. *Feminist Economics,* 15(3), 91–132.
Knowles, S., & Lorgelly, P. (2002). Are Educational Gender Gaps a Brake on Economic Development? Some Cross-Country Empirical Evidence. *Oxford Economic Papers,* 54, 118–149.
Krolokke, C., & Sorensen, A. S. (2005). Three Waves of Feminism: From Suffragettes to Grrls. In *Gender Communication Theories and Analyses: From Silence to Performance* (p. 24). Retrieved from https://uk.sagepub.com/sites/default/files/upm-binaries/6236_Chapter_1_Krolokke_2nd_Rev_Final_Pdf.pdf
Lerner, D. (1958). *The Passing of Traditional Society: Modernizing the Middle East.* Glencoe, IL: The Free Press.
Mahmood, S. (2001). Feminist Theory, Embodiment, and the Docile Agent: Some Reflections on the Egyptian Islamic Revival. *Cultural Anthropology,* 16(2), 202–236.
Mir-Hosseini, Z. (1998). Rethinking Gender: Discussions with Ulama in Iran. *Critique: Journal for Critical Studies of the Middle East,* 7(13), 45–59.

Moghadam, V. M. (2002). Islamic Feminism and Its Discontents: Toward a Resolution of the Debate. *Signs: Journal of Women in Culture and Society, 27*(4), 1135–1171.
Moore, L. M., & Vanneman, R. (2003). Context Matters: Effects of the Proportion of Fundamentalists on Gender Attitudes. *Social Forces, 82*(1), 115–139.
Murthi, M., Guio, A.-C., & Dreze, J. (1995). Mortality, Fertility, and Gender Bias in India: A District-Level Analysis. *Population and Development Review, 21*, 745–782.
Plantenga, J., Remery, C., Figueiredo, H., & Smith, M. (2009). Towards a European Union Gender Equality Index. *Journal of European Social Policy, 19*(1), 19–33.
Rashid, A. A. (2014). Islamic Paradigms for Women's Education and Their Roles to Bring Up Tawhidic Ummah (Belived Nation). *Asian Journal of Management Sciences and Education, 32*(2), 136–141.
Redfern, C., & Aune, K. (2010). *Reclaiming the F Word: The New Feminist Movement.* London: Zed.
Schultz, T. P. (1994). Human Capital, Family Planning, and Their Effects on Population Growth. *The American Economic Review, 84*(2), 255–260.
Sedelmeier, U. (2009). Post-Accession Compliance with EU Gender Equality Legislation in Post-Communist New Member States. Retrieved from http://eprints.lse.ac.uk/26598/1/post-accession_compliance_%28LSERO%29.pdf
Self, S., & Grabowski, R. (2004). Does Education at All Levels Cause Growth? India, a Case Study. *Economics of Education Review, 23*(1), 47–55.
Sharma, A., & Young, K. K. (1999). *Feminism and World Religions.* Albany, NY: State University of New York Press.
Shu, X. (2004). Education and Gender Egalitarianism: The Case of China. *Sociology of Education, 77*(4), 311–336.
Starkey, C., & Tomalin, E. (2013). Gender, Buddhism and Education: Dhamma and Social Transformation within the Theravada Tradition. In *Gender, Religion and Education in a Chaotic Postmodern World* (pp. 55–71). Netherlands: Springer.
Stokey, N. (1996). Free Trade, Factor Returns, and Factor Accumulation. *Journal of Economic Growth, 1*, 421–447.
Tallichet, S. E., & Willits, F. K. (1986). Gender-Role Attitude Change of Young Women: Influential Factors from a Panel Study. *Social Psychology Quarterly, 49*, 219–227.
Tohidi, N. (1998). The Issues at Hand. In H. Bodman & N. Tohidi (Eds.), *Women in Muslim Societies: Diversity within Unity* (pp. 277–294). Boulder, CO: Lynne Rienner.
Tomalin, E. (2006). Religion and a Rights-Based Approach to Development. *Progress in Development Studies, 6*(2), 93–108.
World Bank. (2001). *Engendering Development.* Washington, DC.
Zanan. (1992, February). Issue no. 1, 1370.

CHAPTER 2

Religious Theory vs. Modernization Theory

RELIGIOUS THEORY

Why many females still experience political, social, and economic gender discrimination is a question that can be explained by many theories; however, the religious and modernization theories are the most commonly used. Modernization theorists such as Karl Marx (1859) opened the debate on the influence of religion and the role that modernization plays in social change, and that debate has continued over time. Emile Durkheim (1912), Daniel Lerner (1958), and Daniel Bell (1973) argue that modernization changes culture. They claim that the economic development that leads to modernization can reduce the influence of religion. Other scholars such as Max Weber (1904) and Samuel Huntington (1993) argue that religions are deep rooted in societies and that economic development is unlikely to change culture; but that changing culture can pave the way for modernization. Max Weber (1904) considers religion one of the core forces for society.[1] He argues that the basic tenets of Protestantism led to economic development in the Western world, not vice versa.[2] He claims that the reason China and India did not become capitalist societies is because of their religious culture.[3] He justifies the strong influence of religions by claiming that "traditional religious values have an enduring influence on the institutions of societies."[4] Huntington also challenges the modernization theorists and argues that economic development does not necessarily lead to the social progress that produces stable democracy. He claims that some religious societies are resistant to change, finding that modernization could lead to a clash between religionists and modernists. He suggests that there has been a "religious revival in many poorer societies in recent decades, especially among fundamentalist sects in Muslim societies, perhaps as a backlash against the perceived threats of modern Western values to traditional social norms and sexual mores."[5] However, Ronald Inglehart and Pippa Norris (2003) argue that Muslims are not experiencing a backlash against modernization; they remain unchanged despite the change in their lifestyle. They believe that some agrarian societies, such as Muslim societies, remain largely unchanged in terms of their religiosity and cultural beliefs, and that the changes that have occurred due to industrialization and mobilization remain minor.

Another important aspect of this debate is the impact of religion on gender equality in education. Scholars have investigated the reasons behind the high and low performance of countries in educating females. Many scholars in the field of world politics attribute gender inequality in education to religious or economic factors. For example, even though many countries in the world have already achieved educational gender equality or are close to doing so, several Muslim countries still struggle with closing the gender gap in education. Some scholars attribute the educational gender gap to the Islamic religion, others to the lack of modernization. This ongoing debate over whether Islam has a negative impact or no impact on educational gender equality is one of the main drivers of this book.

Several religions, such as Islam, Christianity, and Judaism, are historically well known for their patriarchal structure and their belief that females are inferior to males. Guiso et al. (2003) used the World Value Survey (WVS) and found that "all religious denominations are associated with a more conservative attitude toward women. However, the effect is much stronger for Muslims."[6] The statistical results support the idea that religion could discourage societies from investing in female education and encourage religious societies to invest in education for males instead. Several scholars, such as David Dollar and Roberta Gatti (1999), Seth W. Norton and Annette Tomal (2009), and Arusha Cooray and Niklas Potrafke (2011), argue that women in Muslim countries do not go to school as much as women in other countries, or even males in Muslim countries, because of religion and culture. Dollar and Gatti (1999) use a panel-data analysis of 400[7] observations for 127 countries over five years. They control for region and GDP per capita, and find that low female attainment at secondary level is weakly associated with Islam and Hinduism.

Norton and Tomal (2009), in a cross-sectional study of 97 countries, also find a negative association between female educational attainment and Muslim countries.[8] They control for British colonial history, tropical climates, urbanization, young adult mortality, and female labor-force participation. They find a significant effect in some of their models for British colonial status and mortality, but a positive effect, although not statistically significant, for urbanization.[9] They declare that it is not clear why Muslim countries have negative female educational attainment, but they suggest that further analysis should examine the link between religion, institutions, and human capital,[10] which is also one of the purposes of this book.

Other scholars, such as Mandana Hajja and Ugo Panizza (2009) and Shawn Dorius and Glenn Firebaugh (2010), find no relationship between religion, particularly Islam, and gender inequality in education. Hajja and Panizza (2009) use local data from the 1996 Lebanese Population and Housing Survey (PHS), which covers 61,580 households and 290,000 individuals, and find that, "other things equal, girls (both Muslim and Christian) tend to receive more education than boys and that there is no difference between the education gender gap of Muslims and Christians."[11] Dorius and Firebaugh (2010) examine the trend in key indicators of gender inequality—education, mortality, political representation, and economic activity—in Buddhist, Chinese Universalist, Christian, Hindu, and Muslim societies. They find that "gender inequality is declining across diverse religious and cultural traditions," but that "women's relative progress generally has been slowest in Buddhist, not Muslim, societies."[12]

It is clear from this brief literature review that most of the current literature accuses Muslim countries of having a higher educational gender gap than other countries with different religions. The limitation of females' schooling and professional development in some Muslim countries over time could be the reason for some scholars finding that Muslim countries have high gender inequality in education. Scholars such as Dollar and Gatti (1999), Forsythe et al. (2000), Norton and Tomal (2009), and Cooray and Potrafke (2011) have tested the association between religion and gender inequality in education. They have correlated societies' major religions with female education using the datasets of Barro and Lee (2013) or the World Bank. They find that, compared to other religions, Muslim societies are associated with higher gender inequality in education. Such results indicate that the majority of Muslim societies discourage the education of females or favor the education of males over females. The common problem with this approach is that none of the scholars who conclude that religion is the reason behind gender inequality in Muslim countries differentiates between religiously conservative and liberal Muslim countries. The variation in the level of religious conservativeness is usually due to governments' weak/strong enforcement of religious values or to different interpretations of the Holy Qur'an and *Hadiths*. In general, as I mentioned in the previous chapter, there is nothing in the Holy Qur'an or *Hadiths* that directly restricts females from obtaining education, so this debate over educational gender inequality in Muslim countries cannot be explained by referring to a particular statement in the Holy Qur'an. In fact, the Qur'an and *Hadiths* are sometimes used by supporters of gender equality to enhance their beliefs and defend their position.

For instance, it is stated in the Holy Qur'an that men and women are equal in humanity—"O mankind! Be dutiful to your Lord, Who created you from a single person (Adam)"[13]—and equal in all religious duties and rewards—"whoever works righteousness, whether male or female, while he (or she) is a true believer verily, to him We will give a good life, and We shall pay them certainly a reward in proportion to the best of what they used to do (i.e. Paradise in the Hereafter)."[14] The Holy Qur'an also encourages both genders to seek education—"And say: "[M]y Lord! Increase me in knowledge"[15]—and the Prophet Mohammed said, "every Muslim male and female, is requested to seek for knowledge." He also said, "he who has a daughter and who teaches her good manners and improves her education and then manumits and marries her, will get a double reward."[16]

However, many male conservative religious Muslim scholars interpret the Holy Qur'an and *Hadiths* based on their values, and in a way that puts restrictions on females' movement and social role. These scholars argue that in the Holy Qur'an, God instructed females to stay at home and not to mingle with men: "and stay in your houses. Bedizen not yourselves with the bedizenment of the Time of Ignorance."[17] Hassan (1999) mentions:

> Muslims, in general, tend to believe that it is best to keep men and women segregated—in their separate, designated spaces. The intrusion of women into men's space is seen as leading to the disruption, if not the destruction, of the fundamental order of things. If some exigency makes it necessary for women to enter into men's space, they must make themselves "faceless," or at least as inconspicuous as possible. This is achieved through "veiling," which is, thus, an extension of the idea of the segregation of the sexes.[18]

Such an interpretation encourages females to stay at home and reduces the incentive to send girls to school or into the work force. In addition, women in Muslim countries are well known for their dependence on men. This is because some religious scholars refer to this statement in the Holy Qur'an: "and they (women) have rights similar to those (of them) over them in kindness, and men are above them."[19] So for centuries, women in Muslim countries such as Saudi Arabia have been required by law, and in other countries such as Yemen by custom, not to leave the house without permission from their family, and they must be accompanied by a male relative if they want to go anywhere in public.

A male relative is an important companion for females because of the presumed need for protection from foreign males, with whom a female, by her religion, is not supposed to have any communication. A female could be denied her right to go to school, if the school is far from home and no male relative is available to accompany her. She can also be denied her right to go to school if the only local school is coeducational, or if no female teachers are available. The order of segregation was inferred from this statement in the Holy Qur'an:

> [S]ay to the believing women that they should not display their beauty and ornament except what must ordinarily appear thereof; that they should draw their veils over their bosom and not display their beauty, except to their husbands, their father, husbands' fathers, sons, their husbands' sons, their brother's sons or sister's sons, their women, their slaves or male attendants who lack vigor, or children who know naught of women's nakedness. And let them not stamp their feet so as to reveal what they hide of their adornment.[20]

This condition of male accompaniment limits the ability of women to move freely, which is necessary for attaining an education and, in turn, a successful career.

Another reason that could reduce the incentive to send girls to school in Muslim countries is the restriction of females' future careers. In most Muslim religious countries, such as Saudi Arabia, Yemen, Iran, and Afghanistan, it is acceptable, by law and custom, for a woman to be a teacher or a doctor, but not a judge, a politician, an engineer, or a soldier. These jobs are sometimes officially not open to females, or women do not consider them as a future career because of social pressure. These restrictions came from the interpretation of a *Hadith* claimed to be said by the Prophet Mohammed: "never will succeed such a nation as lets their affairs carried out by a woman."[21] For example, at present, Saudi Arabia and Iran officially do not allow women to become judges. In Yemen, although there is no *legal* restriction on a female's social activities with males, *socially* a female is not allowed to interact with males, so she cannot be a businesswoman, unless she will only have contact with women. If she decides to break this social rule, then she will have to expect harassment. The limitations imposed on a woman's future career could make her more enthusiastic about getting married, rather than going to school and preparing herself for the work force. All these restrictions have a religious foundation based on the interpretation of some Muslim religious scholars.

However, if Islam is the cause of educational discrimination, then we must assume that the majority of Muslim people and countries practice and enforce Islamic law, Sharia. In reality, someone who is a Muslim or a Christian or anything else is not necessarily a *devoted* Muslim or Christian. Also, not all Muslim countries enforce Islamic law. In fact, there are countries with a high Muslim population that do not emphasize the use of Islamic law in their legislation, such as Jordan and Algeria. There are also countries where a high percentage of the population is Muslim that do not even identify themselves as Muslim countries, such as Turkey. Even if Islam has an impact on gender equality in education, then the variation of countries' commitment to Islamic law should lead to a variation in the impact of Islam on gender equality in education.

The probability of the negative impact of Islam on educational gender equality, to a certain degree, should also apply to other religions as well. In almost all religions, education was formerly perceived as a major means of secularization, emancipation, and social mobility; thus, it was limited to men. Education was restricted to men on purpose, because men did not want to jeopardize the social order. However, currently education is accessible to many women and the social order has changed toward more gender egalitarianism. Yet, like Islam, major religions such as Christianity, Judaism, and Buddhism still have some sort of inherent gender discrimination that is not directly linked to education, but could lower women's incentive to obtain education. For example, one of the main features of education in the religious Zionist school system in the twenty-first century is "the allocation of woman to the domestic sphere while excluding her from the public arena." El Or (1998) states that in the traditional Jewish culture, knowledge and study were limited to males and anyone "teaches his daughter sacred lore was said to be 'teaching her folly.'"[22] At present:

most little girls in Jewish kindergartens still continue to assume the traditional feminine role of lighting the candles to welcome the Sabbath, while their brothers take on the ritual task of reciting the blessing over the wine. Post high-school male and female students still pursue traditionalist Torah learning in separate study halls, despite the fact that they routinely meet each other in co-ed university classes. Orthodox synagogues still insist upon conducting prayers with a *mehitza* (a physical divider between men and women), although many of their members no longer regard the very sight of women as a serious erotic distraction.[23]

Additionally, the "representation of women in the public sphere has been low relative to their level of education and their evident intellectual and organizational capacities. Their representation in the Knesset (the Israeli parliament), in the different political parties, in the municipal arena, in the universities, and in the business world remains relatively small. This gap is undoubtedly a form of silencing and reflects the discrimination against women in Israel."[24] Education in Christianity too used to be limited to males, but recently women have begun to penetrate this previously male world. Currently, Christianity does not have restrictions on public movement for women, like in Islam; nevertheless, according to the Bible females have to obey males, particularly their husbands, which means that a man has the right not to allow his female relative (wife or daughter) to go to school or work.[25] As in Islam, women are still excluded from top leadership positions. For instance, in Roman Catholicism a female is still not allowed to become a priest, and in Orthodox Judaism she cannot become a rabbi. The Church of England did not allow women to serve as priests until 1999, and only in 2008 were women accepted as bishops. In 1972, women started to serve as rabbis in Reform Jewish congregations; not until 1999 were Orthodox Jewish women allowed to become *halakhic* consultants, a leadership position in the religious community. In Hinduism, a women is not widely accepted to become a *guru*.[26] In Buddhism, only men are allowed to be priests, with nuns being subordinate to both priests and monks. A high level of commitment to any of these religions could weaken female empowerment and have an impact on females' ability and incentives to go to school or join the labor force. However, unlike the majority of Muslim countries, the variation of the commitment to religion is limited to the individual level, and religious roles are not enforced by Western secular governments. This means that individuals in a liberal country can choose whether or not to be committed to their beliefs, and the rules that religions impose on committed religious people with regard to recognizing the difference between males and females are not necessarily sponsored or adopted by governments. Women in most non-Muslim countries have no restriction on participating in any non-religious field of work, and by law females and males have equal rights. The separation between a religion's and a government's institutions, which seems to mitigate the negative influence of religion, is called secularism.

The conflict between the secular and the sacred is not new: it started in the ancient world. In the West, it could be traced to over two millennia ago, when the state was the only religion and other thoughts were considered philosophy. Philosophers, who used to be atheists, were condemned for questioning polytheism and challenging the polis (city-state), not the church, since there was no church at that time.[27] However, the conflict became more intense with the appearance of Christianity. The conflict between religious and political institutions caused the majority of Western wars. The European wars of religion came to an end when Western countries signed the Westphalia agreement in 1648. The purpose of the agreement was to ensure peace not just among religious and non-religious institutions, but also between the different religious institutions in Western countries. The agreement had indeed created peace, but did not end the conflict between the secular and sacred, since each Western country has its own interpretation of secularism that matches the country's social, political, and religious history. Some countries have seen secularism as freedom of religion and religion-free politics. This means that religious institutions cannot directly get involved in politics, and people can be as committed to their religion as they want as long as they are not hurting others. Such an approach can be found, to a certain extent, in the United States and Canada, and in Germany, Sweden, and many other European countries. However, there are countries that have interpreted secularism in a stricter way, such as France, the Soviet Union, and some Asian countries. They lean more toward banning religious education and/or practice. Generally, Westphalia ended the violent conflict, but the peaceful political-social conflict still exists today. Western countries still struggle with some of their citizens' embedded religious beliefs, which can be seen in the conflicts over, for example, women's rights, gay rights, and the appropriate public dress code.

The situation in the Middle East was different. The conflict between secular and sacred was not as clear as it was in the West, because Israel was a theocratic state. There was a conflict between prophets, such as Isaiah and Jeremiah and the rulers of ancient Israel, but there was no clear separation between these two powers as there was in Europe. The fight between the different religions in the Middle East and the different sects within religions has been escalating over the years and has become more persistent. Most Middle Eastern countries still struggle with the heavy control or involvement of religious institutions in politics and people's familial and social lives. These countries have failed to create secular countries where "religion and politics ought to be separated—and be protected against one another in order to ensure freedom of religion as well as religion-free politics."[28] Several Muslim countries have tried to follow the steps taken in the West, but they all ended up with a different doctrine for how secular and religious society ought to be.

Currently, religious conflicts in the world can by categorized into three types in relation to religion: "the secular state fears religious politics; religio-political movements fears the secular state; and religion fears religion."[29] The first type can be found in Western countries, since they are secular, but some religious people still try to challenge the system by working within it, such as using democracy to pass or block policies they are against or in favor of. Some religious people also work outside the system through creating or joining terrorist groups. The second type— where religio-political movements fear the secular state—can be found in religious states, such as most of the countries in the West of Asia, and particularly Middle Eastern countries. These countries are struggling with maintaining the society's religious identity and coping with modernization. The last type can be found in both worlds—Eastern and Western— and it represents the conflict between religions, such as the conflict between the different Islamic terrorist groups and the West, or the battle between Sunni and Shia. All these conflicts put pressure on the establishment of a fully implemented secular or religious state. This pressure affects the level of implementation of secular or religious rules, and the variation is also affected by countries' path dependency.[30] Therefore, one of the major mistakes that scholars who advocate for religious theory are making is investigating only the relationship between gender inequalities in education and major religions. They do not account for the level of religious commitment and the impact of variation in religious commitment on females' education.

Measuring an individual's and a country's level of religiosity is difficult. As I have shown before, several scholars attempt to measure the individual's level of religiosity by doing a survey asking people questions about their religious beliefs and their commitment to religious instructions. This approach is suitable for some research questions, but not for this study. This study argues that governments have strong power over citizens, which applies to both democratic and autocratic regimes. In fact, non-democratic governments could have more power over their citizens than democratic governments. The government's preference can be imposed on society more easily than when citizens are trying to impose their preference on their government. Individuals' level of religiosity could matter if the demands for policies that support their preference increase, but this process is slow and depends on the type of political regime in place. For example, in democratic countries it takes a few years to establish or change policies depending on the timing of the election, but in non-democratic countries it may take decades to establish or change laws. The change usually occurs after a revolution, coup d'état, or the death of a king. Therefore, if the state believes in gender equality, it is likely to adopt policies that could help improve gender equality. This approach is called "top-down" policy initiatives. Governments that believe in gender equality are more likely to run ahead of public opinion and introduce policies that could support improving gender equality. An example is the introduction of gender quotas to get women into parliament by many communist regimes, even Muslim countries such as Afghanistan, Iraq, Jordan, Algeria, and Morocco.[31]

Therefore, in this book I focus on the status of religion as stated in each country's constitution, to test whether the high/low involvement of religion in government affects educational gender equality. A constitution is a suitable measurement of a country's religiosity because it is "a written or generally agreed body of law, equally applied to all adult members of society. Furthermore, it reflects the cultural values and civilizational goals of its citizens, establishing both the boundaries of the state's role in society as well as the scope of action of the various institutional organs of the state."[32] Constitutions are used in this study because they represent a society's values and its political/institutional culture. If the state indicates in its constitution that it is secular, then it will operate based on that principle. Also, if the constitution indicates that the state follows a particular religion and it implements a certain law, then the political institution's actions will be grounded in that principle. The constitutional religious status should be able to measure the government's level of commitment to religion. In order for a religion to have an impact on people's lives, people have to practice the religion. When a country has a constitution that emphasizes the importance of using a particular religion as the main source of legislation, it is likely that the country is more committed to its religion's instructions, in contrast to a country or state that does not associate itself with a specific religion, or a state or country that identifies itself as secular. In turn, if the state's level of commitment to religion is associated with educational gender inequality in Muslim religious states, such states, such as Iran and Saudi Arabia, should have high gender inequality in education, when compared to Muslim religiously liberal and secular countries, such as Tunisia and Turkey. Also, if religious states educate fewer females than males, non-Muslim religious states, such as Malta and Thailand, also should have fewer females than males in school, when compared to states with no particular religion or secular countries such as the Netherlands or China.

However, some scholars may debate the use of countries' constitutions as a measure of the level of religious conservativeness, because the implementation of the constitution could be weak. Roger Myerson (2008) states that "constitutional rules are enforced by actions of political leaders and government officials, who must be motivated by an expectation of rewards and privileges as long as they fulfill their constitutional responsibilities."[33] This indicates that if politicians do not expect a reward from improving gender equality in education, they may not support it. This could be true; however, it gives more reason to use the constitution as a measure of the country's level of conservativeness. If Myerson's conclusion is correct, scholars in religiously conservative countries, such as Iran, Saudi Arabia, and Yemen, should advocate more for females' traditional social roles than those in less religiously conservative countries. In religiously conservative countries, politicians, who discuss and recommend policies, are likely to target religious interest groups and their supporters, since those are the ones that can punish or reward them. In contrast, religious interest groups are not the main constituencies of political leaders in less conservative countries; therefore, politicians would not see a reward for advocating the traditional social role of women. Politicians in less religious countries are more likely to promote gender equality in general, and in education in particular, since liberal states are usually built based on the concept of gender equality. Therefore, the constitution is still a good measure of a country's level of religiosity, even under the assumption of the weakness of some constitutions.

In summary, tracking the real reason behind gender inequality in education could inform better policy-making. It would help with the choice of the right policies to improve female education, which has a positive impact on the economy. However, scholars who study the impact of religion on gender equality in education do not seem to agree on whether religion affects educational gender equality or not. In addition, scholars who have found a result that supports religious theory[34] do not seem to agree on which religions have the most negative effect on gender equality in education, although most of them found supportive results against Islam. These conflicting results among the advocates of religious theory could be due to the lack of differentiation between the levels of countries' religious conservativeness and to a lack of consideration of modernization factors. Being able to differentiate between Muslim countries, such as Turkey and Iran, or Tunisia and Saudi Arabia, should make a difference in the results. This is important, because if Islam is the single factor that leads to gender inequality in Muslim countries, then why does gender equality in education vary from one Muslim country to another? It would be important to answer why, for example, total school enrollment in Yemen in 2010 was 45.21 percent, while in Turkey it was 82.35 percent, and in Iran it was 96.32 percent. Lerner (1958) argues that modernization is the answer. Several scholars who are interested in religious theory and who found a relationship between gender equality in education and GDP per capita, urbanization, and the fertility rate did not attempt to create an association between these variables and modernization theory. Thus, in this book I study modernization and the different level of states' religiosity as the two main factors that could explain most of the variation in gender inequality in education.

Modernization Theory

Following the above argument, there are many scholars who study the relationship between gender equality, religion, and modernization. Modernization theorists can be divided into two groups: Marxists and capitalists. Marxist scholars believe in adopting the communist way of governing in order to achieve economic and cultural change. Such a change is needed to achieve modernization. This approach promotes governments' direct involvement in changing the economic structure of the country and the religious beliefs of society. The Marxist approach inspired advocates of secularism. The other group of modernization theorists argues that economic growth can change culture and lead to modernization. Economic growth can occur in many ways, such as by an increase in urbanization, entrepreneurial activities, or even a natural resource revolution. Since the

Marxist approach has failed through the failure of the communist model, this book concentrates on the capitalist approach.

The capitalist model of modernization became popular during the late 1950s and early 1960s. The leading scholars in this theory are Daniel Lerner (1958), Seymour Martin Lipset (1959), Walt Rostow (1960), and Karl Deutsch (1964). Current scholars who study the capitalist model of modernization include Inglehart (1977, 1990, 1997, 2003). In their book *Rising Tide: Gender Equality and Cultural Change around the World*, Inglehart and Norris (2003) extensively study the impact of modernization on cultural change. They argue that cultural change is an interactive process, in which human development and societal modernization lead to a shift in values and attitudes. They find that modernization leads to secularization and the decline of religious beliefs.[35] They propose that "the process of secularization has gradually accompanied societal modernization, weakening the strength of religious values in postindustrial societies, particularly among the youngest generation and fueling the rising tide of gender equality."[36] However, they argue that not all societies change by modernization. They state that the level of cultural change can vary from one culture to another, depending on the "cultural legacy and institutional structure of any given society, as exemplified by the role of an Islamic heritage in the Middle East, the legacy of Communism in Central Europe, and the egalitarian transition in Scandinavia."[37] They maintain that "despite the roles of human development, attitudes toward gender equality were still found to vary even among societies at similar levels of human development, according to factors such as religious traditions."[38] They claim that changes due to modernization are less visible in religiously conservative countries such as Saudi Arabia and Yemen, and therefore views on gender roles and equality remain almost the same. They explain that "societies whose people live with high levels of insecurity tend to develop cultures mistrustful of rapid changes, emphasizing the values of traditional authority and strong leadership, inherited social status, and communal ties and obligations, backed up by social sanctions and norms derived from religious authorities."[39] Inglehart and Norris's (2003) book seems to be an extension of Lerner's (1958) study; however, their results contradict Lerner's findings, since they established that Muslim countries are resistant to change.

Lerner's (1958) study focuses on seven Muslim countries, on which he finds that modernization has a positive effect, while Inglehart and Norris's (2003) study seems to be a test and extension of Lerner's modernization theory. Inglehart and Norris (2003) study 70 nations with different religions and find that modernization changes culture, but that certain cultures such as Islamic cultures are resistant to change. The difference in their conclusions could be due to differences in the study sample, time period, and statistical method. Lerner's (1958) study concentrated on the impact of modernization on seven Muslim countries using a survey that was done in 1950. Inglehart and Norris's (2003) study examines the effect of modernization on changing cultures using data collected for 70 nations from 1980 to 2000. Moreover, the number of Muslim countries in Lerner's (1958) study was bigger than the number of Muslim countries in Inglehart and Norris's (2003) study. In this book, I focus on Lerner's (1958) study, because he was the first scholar to test modernization theory on Muslim societies, and because he is one of the few scholars who have found empirical evidence of the positive effect of modernization on Muslim societies.

This book examines whether a country's tendency toward less traditional, religious, and patriarchal values, such as favoring male education more than female education, is due to moving from being very religiously conservative to being more liberal or secular, and/or because the country is becoming more modernized. There are several definitions of modernization; for the purpose of this study, Lerner's (1958) definition is used. In his book *The Passing of Traditional Society*, Lerner (1958) defines modernization as "the social process of which development is the economic component."[40] He uses 1600 interviews that were conducted in 1950 in seven Muslim countries (Turkey, Lebanon, Jordan, Egypt, Syria, and Iran) to argue that even "Islam is absolutely defenseless" against modernization.[41] He believes that all countries will eventually become modernized after passing through the three phases of urbanization, literacy, and media participation.[42][43]

Lerner (1958) argues that Western modernization went through several historical phases until it reached its current position. He believed that Middle Eastern countries or Muslim countries are no different from Western countries; they are merely still going through the historical sequences through which most Western countries have already passed. He argues that eventually Muslim nations will reach the point at which they realize that they have to give up their old, traditional ways of living and thinking, because these no longer satisfy the new needs.[44] He claims that social change, brought about by great historical events, will change individuals' daily lifestyles and bring modernization to the Middle East, as it did in the Western world. He suggests that it is a historical fact that Western modernization started with increases in urbanization that raised literacy and then media exposure, which was accompanied by wider economic and political participation.[45]

Based on Lerner's modernization theory (1958), urbanization is a necessary condition to start modernization and stimulate education. He assumes that a person who moves from his/her hometown to somewhere else out of personal choice is seeking a better life. However, this physical mobility requires new skills and a higher level of merit. Unlike the traditional person, who still lives in a small town, accepts everything as it is, and rejects innovation, a mobile person "comes equipped with mechanisms needed to incorporate new demands upon himself that rise outside his habitual experience."[46] Therefore, mobile people demand to gain from their mobility and the system responds to the demand, so more schools open to help improve people's skills, banks open to secure people's wealth, and legal and police regimes form to maintain order in the neighborhood. A mobile person is more willing to be tenacious and learn from others and become like them; Lerner uses the psychoanalytic term "empathy" to describe this behavior.[47]

Empathy is the ability to see oneself in another person's situation. Empathy is a skill that a mobile person has to have in order to be able to adjust to his or her new environment. She or he needs to get to know new people, learn how to socialize with them, and understand them and their roles and rules. Therefore, a person in an urban area has to go to school in order to be able to read the newspaper, understand news on the radio, and have common interests to share with others. So, social mobility leads to social change. However, empathy is only one component of modern societies, because, unlike a person in a modern society, a person in a traditional society (a village) does not need to learn much to survive. The lifestyle in a traditional society does not demand much knowledge or skills, since a person grows up knowing all the living people, their roles, and the rules in the surrounding environment. The familiarity with people and rules in a traditional society does not force a person to seek education in order to be able to give an opinion on public issues or matters that are not his/her personal business. People in a participating society are expected to have opinions and they expect their opinions to matter. Lerner (1958) finds high correlations between urbanization and literacy, and suggests that literacy may be a supply-and-demand reciprocal that can only occur in urban locations.[48]

Besides the social pressure that demands that an urbanized person gain an education, career pressure also requires education and skills different from those needed in rural areas. Boserup Ester (1970) argues that migrating families who decide to give up farming to move to a town to find work other than agriculture are faced with a change not just in occupation, but also in their way of life. They have to deal with the higher cost of living that comes from replacing subsistence agriculture with store-bought food, for example. However, buying the basic products that the family used to produce could leave no money for purchasing the goods and services the family had hoped to obtain in the town.[49] Economic interdependence forces a person to become a specialist, in order to be able to contribute in such an interdependent and economically competitive environment. Yet life in an urban environment requires more than agricultural skills, thus both men and women will try to acquire new skills. Ester argues that the first generation of migrant families may find themselves working in low-skilled jobs. Moving to a town would force people to move from working in agriculture to working in a bazaar or the service sector, while modern jobs will be limited to those who have acquired a decent level of education.[50] However, as Lerner (1958) already identified, just moving to a city in and of itself requires some level of literacy, in order to be able to read labels, sign checks, and ride public transportation. The demand for literate people in the city encourages migrants at least to learn to read and write and join a training school. The second generation of migrants is more likely to go to school than children in villages, who are not faced with the same future career challenges.

Lerner stresses the importance of urbanization as the main driver of modernization. However, there are several problems with his assumptions. First, scholars who study the impact of urbanization argue that urbanization could hinder development if the government is not able to respond to people's demands for many basic services. Such a problem occurs in countries that have high population density and low economic growth,[51] which applies to the majority of Muslim countries. The government might not be able to provide enough schools and the good-quality education that are needed for modernization. Also, Lerner assumes that urbanization has the same impact on both genders. Yet in practice, females may not be able to benefit from urbanization if culture restricts their movement and social role, or if women "willingly adhere to the traditional division of sex roles in the home, family, and workplace."[52] If a woman's social role is limited to marriage and having children, she might not be able to move to an urban area without her family. She would have to move with her family or husband, and the priority for education would be for the male, since the male would be considered the family breadwinner.[53] In addition, the woman would not need to be able to read, as her mobility would be restricted by having a male companion, who could likely read. Females in traditional societies are forced to depend on their male relatives for everything outside of the home. Females are not expected to work, and getting an education becomes a luxury, not a necessity. Furthermore, a female's social communication in these societies is usually limited to females from the same social class, who are not educated and living a simple life; thus, keeping up with up-to-date news is not a necessity.

Women in traditional societies are expected to get married at an early age, and married women are likely to have children, further restricting their mobility.[54] The more children a woman has, the more likely she is not to have the chance to study and/or work outside her home. Children could also reduce a family's ability to be mobile and lower its standard of living. So the more children the family has, the less likely the girls are to go to school. However, if a woman is not married and does not have children, then she has a good chance of benefiting from urbanization and the services that are provided for citizens in urban areas. Also, having a high rate of urbanization and a low rate of fertility could increase a woman's incentive to spend her leisure time improving her skills and standard of living. A decrease in the fertility rate also helps governments provide enough services to people, and it helps people pursue their goals with less of a burden. Therefore, a declining fertility rate, although not mentioned by Lerner (1958), is a very important sign of modernity.

Scholars have already confirmed the positive relationship between fertility and education.[55] Developed countries, such as those in Europe, are associated with low fertility rates, while developing countries, such as those in the Middle East and Africa, are associated with high fertility rates. In developing countries, particularly Muslim countries, females still get married and have children at an early age. Because of low incomes and the rare availability of childcare, mothers have to stay at home with their children until the children go to school. By the time the first child begins education, the mother may have a second, and going back to school becomes very unlikely for her. Therefore, the lower the fertility rate, the less gender inequality exists in education.

In Chap. 3, I test Lerner's modernization theory (1958) using urbanization while controlling for the fertility rate. The test shows that the association between urbanization and educational gender equality is strong in non-Muslim countries, but weak in Muslim countries. Since I am controlling for the fertility rate, readers will be able to see that the effect of a decrease in fertility is bigger and more significant on educational gender equality than the effect of an increase in urbanization. This result applies to both Muslim and non-Muslim countries. However, omitting urbanization from the models and using only the fertility rate reduces the overall fit. In addition, urbanization cannot be deleted, because the correlation between urbanization and the decrease in the fertility rate is only 59, which is considered moderate. Thus, including urbanization in any model used to study the effect of modernization is still essential. The result illustrates that, depending on the research, for an independent variable that represents modernization the fertility rate is better than urbanization, which still should be used as a control variable. The fertility rate seems to work better as an indicator of modernization in this study because the variable is more relevant to gender equality studies, and it accounts for both social and economic changes in societies.

Conclusion

This chapter briefly covers the literature on the religious and modernization theories. Religious theorists argue that religion has a strong influence on governmental institutions and societies. Some scholars maintain that all religions are the enemy of modernization, and that the solution is in secularizing societies. Other religious theorists claim that the impact of modernization on gender equality varies depending on the religion's values, and that the solution is in adopting Western culture. On the other hand, modernization theorists argue that a country does not need to go to the extreme of secularizing society or adopting Western culture to achieve gender equality. They maintain that modernization can defeat the influence of religion on people. Urbanization, which is the main driver of modernization, forces religious societies to change because modernized life brings with it different values and cultures. Those values conflict with the values in traditional, and often religious, societies. Urban people have to educate themselves and to learn how to rationalize. They are individualists and materialists, and they build a small family so they can handle the cost of living. However, some modernization theorists believe that modernization can change a culture, but not all cultures. They claim that some cultures such as the Muslim culture are resistant to change, and that modernization does not influence Muslim societies' cultural values.

This chapter shows that there are two problems that need to be investigated. The first is to understand whether religion affects gender equality in education, which can be done by adding a variable that differentiates the level of conservativeness within each religion. The second issue is whether any effect of the level of religious conservativeness will disappear once urbanization interacts with a Muslim country. Based on modernization theory, urbanization is the main element that stimulates education regardless of a country's religion, so the impact of religion on education should be reduced or non-existent in urban societies. If fertility rate is a better indicator of modernization, the same result should apply, but with a higher effect. The decrease in the fertility rate should indicate a higher increase in female education than urbanization in both traditional and modern societies.

This book is different from those of previous scholars in several respects. First, this study concentrates on the impact of modernization and religion on educational gender equality. Thus, it is more focused on education than on any other aspect of gender equality. This is different from previous studies, because education was only a small part of those studies. Also, unlike Lerner (1958), this study is not limited to Muslim countries; it has been expanded to 26 non-Muslim countries as well. It also includes 29 Muslim countries, which is the biggest sample that has been used for such a study. In addition, I cover a longer time period, from 1960 to 2010, which allows us to see the impact of modernization and the change in culture better than previous studies. Finally, unlike previous studies, this study attempts to differentiate between the levels of conservativeness within each religion. Such an attempt has not been tried by the other two scholars.

In the next chapter, I introduce the variables I use to analyze religious theory and modernization theory in relation to educational gender equality, and provide a justification for using these variables in the statistical models. I also explain the method I use to categorize the level of governments' religious conservativeness and the panel-corrected standard error method that is employed in order to analyze 55 Muslim and non-Muslim countries from 1960 to 2010.

Notes

1. Allan, Kenneth D. (2005, 2 November). *Explorations in Classical Sociological Theory: Seeing the Social World*. Pine Forge Press, p. 153.
2. Weber, Max. *The Protestant Ethic and "The Spirit of Capitalism"* (1905). Transl. by Stephen Kalberg (2002), Roxbury, pp. 19, 35.

3. Reinhard Bendix (1977). Max Weber: an intellectual portrait. University of California Press. p. 90. ISBN 978-0-520-03194-4. Retrieved 5 April 2011.
4. Inglehart and Baker (2000: 22).
5. Inglehart and Norris (2003: 59).
6. Guiso et al. (2003: 228).
7. They ended up with 400 observations because they had some missing data.
8. Norton and Tomal (2009: 901).
9. Norton and Tomal (2009: 974).
10. Norton and Tomal (2009: 981).
11. Hajj and Panizza 2009: 337).
12. Dorius and Firebaugh (2010: 2 and 18).
13. *Qur'an*, Al Nisaa (4: 1).
14. *Qur'an*, Al Nahl (16: 97).
15. *Qur'an*, Taha (20: 114).
16. Hadith, Abu Musa al-Ashari (733).
17. *Qur'an* Al-Ahzab (33: 33).
18. Hassan (1999: 252).
19. *Qur'an* Al-Baqra (2: 228).
20. *Qur'an* an-Nur (24: 31).
21. Bukhari, Maghazi (82), Fitan (18), Tirmidhi, Fitan (75), Nasai, Qudat (8), Ahmad b. Hanbal (V, 43, 51, 38, 47).
22. Gross (2012: 96).
23. Ross (2012: 9).
24. Gross (2012: 96).
25. Genesis (3: 16) and Ephesians (5: 22–24).
26. Redfern and Aune (2010: 159).
27. Kennedy (2000: 31).
28. Wæver (2008: 210).
29. Wæver (2008: 211).
30. It refers to the country's history, which could have an influence on the present and the future.
31. Inglehart and Norris (2003: 163).
32. Kleidosty (2016: 8).
33. Myerson (2008: 135).
34. There is no specific theory named religious theory, but I will refer to studies that focus on the relationship between education and religion as religious theory.
35. Inglehart and Norris (2003: 58).
36. Inglehart and Norris (2003: 3).
37. Inglehart and Norris (2003: 9).
38. Inglehart and Norris (2003: 48).

39. Inglehart and Norris (2003: 16).
40. Lerner (1958: 21).
41. Lerner (1958: 45).
42. Media participation is a stage where a person will seek information through the media that will help him/her handle the new experience caused by leaving his/her town.
43. Lerner (1958: 61–62).
44. Lerner (1958: 44).
45. Lerner (1958: 46).
46. Lerner (1958: 49).
47. Lerner (1958: 48–49).
48. Lerner (1958: 60).
49. Ester (1970: 160).
50. Ester (1970: 179).
51. See, for example, Ehrlich (1968), Malthus (1798), and Bloom et al. (1999).
52. Inglegart and Norris (2003: 42).
53. Inglegart and Norris (2003: 68).
54. Inglehart and Norris (2003: 2).
55. See Holsinger and Kasarda (1976), Cochrane et al. (1979), Cochrane (1983), Graff (1979), Jain (1981), Cleland and Rodriguez (1988), Jejeebhoy and Rao (1992), Teresa Castro Marti (1995), and Ainsworth et al. (1996).

References

Ahadith. (2010–2017). Chapter No: 48, Book of Manumission of Slaves. Retrieved from http://ahadith.co.uk/chapter.php?cid=134&page=4

Ainsworth, M., Beegle, K., & Nyamete, A. (1996). The Impact of Women's Schooling on Fertility and Contraceptive Use: A Study of Fourteen Sub-Saharan African Countries. *The World Bank Economic Review, 10*(1), 85122.

Barro, R. J., & Lee, J. W. (2013). A New Data Set of Educational Attainment in the World, 1950–2010. *Journal of Development Economics, 104*, 184–198.

Becker, H. (1931). *Weber, Max. The Protestant Ethic and the Spirit of Capitalism* (T. Parsons, Trans., with a Foreword by R. H. Tawney, pp. xi, 297). New York: Charles Scribner's Sons, 1930. (The Actually Meterial Was Writen in 1904 and Some Scholar Wrote 1905).

Bell, D. (1973). *The Coming of the Industrial Society.* New York, NY: Basic Books.

Bloom, D. E., Canning, D., & Malaney, P. N. (1999). *Demographic Change and Economic Growth in Asia.* CID.

Cleland, J., & Rodriguez, G. (1988). The Effect of Parental Education on Marital Fertility in Developing Countries. *Population Studies, 42*(3), 419–442.

Cochrane, S. H. (1979). *Fertility and Education: What Do We Really Know?* Baltimore: Johns Hopkins University Press for the World Bank.

Cochrane, S. H. (1983). *Effects of Education and Urbanization on Fertility.*

Cochrane, S. H., Pandey, G. D., Pandey, J., Rice, F. J., Lanctot, C. A., Garcia-Devesa, C., et al. (1979). Fertility and Education: What Do We Really Know? *Pop Cen News Letter, 5*(4), 1–5.

Cooray, A., & Potrafke, N. (2011). Gender Inequality in Education: Political Institutions or Culture and Religion? *European Journal of Political Economy, 27*(2), 268–280.

Deutsch, K. W. (1964). Social Mobilization and Political Development. *American Political Science Review, 55*, 493–514.

Dollar, D., & Gatti, R. (1999). *Gender Inequality, Income, and Growth: Are Good Times Good for Women?* Development Research Group, The World Bank.

Dorius, S. F., & Firebaugh, G. (2010). Trends in Global Gender Inequality. *Social Forces, 88*(5), 1941–1968.

Durkheim, E. (1912). *The Elementary Forms of the Religious Life [1912].* London: Allen & Unwin.

Ehrlich, P. (1968). *The Population Bomb.* New York: Ballantine.

Ester, B. (1970). Women's Role in Economic Development. *American Journal of Agricultural Economics, 53*(3), 536–537.

Forsythe, N., Korzeniewicz, R. P., & Durrant, V. (2000). Gender Inequalities and Economic Growth: A Longitudinal Evaluation. *Economic Development and Cultural Change, 48*(3), 573–617.

Graff, H. J. (1979). *The Literacy Myth: Literacy and Social Structure in the Nineteenth-century City* (p. xix). New York: Academic Press.

Gross, Z., Davies, L., & Diab, A. K. (Eds.). (2012). *Gender, Religion and Education in a Chaotic Postmodern.* Springer Science & Business Media: World.

Guiso, L., Sapienza, P., & Zingales, L. (2003). People's Opium? Religion and Economic Attitudes. *Journal of Monetary Economics, 50*(1), 225–282.

Hajj, M., & Panizza, U. (2009). Religion and Education Gender Gap: Are Muslims Different? *Economics of Education Review, 28*(3), 337–344.

Hassan, R. (1999). Feminism in Islam. In A. Sharma & K. K. Young (Eds.), *Feminism and World Religions* (pp. 248–279). Albany, NY: State University of New York Press.

Holsinger, D. B., & Kasarda, J. D. (1976). Education and Human Fertility: Sociological Perspectives. In R. G. Ridker (Ed.), *Population and Development: The Search for Selective Interventions* (pp. 154–181). Baltimore: John Hopkins University Press.

Huntington, S. P. (1993). The Clash of Civilizations? *Foreign Affairs, 72*, 22–49.

Inglehart, R. (1977). *The Silent Revolution: Changing Values and Political Styles Among Western Publics.* Princeton, NJ: Princeton University Press.

Inglehart, R. (1990). *Culture Shift in Advanced Industrial Society*. Princeton, NJ: Princeton University Press.

Inglehart, R. (1997). *Modernization and Postmodernization: Cultural, Economic and Political Change in 43 Societies*. Princeton, NJ: Princeton University Press.

Inglehart, R., & Baker, W. E. (2000). Modernization, Cultural Change, and the Persistence of Traditional Values. *American Sociological Review*, 65, 19–51.

Inglehart, R., & Norris, P. (2003). *Rising Tide: Gender Equality and Cultural Change Around the World*. Cambridge University Press.

Jain, A. K. (1981). The Effect of Female Education on Fertility: A Simple Explanation. *Demography*, 18(4), 577–595.

Jejeebhoy, S. J., & Rao, S. R. (1992, January). Unsafe Motherhood: A Review of Reproductive Health in India. In *Workshop on Health and Development in India, National Council of Applied Economic Research and Harvard University Centre for Population and Development Studies* (pp. 2–4). New Delhi.

Kennedy, E. (2000). The Tangled History of Secularism. *Modern Age*, 42(1), 31. Retrieved from https://isistatic.org/journalarchive/ma/42_01/kennedy.pdf.

Kleidosty, J. (2016). *The Concert of Civilizations: The Common Roots of Western and Islamic Constitutionalism*. Routledge.

Lerner, D. (1958). *The Passing of Traditional Society: Modernizing the Middle East*. New York: The Free Press.

Lipset, S. M. (1959). Some Social Requisites of Democracy: Economic Development and Political Legitimacy. *American Political Science Review*, 53(1), 69–105.

Malthus T. R. (1798 [1986]). *An Essay on the Principle of Population*. London: W. Pickering.

Martin, T. C. (1995). Women's Education and Fertility: Results from 26 Demographic and Health Surveys. *Studies in Family Planning*, 26, 187–202.

Marx, K. (1859). Prólogo de la contribución a la crítica de la economía política. *Obras escogidas*, 1, 518.

Myerson, R. B. (2008). The Autocrat's Credibility Problem and Foundations of the Constitutional State. *American Political Science Review*, 102(1), 125–139.

Norton, S. W., & Tomal, A. (2009). Religion and Female Educational Attainment. *Journal of Money, Credit and Banking*, 41(5), 961–986.

Redfern, C., & Aune, K. (2010). *Reclaiming the F Word: The New Feminist Movement*. London: Zed.

Rostow, W. W. (1960). *The Process of Economic Growth*. No. HB199 R65 1960.

Wæver, O. (2008). World Conflict Over Religion. Secularism as a Flawed Solution. In *Constituting Communities* (pp. 208–235). London: Palgrave Macmillan.

CHAPTER 3

Research Design and Methodology

As noted previously, the current literature still debates whether Muslim countries are associated with a lower ratio of female-to-male school enrollments. Some scholars, such as Dollar and Gatti (1999), Forsythe, Korzeniewicz, and Durrant (2000), Norton and Tomal (2009), and Cooray and Potrafke (2011), find that Muslim countries are associated with high gender inequality in education in comparison with countries dominated by other religions such as Christianity. Other scholars, such as Ross (2008), Hajj and Panizza (2009), and Dorius and Firebaugh (2010), find no relationship between Muslim societies and the gender gap in education. These conflicting results could be due to the inability of these scholars to control for variation in countries' commitment to religion. Also, the difference in the countries sampled and the time period used in the empirical tests could lead to different results.

For example, Hajj and Panizza (2009) examined the difference between Muslim and Christian females' school enrollment in Lebanon and found no statistical difference. However, if he had done the same test in a more conservative country such as Egypt in the last few years, he might have found that Christian girls in Egypt go to school more than Muslim girls. Although both Lebanon and Egypt are popularly considered less traditional societies and less restricted by religion than Arabian Gulf countries, Lebanon is far less traditional and much less restricted by religion than Egypt. This book contributes to the literature by adding a measure of religious commitment

© The Author(s) 2018
S. A. Al-Kohlani, *Improving Educational Gender Equality in Religious Societies*, https://doi.org/10.1007/978-3-319-70536-1_3

to empirical analysis, and also by using a more relevant measure of modernization.

The other main problem that scholars experienced in their studies is that they used short-panel or cross-sectional data and assigned dummy variables for the major religions in each society in their sample to make the comparison between religions and female education. In contrast, this book uses panel data gathered over a 50-year period, which is more extensive than previous studies. In addition, in this examination all of the countries with a Muslim population above 45 percent are included and matched based on the total population size in accordance with a random sample of non-Muslim countries.

This matching is important, because it facilitates the comparison of Muslim countries to the same number of non-Muslim countries, which share a common characteristic with Muslim countries. Most Muslim countries, particularly Middle Eastern countries, have a very small population.[1] It would be unfair to compare countries with a population over 100 million, such the United States, India, and China, to countries that barely have 2 million people, such as Qatar, Bahrain, and Kuwait. Educating a small population is easier and less expensive than educating a large population. The technique of matching Muslim and non-Muslim countries renders their shared characteristics more discernable. Table 3.1 exhibits the matched Muslim and non-Muslim countries, with details on population size and the major religion in each country.[2]

The second difference between this study and those of other scholars is that, while other scholars compare Muslim countries as one group and other major religions as another group, this examination distinguishes between the level of governments' religious conservativeness within both Muslim and non-Muslim countries. Jonathan Fox's Religion and State Project Constitutions Dataset, 1990–2008, is used in order to differentiate between religiously conservative, less conservative, moderate liberal, liberal, and secular countries. Since Fox's data were available only from 1990 to 2008, additional data were collected in order to extend the constitution database up to 2010 and back to 1960. Using the status of religion in the countries' constitutions shows how involved religions are in countries' regulations and identity for both Muslim and non-Muslim governments.

The differentiation between conservative, less conservative, less liberal, liberal, and secular countries captures the differences between Muslim and non-Muslim countries and does so across these groups. If Muslim countries

Table 3.1 The list of countries in my sample

Muslim countries	Muslim population (1990 data)[a]	Average of total population from 1960 to 2010 (in thousands)[b]	Non-Muslim countries	Dominant religious populations (1990 data)	Average of total population from 1960 to 2010 (in thousands)
Afghanistan	99.8	16,488.22	Australia	67.3 CH	15,840.91
Albania	70	2682.85	Austria	80.4 CH	7715.74
Algeria	98.3	22,169.89	Benin	53.0 CH	4581.41
Bahrain	81.8	480.13	Cameroon	70.3 CH	11,000.72
Bangladesh	88.3	101,096.14	Ghana	74.9 CH	14,208.86
Egypt	93.2	49,912.20	Italy	83.3 CH	56,044.52
Gambia	87	897.48	Japan	57.0 UNAF, 36.2 BU	116,511.65
Indonesia	87.2	167,934.31	Netherlands	50.6 CH	14,445.29
Iran (Islamic Republic of)	99.6	48,882.89	Lao People's Democratic Republic	66.0 BU	4016.29
Jordan	96.8	3049.34	Mongolia	55.1 BU	1956.53
Kuwait	91.7	1430.42	Republic of Korea	46.4 UNAF, 29.4 CH, 22.9 BU	39,446.28
Malaysia	49	16,778.13	Thailand	93.2 BU	49,657.74
Maldives	99.9	204.43	Romania	99.0 CH	21,532.18
Mali	93.6	8074.63	Russian Federation	73.3 CH	139,390.21
Mauritania	99	1884.35	Barbados	95.2 CH	257.18
Morocco	99	21,896.40	Chile	89.4 CH	12,196.69
Niger	98.7	7884.38	Paraguay	96.9 CH	3885.02
Pakistan	97	108,699.59	Uruguay	57.9 CH	2994.07
Qatar	90.6	376.92	Malta	97.0 CH	356.86
Saudi Arabia	99	13,719.12	Sri Lanka	69.3 BU	15,801.47
Senegal	94	6891.23	Switzerland	81.3 CH	757
Sudan	72	24,058.80	Malawi	82.7 CH	8219.48
Syrian Arab Republic	87	4476.31	Uganda	86.7 CH	16,688.21
Tunisia	99	7314.44	Tanzani	61.4 CH	51,609.59
Turkey	98.3	51,609.59	Zambia	97.6 CH	7260.98
United Arab Emirates	87	1747.35	Papua New Guinea	99.0 CH	3482.21
Yemen	99	12,125.63			

(*continued*)

Table 3.1 (continued)

Muslim countries	Muslim population (1990 data)[a]	Average of total population from 1960 to 2010 (in thousands)[b]	Non-Muslim countries	Dominant religious populations (1990 data)	Average of total population from 1960 to 2010 (in thousands)
Sierra Leone	50	3597.22			
Iraq	96	16,176.02			

CH Christian, *BU* Buddhist, *UNAF* Unaffiliated

[a]The data for religious affiliation of the population was obtained from the Pew Research Religion & Public Life Project (2012). Religious Composition by Country, in Percentages. http://features.pewforum.org/grl/population-percentage.php#

[b]The data for total population was obtained from Alan Heston, Robert Summers, and Bettina Aten (2011), Penn World Table Version 7.0, Center for International Comparisons of Production, Income and Prices at the University of Pennsylvania. https://pwt.sas.upenn.edu/php_site/pwt70/pwt70_form.php

are not educating as many females as males because they are religiously conservative, then non-Muslim countries that are conservative should also have fewer females than males in school compared to Muslim and non-Muslim liberal or secular countries. As mentioned before, within all major religions there is some level of discrimination against females, and religious discrimination against females can decrease the incentive to send girls to school. These restrictions are not limited to Muslim societies; as discussed in Chaps. 1 and 2, it is a problem that all religiously conservative societies have, but with some difference in scope.

The last reason this book is different from previous studies is that it examines the impact of modernization factors on educational gender equality in conservative countries. If religiously conservative governments educate fewer females than males, then could modernization lower the negative impact of religion? In traditional societies, women's roles are limited; modernization reduces these limits. Previous studies (e.g., Dollar and Gatti 1999; Norton and Tomal 2009) looked at the effect of the Muslim religion on educational equality controlled for variables like GDP per capita, urbanization, mortality, or fertility, and most of the time these variables were statistically significant. However, none of these studies tries to examine Lerner's modernization theory (1958) and create a variable that interacts urbanization or fertility with Muslim countries to test Lerner's argument that urbanization is a factor that stimulates education.

Research Questions

There are four research questions that guide this study:

1. Does religion have a negative association with educational gender equality?
2. Do Muslim countries have higher gender inequality in education than non-Muslim countries, holding constant other related factors?
3. Is the variation of gender inequality in education due to the countries' levels of religious conservativeness?
4. Does modernization, as reflected by urbanization, reduce the impact of religion?

First Hypotheses

H_{01} All else being equal, Muslim and non-Muslim countries **have similar** gender equality in education.

H_{a1} All else being equal, Muslim and non-Muslim countries **do not have similar** gender equality in education.

H_{02} All else being equal, religiously conservative and less conservative Muslim countries **have similar** gender equality in education.

H_{a2} All else being equal, religiously conservative and less conservative Muslim countries **do not have similar** gender equality in education.

H_{03} All else being equal, religiously conservative and less conservative non-Muslim countries **have similar** gender equality in education.

H_{a3} All else being equal, religiously conservative and less conservative non-Muslim countries **do not have similar** gender equality in education.

H_{04} All else being equal, modernization factors such as urbanization and countries' available resources **have no effect** on gender equality in education.

H_{a4} All else being equal, modernization factors such as urbanization and countries' available resources **increase** gender equality in education.

My main hypothesis is that religion may not be associated with the increase or decrease of female school enrollment or attainment. When societies move from being traditional to being modernized, government gender inequality policies that were built based on traditional values may have no impact or only a weak impact on increasing/decreasing females' school education. Modernization factors, represented by the increase of urbanization and decrease of fertility, may have a major impact on increasing the number of girls and women who go to school and university.

Alternative Hypotheses

Alternative hypotheses prevalent in the literature suggest that Muslim countries may have lower levels of female school enrollment than non-Muslim countries, because Muslim countries are still more religiously conservative than non-Muslim countries or because they are less modernized. In addition, religiously conservative Muslim countries may have fewer females than males in school, when compared to religiously liberal Muslim countries. Furthermore, religiously conservative non-Muslim countries also have lower female-to-male total school enrollment than less religious non-Muslim countries. However, modernization factors may reduce the negative impact of religion on religiously conservative countries, both Muslim and non-Muslim.

H_{01} All else being equal, Muslim and non-Muslim countries **have similar** gender equality in education.

H_{a1} All else being equal, Muslim countries **have less** gender equality in education than non-Muslim countries.

H_{02} All else being equal, religiously conservative and less conservative Muslim countries **have similar** gender equality in education.

H_{a2} All else being equal, religiously conservative Muslim countries **have less** gender equality in education than less religiously conservative Muslim countries.

H_{03} All else being equal, religiously conservative and less conservative non-Muslim countries **have similar** gender equality in education.

H_{a3} All else being equal, religiously conservative non-Muslim countries **have less** gender equality in education than less religiously conservative countries.

H_{04} All else being equal, modernization factors such as urbanization and countries' available resources **have no effect** on gender equality in education.

H_{a4} All else being equal, modernization factors such as urbanization and countries' available resources **increase** gender equality in education.

Data

There is a total of 55 countries in the study, with 29 Muslim and 26 non-Muslim countries spanning the time period from 1960 to 2010. All countries with a Muslim population of 45 percent or above as of 1990 were included, except those for which Barro and Lee (2013) do not provide education data, or those that did not gain their political independence from the Soviet Union until the 1990s. I also had to drop some non-Muslim countries that gained their independence in the 1990s, because countries that were still not independent had adopted constitutions that did not represent their cultures and religion. Muslim countries were matched with non-Muslim countries based on population size.[3]

Dependent Variable

There are two common education datasets that scholars who are interested in this area of study typically use. The first is Barro and Lee's (2013) education database, which is the most commonly employed, and the second is the World Bank education indicator (2013). This study uses Barro and Lee's total ratio of female-to-male school enrollment, which is the average of the ratios of female-to-male primary, secondary, and tertiary school enrollments. Using the ratio of female-to-male total education is a good measure, since it is a direct measurement of equality. However, the ratio, which is from 0 to 100, is altered to a percentage from 1 to 100 by multiplying the education values by 100. This change was implemented due to its simplicity and also in accordance with the practices of the World Bank indicator. Some countries have female-to-male school enrollment that exceeds 100, such as Australia, Switzerland, Italy, and South Korea, because they have many more girls than boys in school. There are also countries that have very small female-to-male total school enrollment, which in some years goes lower than 15 percent, such as Yemen and Afghanistan. This indicates that the average of female-to-male primary, secondary, and tertiary enrollment is very low.[4]

Barro and Lee's (2013) education database was selected over the World Bank education indicator for two reasons. First, the World Bank's education data have many missing observations, and it is difficult to impute those missing observations because some countries do not have data for more than 10 years, and do not have a value that the imputation could start and end with. Barro and Lee's dataset starts from 1950, but they report the data only every five years. Therefore, for the 55 countries that start from 1960 in the sample, in order to expand the number of observations from 605 before imputation to 2805, it was necessary to impute the data between the five years.[5] The method I used to impute the data between each five-year period was the linear interpolation method.

Figure 3.1 is an example of why Barro and Lee's dataset is more viable than the World Bank dataset. Look to Fig. 3.1, graph One and Three in the left column for Albania and Algeria, which are two examples of the countries in the sample, before the imputation of the data.[6] For Albania, the World Bank's data start from somewhere in the 1990s and end before 2010, and before imputation seem to have higher values than those in Barro and Lee's data. For Algeria, the World Bank's data start from somewhere in the 2000s and end before 2010, and before imputation have higher values than those in Barro and Lee's data. This situation is not limited to these two countries. The World Bank–reported data for several countries, particularly Arabian Gulf countries, seem to be inflated.

This could be the case because the World Bank dataset is based on self-reporting. These data may not be as reliable as those in the Barro and Lee education database, which are collected from countries' censuses and surveys. Barro and Lee gathered their data from 621 censuses and surveys as compiled by the UN, the United Nations Educational, Scientific and Cultural Organization (UNESCO), Eurostat, and other sources. They used forward and backward extrapolation of the census/survey observations on attainment to fill in the missing observations. Their data are available for every five years from 1960 to 2010.

The second problem is that the extrapolation method does not seem to work well for the World Bank data. In Fig. 3.1, when the data for Albania were imputed, the World Bank data remain higher than Barro

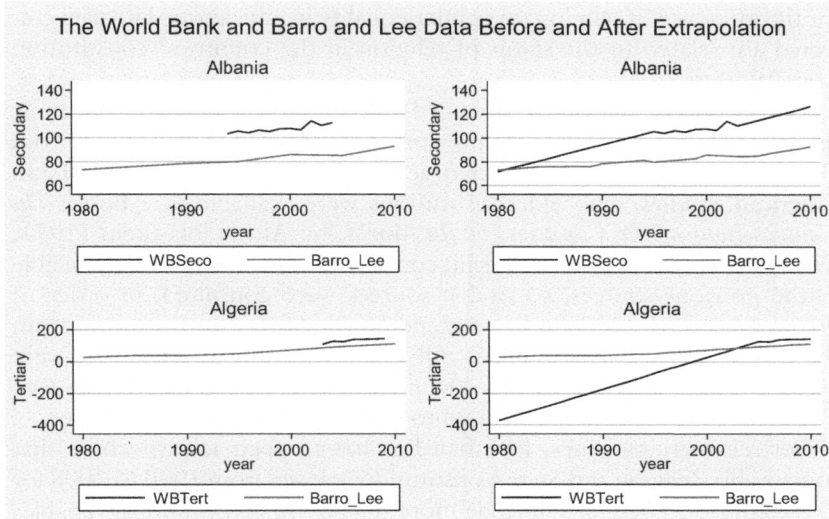

Fig. 3.1 Comparison between the educational dataset in Barro and Lee's and World Bank datasets

and Lee's data and the gap between the observations became bigger. For Algeria, when the data were imputed, the World Bank data reversed and became negative, which is not even possible. These two problems do not apply to Barro and Lee's dataset. Even if there were a conditional command to order the program not to impute anything lower than zero, the data would still be problematic. This problem does not exist in Barro and Lee's dataset, and these circumstances are not limited to these two cases. Therefore, Barro and Lee's total ratio of female-to-male school enrollment is used instead of the World Bank dataset.

Key Independent Variables

For the independent variable measuring religiousness, an indicator was created based on the role of religion in the countries' constitutions, while the traditional method used by scholars, which differentiates between Muslim and non-Muslim countries by creating a dummy variable of either zero or one, was also employed. To create the religiousness indicator, the status of religion in countries' constitutions was utilized in order to test for the influence of religion on gender equality in education. The data collected are related to the status of religion in the countries' constitution from 1960 to 2010.

Constitutional data were obtained from several resources. The most recent constitutions and some previous ones were available online from Constitution Finder and from Georgetown University's Center for Latin American Studies. The old constitutions were available in a book, *The Constitutions of the Countries of the World*, by Albert Blaustein (1971, 1988, 1994). Not all of the Muslim countries' constitutions were available in the previous sources, so Arabic sources were consulted, in order to obtain most of the Middle Eastern and North African constitutions from the official government websites. All statements and websites that were used to obtain information are documented and available upon request. Table 3.2 shows the method I used to code the Constitution variable.

For reliability purposes, Jonathan Fox has an open-access website that contains his Religion and State Constitutions dataset from 1990 to 2008 for 177 countries. These data include more than 2900 constitutional variables collected from the Religion and Law International Document database, the International Constitutional Law project, the Political Database of the Americas, and the University of Richmond Constitution Finder. When documents were not translated into English, he used Google Translate.[7] Out of the 2000 variables, there were 12 variables that can be used to test for the reliability of the data I collected for the Constitution variable. Table 3.3 includes Fox's variables that were used to test for coding reliability.

Table 3.2 Constitution coding and the variables used for coding

Al-Kohlani's Constitution Religiousness Index

Coding	Statement
.	No constitution
2	The country has an official religion and that religion is the only source of legislation
4	The country has an official religion, but religion is one source of legislation
6	The country has an official religion or religion has a specific place or the king is the protector of religion, but religion is not mentioned as a source of legislation
8	A country has no official religion; so there is tolerance for religion and the name of god or a religion is mentioned somewhere in the constitution
10	The country explicitly says that it is a secular country, or there is no tolerance for any religion

Table 3.3 This study's constitutional coding, with Fox's variables

Coding	Variable	Statement
2[a]	claws01x	Religious law is declared a principle or the main source of legislation.
4	coffestab01x	A religion is declared the state religion, official religion, or established religion.
4	coffestab02x	The state is declared a religious state (e.g., "X is an Islamic state")
4	claws02x	Laws may not be contrary to the principles or law of a designated religion.
6	coffestab03x	The state supports, upholds, or recognizes a specific religion as the state religion.
6	cother01x:	The head of state is described as the protector or defender of the state religion or is required to protect or defend the state religion.
6	cother02x:	Declaration that a religion or religions have a special place in the country's history, culture, or government or that a specific religion has a special relationship with the government.
6	cother03x	Recognizes a specific religion or religions as legal personalities or recognized (but not official) religions.
8	coffsras01x	The state may not (shall not, etc.) establish/institute/adopt/recognize a religion.
8	coffsras02x	There is no state religion (code similar language such as "no religion will have a state character").
8	csymbol01x	General references to God (includes other names for God such as Allah or other deities), other than oaths of office, such as "in the name of God Almighty."
8	csymbol02x	General references to religion other than references to God.
8	csymbol03x	General references to or quotes from the Bible, Qur'an, or similar religious documents.
8	csymbol04x	Oaths of office which include optional religious references to God or religion.
8	csymbol05x	Oaths of office which include mandatory references to God or religion.
8	csymbol06x	Oaths of office which require one to respect, glorify, protect, defend, uphold, or safeguard a religion (or other similar terminology).
10	coffsras03x	The state is secular (code similar words such as "lay").
10	coffsras04x	The state is separate/autonomous/independent from religion or religious organizations (or vice versa). (This includes similar language such as the state is not bound by a religion, not linked to a religion, etc.).

Note: The statements in column three were taken from Fox's codebook 2012

[a]See Appendix A, Point 3

The difference between Fox's data and the data in this study rests in the fact that his data were gathered from 1990 to 2008, while the data in this study were generated from 1960 to 2010. The time-matched data in this study were compared with Fox's data (from 1990 to 2008). The correlation between his coding and that of this examination for that period (1990–2008) was 74 percent. One cause of the reduced intercorrelation is that Fox's Muslim dataset was not very accurate when it comes to whether Islam is the *main* source or simply *one* source of legislation. For example, Fox's database indicates that in the constitutions of Yemen, Qatar, Saudi Arabia, and Sudan, Islam is not the main source or a source of legislation, but this is not true. Islam is mentioned in the constitution of those countries as either *the* source or *a* source of law. Although the correlation between the two coding methods is not as high as one might ideally hope, for Muslim states the coding used in this study is more accurate and precise than Fox's coding.

In general, the main problem with the Constitution variable is that it does not vary much for each country over time. Table 3.4 shows the coding for each country in the sample, and demonstrates how limited the variation is of religion's role over the 50 years for each country. For example, Afghanistan was conservative for 24 years and moderately conservative for another 24 years. Some countries, such as Austria and Australia, have been liberal for the last 51 years. Of course, the cross-sectional element of the analysis allows for more variation than does the cross-time element. The standard deviation for the Constitution variable in non-Muslim countries is 1.5, which is smaller than the standard deviation for Constitution in Muslim countries, which is 2.45 (for more details, see Table 4.2).

The other important independent variable is Urbanization. The early and continued research has shown that there is an association between urbanization and modernization. Urbanization was used by several scholars, such as Lerner (1958) and Inglehart and Norris (2003), as one of the main indicators of modernization. Lerner proposed that urbanization helps change traditional societies to modern societies, in which individuals are open to new ideas and seek to operate effectively in a changing world. Education becomes essential for an individual to survive in a multicultural society with a high cost of living that demands paid employment (Lerner 1958). Urban areas also provide cheaper education, since pupils live in close proximity and transportation is more available than in rural areas. The evidence presented by Daniel Lerner (1958) demonstrating that urbanization transfers traditional societies to modern societies, with an

Table 3.4 The frequency of the constitutional religious levels per year from 1960 to 2010

Country	Conservative (2)	Moderate conservative (4)	Moderate liberal (6)	Liberal (8)	Secular (10)	Total
Afghanistan	24	24	3	0	0	51
Albania	0	0	0	13	38	51
Algeria	0	0	48	0	0	48
Australia	0	0	0	51	0	51
Austria	0	0	0	51	0	51
Bahrain	10	28	0	0	0	38
Bangladesh	0	0	23	9	7	39
Barbados	0	0	0	51	0	51
Benin	0	0	0	0	51	51
Cameroon	0	0	0	0	51	51
Chile	0	0	39	12	0	51
Egypt	0	40	11	0	0	51
Gambia	0	0	0	19	32	51
Ghana	0	0	0	29	22	51
Indonesia	0	0	10	41	0	51
Iran (Islamic Republic)	31	0	20	0	0	51
Iraq	0	8	43	0	0	51
Italy	0	0	24	27	0	51
Japan	0	0	18	17	16	51
Jordan	0	0	51	0	0	51
Kuwait	0	31	18	0	0	49
Lao People's Democratic Republic	0	20	5	26	0	51
Malawi	0	0	0	45	0	45
Malaysia	0	0	51	0	0	51
Maldives	3	10	30	8	0	51
Mali	0	0	0	0	37	37
Malta	0	47	0	0	0	47
Mauritania	26	0	25	0	0	51
Mongolia	0	0	0	19	32	51
Morocco	0	0	51	0	0	51
Netherlands	0	0	23	28	0	51
Niger	0	0	18	33	0	51
Pakistan	0	44	2	0	0	46
Papua New Guinea	0	0	0	51	0	51
Paraguay	0	0	32	19	0	51

(*continued*)

Table 3.4 (continued)

Country	Conservative (2)	Moderate conservative (4)	Moderate liberal (6)	Liberal (8)	Secular (10)	Total
Qatar	0	51	0	0	0	51
Republic of Korea	0	0	0	51	0	51
Romania	0	0	0	51	0	51
Russian Federation	0	0	0	33	18	51
Saudi Arabia	51	0	0	0	0	51
Senegal	0	0	0	0	51	51
Sierra Leone	0	0	0	47	0	47
Sri Lanka	0	5	34	0	0	39
Sudan	0	25	13	13	0	51
Swaziland	0	0	0	18	0	18
Syrian Arab Republic	0	38	0	13	0	51
Tanzania	0	0	0	15	34	49
Thailand	0	6	30	15	0	51
Tunisia	0	4	47	0	0	51
Turkey	0	0	10	0	41	51
Uganda	0	0	0	48	0	48
United Arab Emirates	0	51	0	0	0	51
Uruguay	0	0	0	51	0	51
Yemen	47	4	0	0	0	51
Zambia	0	0	20	27	0	47
Total	192	436	699	931	430	2688

increase in literacy, inspires and informs this discussion. Therefore, in this study, Urbanization is used as an independent variable to represent modernization. The study used the World Bank data for urbanization, which refer to the percentage of people living in urban areas as defined by national statistical offices.

Control Variables

This examination controls for the rate of fertility. Although Lerner (1958) argues that urbanization is the main driver of modernization, his assumption was challenged by the problems of high density and governments' inability to meet the high demand for basic services. Also, urbanization in traditional societies seems to have a different impact on men and women. Unlike males, females' ability to benefit from urbanization is restricted by the family's financial status, marital status, and cultural gender norms. A low/middle-income family that has several children is more likely to give the priority for education to a male, and females would be expected to marry early. Societies that still have high fertility rates are more likely to have fewer females both in school and in the labor force, because these societies may still believe that a female's priority is to be a mother and take care of her husband and children. The fertility rate is a good indicator of modernization because traditional societies are more likely to have a high fertility rate than modernized societies[8]; therefore, I am using the Fertility rate as a control variable in my test for Lerner's modernization theory, to offset the weakness of the Urbanization variable. The test would use Urbanization as well as Fertility rate, because both are essential for measuring modernization when studying gender equality issues. Urbanization will be used as an independent variable and Fertility rate as a control variable. These two variables do not highly correlate and omitting Fertility would reduce the fit of the overall model. In any case, the data for fertility were also obtained from the World Bank, and they are from 1960 to 2010. Fertility is measured as "the number of children that would be born to a woman if she were to live to the end of her childbearing years and bear children in accordance with current age-specific fertility rates."[9]

The study also controls for the impact of time by creating a dummy variable that runs from 0 (1960) to 50 (2010). This variable is used when the test covers a long period over many countries that have different characteristics. Education can improve over time for many reasons that cannot be tested. So, this variable should be able to capture the effect of time, since it helps reduce omitted variable bias due to within-country (and also worldwide) factors that cannot be captured by systematic variables. It is normally used when the fixed-effects model cannot be employed, and there is a need to control for panel data autocorrelation.

GDP per capita is an important variable that was supposed to be used in the model because of the expected relationship between GDP per capita and the improvement of education. However, because of the high correlation between Urbanization and GDP per capita in this sample, which was more than 81 percent in most models, GDP per capita was dropped. Other variables that could be related to modernization, such as Oil, Oil/GDP per capita, Balance of Budget, Immigration, Education Aid, Relative

Political Extraction (RPE), and Relative Political Reach (RPR) were also used, but were dropped because they were not significant.[10] Moreover, other variables that scholars typically use to measure gender equality, such as Women in Parliamentary Lower House, and UN Treaty (CEDAW), were used in this study to measure the level of the countries' religiosity, but they were also dropped because they were not statistically significant or the sign of the coefficients was inconsistent.[11]

Interaction Variables

To follow other scholars in answering the first question that concerns this study—whether Muslim countries have the same gender equality in education as non-Muslim countries—all that is needed is a dummy variable for Muslim countries that allows for the estimation of their impact on female-to-male total school enrollment. However, since the impact on Muslim countries of the religious structure contained in the constitution is desired, there is a need to create an interactive variable that allows for estimation of the marginal effect of the interaction between Muslim countries and the constitution. Would a liberal constitution (measured as a higher number on Al-Kohlani's Constitution Religiousness Index) help Muslim countries increase gender equality in education? Also, the creation of an interactive variable between Muslim countries and Urbanization is recommended. Table 3.5 presents the statistical description of the data.

The purpose of the first interaction variable is to measure the marginal effect of the level of the constitution's inclusion of religion on Muslim countries in comparison to non-Muslim countries. The purpose of the

Table 3.5 Descriptive data for the main variables

Variable	Obs	Mean	Std. dev.	Min	Max
Year	2805	1985	14.72223	1960	2010
Total F/M education	2805	67.37826	30.99614	8.6567	199.46
Urbanization	2805	45.29217	25.50628	3.415	98.655
Constitution	2688	6.72247	2.283984	2	10
Fertility	2805	4.745166	2.075379	1.076	9.223
Time	2805	24.60784	14.5157	0	50
Muslim	2805	0.5090909	0.500007	0	1
Muslim × Constitution	576	2.982639	3.418575	0	10
Muslim × Urbanization	605	22.29073	28.05813	0	98.655

Table 3.6 Variables and expected results

Variables	Expected results
Dependent variable	
The total percentage of the ratio of female-to-male school enrollments from 1960 to 2010	
Independent variables	
Constitution	The more religiously liberal the constitution is (the higher the value on the index), the less gender inequality in female-to-male total school attainment
Urbanization	The greater the urbanization of a country's population, the less gender inequality in education
Muslim × Constitution	Muslim states are particularly sensitive to the structure of the constitution
Muslim × Urbanization	Muslim states are particularly sensitive to the level of urbanization
Control variables	
Fertility rate	The lower the fertility rate, the higher the percentage of girls who go to school
Time	Time should have a positive impact on females' education
N	2805

second interaction variable is to estimate whether urbanization has a different impact on Muslim and non-Muslim countries. The following are the main five statistical models that will be applied to Muslim and non-Muslim countries, Muslim countries only, and non-Muslim countries only.[12] Table 3.6 summarizes the results that are expected by the modernization theory.

THE STATISTICAL MODELS

Υ (Female-to-Male Total School Enrollment)

$$= \beta_0 + \beta_1 \text{ Constitution} + \beta_2 \text{ Fertility} + \beta_3 \text{ TimeEffect} + \varepsilon 1 \quad (3.1)$$

$$= \alpha_0 + \alpha_1 \text{ Urbanization} + \alpha_2 \text{ Fertility} + \alpha_3 \text{ TimeEffect} + \varepsilon 2 \quad (3.2)$$

$$= \gamma_0 + \gamma_1 \text{ Constitution} + \gamma_2 \text{ Urbanization} + \gamma_3 \text{ Fertility} + \gamma_4 \text{ TimeEffect} + \varepsilon 3 \quad (3.3)$$

$$= \lambda_0 + \lambda_1 \text{Constitution} + \lambda_2 \text{Urbanization} + \lambda_3 \text{Fertility} + \lambda_4 \text{TimeEffect}$$
$$+ \text{Muslim} \times \text{Constitution} + \varepsilon 4 \tag{3.4}$$

$$= \eta_0 + \eta_1 \text{Constitution} + \eta_2 \text{Urbanization} + \eta_3 \text{Fertility} + \eta_4 \text{TimeEffect}$$
$$+ \text{Muslim} \times \text{Urbanization} + \varepsilon 5 \tag{3.5}$$

Expectations

The first model tests the religious theory, which claims that religion is the main reason behind the high gender inequality in education. The model tests the influence of a religious constitution on female-to-male total school enrollment without controlling for urbanization, which is not considered to be a critical variable from the perspective of the religious theory. In this model, the religious theory expects that the coefficient on the Constitution variable will be positive and statistically significant. So, the more religiously liberal the constitution is (measured as a higher value in the index), the higher the gender equality in education is in both Muslim and non-Muslim countries.

The second model tests for the modernization theory, which claims that urbanization is the main factor in increasing literacy rates. The model tests the influence of urbanization on female-to-male total school enrollment without controlling for the influence of religion, which is considered insignificant (given the existence of high urbanization) from the perspective of the modernization theory. Therefore, in Eq. 3.2, Urbanization is also expected to have a positive impact on gender equality in education.

Equation 3.3 combines religious and modernization variables, because having a less religious constitution and a high urbanization rate may have a significant impact on education. In this model, Constitution and Urbanization are expected to be positively associated with female-to-male total enrollment. This model deals with a potential omitted variable in Models 1 and 2.

The interaction term in Eq. 3.4 estimates whether the constitution has a different impact on Muslim and non-Muslim countries. If the religious theory is correct, the interactive variable between Muslim and Constitution is also expected to be positive, which means that the more liberal the Muslim constitution is, the higher the gender equality in education, with a more powerful effect in Muslim than in non-Muslim countries of the religious liberalness of the constitution.

In addition, Eq. 3.5 estimates whether Urbanization has a different impact on Muslim and non-Muslim countries. If Lerner's (1958) modernization theory is correct, the interactive variable between Muslim states in general and Urbanization should have a positive association. For control variables, the lower the Fertility rate, the higher the gender equality in education. The effect of Time is also expected to be positive, because over the period from 1960 to 2010 the passage of time has had an impact on spreading awareness of the importance of education.

Method

It is expected that the panel data will have a correlation of regression disturbances over time and between subjects (in this case, countries), which could lead to biased standard errors and therefore incorrect statistical inference. Since the dataset used here is panel data, which is cross-sectional and time series, the models were tested by using the panel-corrected standard error (PCSE), which estimates for linear cross-sectional time-series models without bias. This method assumes that the disturbances are not independent, which means that they are assumed to be either heteroscedastic across panels or heteroscedastic and contemporaneously correlated across panels.[13] It may also be assumed that the disturbances may be autocorrelated within the panel, and that the autocorrelation parameter may be constant across panels or different for each panel.[14] These assumptions apply to the current data, since, after testing for previous problems, the data seem to suffer from all of these. Therefore, the method used in this book is robust PCSE.

The problem with PCSE is that it does not account for unobserved omitted variables, as the fixed-effect method does, but fixed-effect data are used when there is a high variation over time, which these data do not have. So, to deal with this problem the Time variable was added, which should reduce the omitted variable bias when the PCSE is used. The other problem with this method is that when N is bigger than T, the results became less precise than if T were bigger than N. In this study, N is 55 and T is 50 years. The other option is to use the feasible generalized least squares method for panel data. However, "this method is infeasible if the panel's time dimension T is smaller than its cross-sectional dimension N."[15] This method also produces "unacceptably small standard error estimates."[16] Thus, since the data suffer from heterogeneity of variances across panels, has serial correlation, and includes dummy variables, these do not work well with the fixed effect method. The PCSE method with first-order serial correlation (AR1) seems to be the most suitable test for these data.

Conclusion

This chapter introduces the data and method that I use in this book to examine the impact of modernization and states' level of religiosity, particularly in Muslim countries, on educational gender equality. It provides an explanation of how the observations (countries) were chosen, and a justification for each variable used in this study. It also explains why some data, such as Barro and Lee's educational data, were used instead of the World Bank's data, and how the missing data of the dependent variable (total female-to-male school enrollment) were imputed. In addition, it explains how Al-Kohlani's Constitution Religiousness Index was constructed and the expected shortcomings of this index.

Notes

1. I thought of matching countries based on GDP per capita, but I substituted it with the total size of population, because I wanted to avoid comparing rich advanced countries to poor developing countries. This was also because GDP per capita was one of my main independent variables, which I deleted due to the high correlation with urbanization.
2. Models that include constitutions have smaller N than models that do not have constitution because of the missing data in the constitution variable.
3. For detailed information on inclusion and exclusion of countries, please see Appendix A, Point 1, and Appendix B, Table B.1.
4. See Appendix A, Figs. B.1, B.2, B.3, and B.4.
5. The tests for the models using the data without imputation are available in Appendix A (Table A.5).
6. It is observable that Stata does not seem to show the missing data for Barro and Lee's dataset, because Stata was capable of forecasting the missing data and connecting the data in Barro and Lee's database. However, Stata could not do that for the World Bank dataset.
7. Fox (2012: 1).
8. Norton and Tomal (2009: 963).
9. World Bank Indicator (2014).
10. See Table 4.6.
11. See Appendix A, Point 4.
12. See more details about other variables I tested but that were not statistically significant in Table 4.6.
13. The data have 55 countries for 50 years, and each country with each 50 years is considered in one panel.
14. Hoechle (2007: 4).
15. Hoechle (2007: 5).
16. Ibid.

References

Barro, R., & Lee, J.-W. (2013). Retrieved from http://www.barrolee.com/data/full1.htm

Cooray, A., & Potrafke, N. (2011). Gender Inequality in Education: Political Institutions or Culture and Religion? *European Journal of Political Economy, 27*(2), 268–280.

Dollar, D., & Gatti, R. (1999). *Gender Inequality, Income, and Growth: Are Good Times Good for Women?* Development Research Group, The World Bank.

Dorius, S. F., & Firebaugh, G. (2010). Trends in Global Gender Inequality. *Social Forces, 88*(5), 1941–1968.

Forsythe, N., Korzeniewicz, R. P., & Durrant, V. (2000). Gender Inequalities and Economic Growth: A Longitudinal Evaluation. *Economic Development and Cultural Change, 48*(3), 573–617.

Hajj, M., & Panizza, U. (2009). Religion and Education Gender Gap: Are Muslims Different? *Economics of Education Review, 28*(3), 337–344.

Heston, A., Summers, R., & Aten, B. (2011). *Penn World Tables 7.0.* Center for International Comparisons of Production, Income and Prices at the University of Pennsylvania.

Hoechle, D. (2007). Robust Standard Errors for Panel Regressions with Cross-Sectional Dependence. *Stata Journal, 7*(3), 281.

Lerner, D. (1958). *The Passing of Traditional Society: Modernizing the Middle East.* Glencoe, IL: The Free Press.

Norton, S. W., & Tomal, A. (2009). Religion and Female Educational Attainment. *Journal of Money, Credit and Banking, 41*(5), 961–986.

Ross, M. L. (2008). Oil, Islam, and Women. *American Political Science Review, 102*(01), 107–123.

Wolfrum, R., Grote, R., Fombad, C. M., Blaustein, A. P., Flanz, G. H., & De Wet, E. (Eds.). (1971–). *Constitutions of the Countries of the World: A Series of Updated Texts, Constitutional Chronologies and Annotated Bibliographies. Bosnia and Herzegowina-Cameroon.* Oceana Publ.

World Bank Indicator. (2014). Fertility. Retrieved from http://data.worldbank.org/indicator/SP.DYN.TFRT.IN

CHAPTER 4

Empirical Testing and Analysis of Data

This chapter is divided into three sections and a summary. In the first section, all the 55 Muslim and non-Muslim countries in the sample are included in all models. The second section includes only Muslim countries, while the third includes only non-Muslim countries. The chapter investigates three main general issues. The first is whether religion affects gender equality in education, which can be done by adding the Constitution variable that differentiates the level of conservativeness within each religion. The second issue is whether Muslim countries have less educational gender equality compared to non-Muslim counties. I introduce a dummy variable to differentiate between Muslim and non-Muslim countries. Finally, I test whether any effect from the level of religious conservativeness will disappear once the Modernization variable interacts with Muslim countries. Based on modernization theory, urbanization is the main element that stimulates education regardless of a country's religion, so the impact of religion on education should be reduced or non-existent in urban societies. The fertility rate is likely to have a higher effect on educational gender equality, since it can directly measure the level of modernization for both sexes, with an emphasis on females' modernization. The decrease in the fertility rate should indicate a higher increase in female education in both traditional and modern societies.

The chapter shows that, based on the religious theory, the ratio of female-to-male total school enrollment is lower in more religiously

© The Author(s) 2018
S. A. Al-Kohlani, *Improving Educational Gender Equality in Religious Societies*, https://doi.org/10.1007/978-3-319-70536-1_4

conservative countries than in less religiously conservative countries, *ceteris paribus*. Religiously conservative countries, regardless of whether they are Muslim or another religion, have less educational gender equality than secular or less conservative countries. Countries that are still conservative are likely to still be influenced by several religious restrictions that are embedded in the system. However, Lerner's modernization theory (1958) argues that an increase in urbanization will have a positive impact on female-to-male total school enrollment, even in religious countries (*ceteris paribus*). The chapter shows that modernization has a modest, positive effect on conservative countries, but a strong, significant effect on less religious countries. A decrease in fertility also has a positive impact on educational gender equality, because a female's chance of going to school would increase if she did not have several siblings and did not get married and pregnant at an early age. Time also has a positive impact, because of the difficulty of controlling for microeconomic and political changes over the years across all countries.

Empirical Testing and Analysis for Muslim and Non-Muslim Countries

Table 4.1 reports the regression results for six models for both Muslim and non-Muslim countries. The first regression model is the basic model that tests for the impact of religious and less religious constitutions without controlling for Urbanization. This model answers the basic general question: Do religiously conservative countries educate fewer girls than boys compared to less religiously conservative countries? It is followed by Model 2, which tests modernization theory by studying the association between urbanization and gender equality in education without considering religion. This model answers whether modernization, represented by urbanization, has a strong and significant effect on educational gender equality. Then, Model 3 combines religious and modernization variables in one model to examine the impact of both religious and less religious constitutions and urbanization on educational gender equality. The strength of the new model is also studied, and whether there is any change in the sign, strength, and statistical significance of the coefficient of Constitution and Urbanization variables is observed. The model shows the strength of the effect of religion and modernization on educational gender equality. Model 4 examines the influence of Muslim countries on

Table 4.1 Muslim/non-Muslim basic regression models

DV: F/M total school enrollment	Model 1 Coef (SE)	Model 2 Coef (SE)	Model 3 Coef (SE)	Model 4 Coef (SE)	Model 5 Coef (SE)	Model 6 Coef (SE)
Constitution	0.25*** (0.10)		0.31*** (0.09)	0.17** (0.10)	0.06 (0.08)	0.17 (0.12)
Fertility	−8.83*** (0.29)	−7.27*** (0.46)	−7.33*** (0.39)	−6.959*** (0.32)	−6.28*** (0.31)	−8.07*** (0.45)
Time	0.09*** (0.04)	0.08*** (0.03)	0.079*** (0.03)	0.10*** (0.04)	0.08*** (0.04)	0.09*** (0.04)
Urbanization		0.27*** (0.06)	0.27*** (0.04)	0.259*** (0.04)	0.35*** (0.041)	0.19*** (0.04)
Muslim				−21.70*** (2.282)	−17.98*** (2.81)	
Arab					−29.25*** (2.21)	
Muslim_conservative						−2.32*** (0.52)
_cons	105.92*** (2.88)	88.27*** (4.83)	86.74*** (4.93)	97.09*** (5.33)	91.80*** (5.40)	94.79*** (5.03)
R^2	0.44	0.38	0.46	0.50	0.49	0.50
Wald Chi^2	1559.13	984.71	1892.37	1882.93	2032.20	2136.15
N	2688[a]	2805	2688	2688	2688	2688

Coef coefficient, *DV* dependent variable, *F/M* female/male, *SE* standard error

***$p < 0.01$, **$p < 0.05$, *$p < 0.1$

[a]Models that include constitutions have smaller N than models that do not have constitutions because of the missing data in the Constitution variable

gender equality in education.[1] This model provides confirmation of the previous literature, which found a negative association between Muslim countries and educational gender equality. However, since Helen Rizzo et al. (2007) find that Muslim Arab countries are less supportive of women's rights than non-Arab Muslim countries, Model 5 tests whether the negative association between Muslim countries and educational gender equality is due only to the influence of Arab culture. Finally, Model 6, in contrast, studies whether the negative effect of Muslim countries is due to the influence of the very conservative Muslim countries. It focuses on the influence of religiously conservative and moderately conservative Muslim countries on educational gender equality.[2] The robust panel-corrected standard errors method was used to estimate all the models.

Starting with the first regression model in Table 4.1 that combines the 55 countries—Muslim and non-Muslim—as the religious theory expects, there is a positive association between female-to-male total school enrollment and Constitution (with higher levels indicating more religious liberalism), and the association is statistically significant at the 99 percent confidence level. However, the coefficient is small, which indicates that the substitutive significance of a country moving from being religious to less religious is small. For example, moving from being a conservative country to a moderately conservative country increases female-to-male total school enrollment by only 0.23 percentage points, which is small compared to the difficulties that political decision-makers may have to go through to reduce the level of religious conservativeness in the constitution. However, the high level of statistical significance of the Constitution variable indicates, in relation to educational gender equality, that religions do indeed matter. This confirms the previous literature, which found that religions in general are an obstacle to achieving educational gender equality.

Fertility rate is negative with a high coefficient, and it is also statistically significant at a 99 percent confidence level. The high coefficient indicates that for 1 percentage point increase in the fertility rate, there is a negative 8.8 percentage point increase in female-to-male total school enrollment. This result indicates that the positive impact of decreasing the fertility rate is bigger than the impact of decreasing the religious level of the constitution. Time is estimated to have a positive effect, and it is statistically significant at the 99 percent confidence level. R^2 is 44 percent for Model 1 (it ranges from 38 to 50 percent across the models), which means that the first model explains 44 percent of the variation in female-to-male total school enrollment. Such a percentage, although less than 50 percent, is still considered good for such a model.

Looking at Model 2, which represents modernization theory, Urbanization is positive and statistically significant at the 99 percent confidence level; Fertility is again negative with a high coefficient, as was the case in Model 1, and it is also statistically significant at the 99 percent level. The coefficient of Urbanization is also small, but a little bigger than the coefficient of Constitution. Like Constitution, this indicates that although urbanization has a positive impact on educational gender equality, the substantive effect is modest. Similar to Constitution, the effect of urbanization on educational gender equality is small, especially if compared to the coefficient of Fertility rate. Fertility still has the biggest substantive significant effect on female-to-male total school enrollment. Time is again positive and statistically significant at the 99 percent level. The coefficient is smaller than the coefficient in the previous model, which indicates that there is a reduction in the omitted variable bias. Although the variables in Model 2 seem to have a higher effect on female-to-male school enrollment than in Model 1, the decrease in R^2 in Model 2 indicates that the religious model explains the variation in female-to-male school enrollment better than Model 2 for modernization. Wald Chi^2 is smaller in Model 2 than in Model 1, which indicates that removing Constitution from the model and substituting it with Urbanization adds less value to Model 2.

So far these two models indicate that there is a positive and significant association between female-to-male total school enrollment and both religious and modernization theories. Moving from being religiously conservative to less conservative or increasing modernization—by increasing urbanization and decreasing fertility—both have a positive impact on female-to-male school enrollment. Therefore, combining the two models becomes a must. So, when Models 1 and 2 are combined in Model 3, both Constitution and Urbanization are still positive and statistically significant at the 99 percent confidence level, but the coefficients have increased a few decimal points. Fertility and Time maintain their signs and statistical significance. R^2 is 46 percent, which is a little higher than for each of the previous two models, meaning that Model 3 explains 46 percent of the variation in female-to-male total school enrollment. It is also worth noting that, controlling for Urbanization, the effect of Constitution becomes greater in this model, with the estimated coefficient increasing from 0.253 to 0.314. Wald Chi^2 also increases by 333.73 points, which indicates that Model 3 fits better than either the religious model or the modernization model alone.

The first three models indicate that, without differentiating between Muslim and non-Muslim countries, less religious (more religiously liberal) constitutions, high urbanization, and a low fertility rate are highly associated with an increase in educational gender equality. Yet the magnitudes of Constitution and Urbanization are small, especially compared to Fertility rate. This indicates that although Constitution and Urbanization have statistical significance, the substantive significant effects of Constitution and Urbanization are modest, while the substantive significance of the decrease in Fertility rate is major. However, to answer the first research question regarding whether Muslim countries have higher gender inequality in education than non-Muslim countries, Muslim countries are controlled by creating a dummy variable coded 0/1 (0 = non-Muslim, 1 = Muslim).

In Model 4, for a Muslim country the predicted female-to-male total school enrollment would be 21.7 points lower than for a non-Muslim country, holding all other variables constant. The estimated magnitude for the effect of Urbanization drops by a few decimal points, but the statistical significance remains the same. Constitution, on the other hand, is somewhat less statistically significant, and its estimated magnitude drops from 0.31 in Model 3 to 0.17 in Model 4. This means that the magnitude of the positive effect of having a less religious constitution in non-Muslim countries decreases when Muslim countries are controlled for. This suggests that half of the negative effect of constitution, 0.14 percent out of 31 percent, is coming from Muslim countries' constitutions.

The signs and the levels of statistical significance for Fertility rate and Time remain about the same as in Model 3. R^2 in Model 4 is 50 percent, which is higher than for all the previous models. This indicates that controlling for Muslim countries leads to a significant increase in R^2, from 44 percent in Model 1 to 50 percent in Model 4. Model 4 seems to explain the variation better than all the previous models. However, since the Wald Chi^2 score in Model 4 is smaller than in Model 3, the increase in R^2 could be just by chance. This means that it could be by chance that the Muslim variable improves the model by less than expected.

However, Model 5 provides evidence that supports Rizzo et al.'s (2007) conclusion regarding the Arab versus non-Arab Muslim attitude to gender equality. In this model, the Muslim variable represents only non-Arab Muslim countries. Arab countries represent the members of the Arab League. The results show that although both Arab and non-Arab Muslim countries have higher educational gender inequality compared to non-Muslim countries, Arab states have higher gender inequality in education than non-Arab states. Separating non-Arabs from Arabs weakens the marginal effect of the Constitution variable and, although it remains positive, it has lost its statistical significance. The marginal effect of Urbanization increases and the positive effect of the decrease in the Fertility rate also remains high and statistically significant. Time remains positive and statistically significant at the 99 percent confidence level. R^2 declines by only 1 percentage point, but Wald Chi^2 increases, which indicates that adding the Arab variable added value to the model.

One could conclude that, even with controlling for other factors, Muslim countries still have less educational gender equality compared to

Table 4.2 Frequency for the levels of religious conservativeness

	CON (2)	MCON (4)	MLIB (6)	LIB (8)	Secular (10)	Total
Non-Muslim						
Freq.	0	78	225	735	224	1262
Percentage	0	5.7	17.8	58.2	17.7	
Mean	0	0.06	0.17	0.55	0.17	
SD	0	0.24	0.38	0.50	0.37	
Muslim						
Freq.	192	350	474	196	206	1426
Percentage	13.5	24.5	33.4	13.74	14.4	
Mean	0.13	0.24	0.32	0.13	0.14	
SD	0.34	0.43	0.47	0.34	0.35	
Total	192	428	699	931	430	

CON conservative, *LIB* liberal, *MCON* moderately conservative, *MLIB* moderately liberal, *SD* standard deviation

non-Muslim countries. Yet, since there are different levels of religious conservativeness, I created dummy variables (0/1) that represent conservative (CON = 1), moderately conservative (MCON = 1), moderately liberal (MLIB = 1), liberal (LIB = 1), and secular (Secular = 1) countries. Looking at Table 4.2, if conservative and moderately conservative Muslim observations are added, both variables represent only 38 percent of Muslim-country observations. Most of the Muslim observations are distributed among other categories. There are 474 Muslim observations in the moderately liberal category, 196 in the liberal category, and 206 in the secular category, with 542 in CON or MCON.

When I combine and control for CON and MCON Muslim observations and remove the Muslim control variable, as I present in Model 6, the Constitution variable loses its statistical significance, which indicates that isolating extremist Muslim countries reduces the precision of estimation of Constitution and the differences between Muslim and non-Muslim countries. It confirms that the negative effect of Constitution is mostly due to the heavy influence of conservative and moderately conservative Muslim countries.[3] However, despite controlling for CON and MCON Muslim countries, the association between Muslim countries and educational gender equality remains negative and high.[4] The coefficient of Urbanization also decreases, but does not lose its significance level, which means that, unlike Constitution, the positive effect of modernization is not significantly affected by the type of religion or the country's level of religiosity.

The negative association between Fertility rate and total female-to-male school enrollment decreased by 1.1 percentage point. This indicates that the conservative and moderately conservative Muslim countries were holding back the marginal positive effect of the decrease in the fertility rate by 1.1 percent. In comparison to less religious Muslim and non-Muslim countries, one unit increase in the level of religious conservativeness leads to a 2.3 percentage point decrease in total female-to-male school enrollment. R^2 remains at 50 percent in Model 6, which indicates that the increase of R^2 in Model 4 was not due to controlling for Muslim countries, but to controlling for Muslim countries that are extremely religiously conservative and committed to religion. However, the coefficient for the Muslim dummy variable in Model 4 is still much bigger than the coefficient for conservative Muslim countries. This indicates that while Muslim countries account for a 21 percentage point decrease in female-to-male total school enrollment, conservative Muslim countries account for only 2.3 percentage points in comparison to the rest of the countries in the sample.

The increase in the Wald Chi^2 score from 1882.93 in Model 4 to 2136.15 in Model 6 shows that controlling for extremist Muslim countries adds value to the model. However, in Model 4, when the Muslim variable is dropped Wald Chi^2 decreases to only 1741. This indicates that the coefficients of conservative Muslim countries are bigger than zero and that the contribution to Model 6 is higher than the contribution of the Muslim variable in Model 4. However, since the estimated magnitude of the Muslim variable is much bigger than the estimated magnitude for the effect of conservative Muslim countries, claiming that Muslim countries in general have gender inequality in education seems to be supported by these results.

Basically, what these six models are saying is that a decrease in the level of a country's religiosity and an increase in urbanization have a positive impact on the increase in females' school enrollment in both Muslim and non-Muslim countries. This section answers the first research question regarding the association between religions and educational gender equality. Model 3 shows that religious countries are associated with negative female-to-male total school enrollment. The decrease in the level of the country's religiosity and the increase in urbanization have a positive impact on both Muslim and non-Muslim countries, but urbanization has a slightly higher positive influence on educational gender equality than the constitution. Table 4.1 also answers the second research question and confirms that Muslim countries explain, to a great extent, the negative association between Muslim countries and gender inequality in education. These results confirm the previous literature that associated Muslim countries with higher educational gender inequality than non-Muslim countries. They also confirm that Arab countries have higher gender inequality in education compared to non-Arab Muslim countries. However, controlling for Muslim conservative and moderately conservative countries reduces the different effect of religion between Muslim and non-Muslim countries on educational gender equality. Moving from moderately liberal to secular remains positive but not statistically significant. In general, this section provides supportive evidence for both theories, religious and modernization, but, unlike religious theory, modernization theory seems to hold in all cases. The results also show that the fertility rate seems to have a stronger positive effect than urbanization, which supports my previous assumption about the strong association between reducing the fertility rate and modernization.

Part of this research is to examine the association between gender inequality in education and the difference at each level of conservativeness of both Muslim and non-Muslim countries. To answer the third research question regarding whether the variation of gender inequality in education is due to the countries' different levels of religious conservativeness, I use dummy variables (0/1) that represent conservative (CON = 1), moderately conservative (MCON = 1), moderately liberal (MLIB = 1), liberal (LIB = 1), and secular (Secular = 1) countries (with higher levels indicating less religious conservativeness). This test could capture the influence of the different levels of religious conservativeness on female-to-male total school enrollment.

As Table 4.2 shows, non-Muslim countries have zero religiously conservative observations, but have some observations in moderately conservative and moderately liberal categories and many observations in the liberal category. I ran a regression with all religious categories and used the CON variable as my reference group. Based on Model 6, I expected that a decrease in the level of religious conservativeness would be associated with an increase in gender equality in education in both Muslim and non-Muslim countries. Table 4.3 shows that there is no significant difference between CON and MCON observations, although the coefficient of MCON is positive. Yet there is a positive and statistical difference between CON and the rest of the religious categories in favor of less religious

Table 4.3 Muslim/non-Muslim regression models with different constitutional religious levels

DV: F/M total school enrollment	Model 7 Coef (SE)
Urbanization	0.192***
	(0.044)
Fertility	−8.024***
	(0.446)
Time	0.088***
	(0.035)
MCON	0.157
	(0.376)
MLIB	2.164***
	(0.544)
LIB	2.993***
	(0.799)
Secular	2.973***
	(0.875)
_cons	92.997***
	(5.066)
R^2	0.496
Wald Chi^2	1989.53
N	2688

Coef coefficient, *CON* conservative, *DV* dependent variable, *F/M* female/male, *LIB* liberal, *MCON* moderately conservative, *MLIB* moderately liberal, *SE* standard error

***$p < 0.01$, **$p < 0.05$, *$p < 0.1$

countries, such that as a state (whether Muslim or not) becomes less religiously conservative, the ratio of females to males in education rises.

Model 7 in Table 4.3 shows that the coefficient for MCON is smaller than the coefficient for MLIB, the coefficient for MLIB is smaller than the coefficient for LIB, and the coefficient for LIB is nearly equal to the coefficient for Secular. This test confirms that, holding all relevant variables constant, the relationship between gender equality in education and the different levels of commitment to religion in Muslim and non-Muslim countries is monotonically positive. Less religious countries in general have significantly higher female-to-male total school enrollment than countries that have higher levels of commitment to religion. However, the increase is not linear, since the coefficient of LIB countries is a few decimal points higher than the coefficient of Secular countries. Wald Chi^2 remains high and R^2 indicates that the model explains 50 percent of the variation in female-to-male total school enrollment.

Table 4.4 Muslim/non-Muslim regression models with interaction terms

DV: F/M total school enrollment	Model 8 Coef (SE)	Model 9 Coef (SE)	Model 10 Coef (SE)
Urbanization	0.267***	0.457***	0.458***
	(−0.04)	(−0.052)	(0.052)
Constitution	−0.072	0.079	−0.114
	(−0.144)	(−0.076)	(0.145)
Fertility	−6.900***	−6.162***	−6.152***
	(−0.315)	(−0.326)	(0.325)
Time	0.091***	0.092***	0.092***
	(−0.036)	(−0.037)	(0.037)
Muslim	−24.299***	−9.690**	−11.972***
	(−2.51)	(−4.104)	(4.201)
Muslim × Constitution	0.368**		0.302*
	(−0.153)		(0.156)
Muslim × Urbanization		−0.295***	−0.291***
		(−0.062)	(0.062)
_cons	98.348***	85.773***	87.168***
	(−5.326)	(−5.864)	(5.842)
R^2	0.490	0.465	0.465
Wald Chi^2	1893.72	1830.96	1845.44
N	2688	2688	2688

Coef coefficient, *DV* dependent variable, *F/M* female/male, *SE* standard error
***p < 0.01, **p < 0.05, *p < 0.1

To answer the fourth research question regarding the impact of urbanization on Muslim traditional societies, which Lerner (1958) expected to have a positive association with education, I created two interactive terms, one for Muslim countries with Constitution and another for Muslim countries with Urbanization, to be able to compare the marginal effect of both terms for Muslim countries alone. Table 4.4, Model 8, shows that the Muslim variable alone is very large, negative, and statistically significant. Holding all relevant variables constant, the interactive term between Muslim and Constitution is positive and significant at the 95 percent confidence level. The coefficient on the interaction term means that for a Muslim country (Muslim = 1), increasing one unit from being a religious country to a slightly less religious country increases gender equality in education by 0.37 percentage points in comparison to non-Muslim countries. This result indicates that Constitution has a stronger effect on Muslim countries than on non-Muslim, but overall the magnitude of the coefficient effect is small.

However, looking at Model 9, the effect of Urbanization is estimated to be 0.457, which is smaller than the estimated coefficient for Constitution, but the interaction term between Muslim and Urbanization is negative and statistically significant at the 99 percent confidence level. This means that Urbanization's effect is less in Muslim countries when compared to non-Muslim countries. Unlike the previous interaction term between Muslim countries and Constitution, when we control for the separate effect of Urbanization on Muslim countries, the coefficient for the Muslim variable is still negative, but decreases from 24.3 in Model 8 to 9.69 in Model 9.

This suggests that, holding all relevant variables constant, in Muslim countries female-to-male total school enrollment is estimated to be 9 points lower than for non-Muslim countries when the Muslim × Urbanization variable is controlled for. Unlike the interaction term between Muslim and Constitution, controlling for interaction between Muslim and Urbanization reduces the estimated difference between Muslim and non-Muslim countries in educational gender equality by 11.96 percentage points, from negative 21.65 in Model 4 to negative 9.69 in Model 9.

Model 10 combines both interaction terms to count for omitted variables, since both interaction terms are significant. This confirms the results in Model 9 and shows that Urbanization has a positive effect on non-Muslim countries. The Constitution variables in all three models are insignificant, with a tiny coefficient indicating that Constitution has no effect on non-Muslim countries in the presence of the interaction terms. However, there is a positive and significant effect of having a less religious constitution in Muslim countries, and Urbanization in Muslim countries has a less positive effect than in non-Muslim countries, although the coefficient is tiny as well.

Figure 4.1 confirms that Urbanization has a positive effect for both Muslim and non-Muslim countries, but the effect is stronger in non-Muslim countries. The y-axes show the marginal effect of Constitution in the left-hand figure and the marginal effect of Urbanization in Muslim countries in the right-hand figure. The graphs show that both the upper and lower estimates have a positive direction. However, in the Muslim × Urbanization interaction term, the upper estimation has a steeper positive marginal effect, but the lower estimation is not as steep as the upper estimation. This situation indicates that, based on the lower estimation, Urbanization has a positive impact on Muslim countries, but

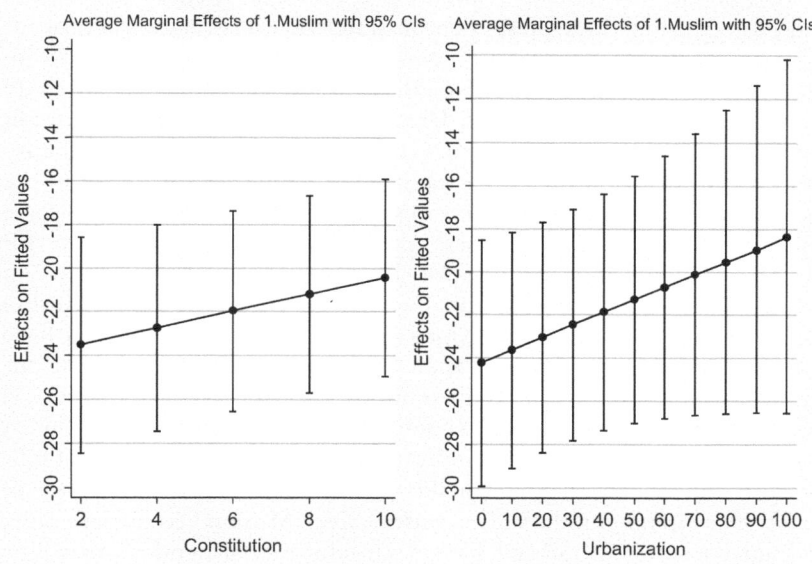

Fig. 4.1 Marginal effect for the interactive terms between Muslim countries and Constitution and Urbanization

once it reaches a certain level the positive impact of Urbanization on Muslim countries seems to stop.[5]

These two graphs estimate that Muslim countries would still be behind non-Muslim countries in educational gender equality even if they became less religious or more urbanized. This is shown by having a negative marginal effect in the y-axis in both graphs. However, having a less religious constitution in Muslim countries and becoming more urbanized reduces the gap between Muslim and non-Muslim countries on gender inequality in education. R^2 for the religious theory with the interaction term of Muslim × Constitution in Model 8 is higher than R^2 for the modernization theory with the interaction term of Muslim × Urbanization in Model 9. The results indicate that in Muslim countries, the level of constitutional commitment to religion explains the variation in educational gender equality better than the increase in the level of urbanization. These results weaken Lerner's (1958) theory, because he argued that the negative influence of religion on gender equality does not stand up against the influence of modernization on gender equality.

To sum up, this section, "Empirical Testing and Analysis for Muslim and Non-Muslim Countries," demonstrates that less religious constitutions for both Muslim and non-Muslim countries and an increase in urbanization both have a positive effect on female-to-male total school enrollment. However, although Urbanization has a positive significant coefficient in all models, the model that is based on the religious theory explains the variation of gender inequality in education better than the model that tests for the modernization theory. In addition, the positive effect of having a less religious constitution is more significant for Muslim countries than for non-Muslim countries, and the increase in urbanization has a stronger positive effect on non-Muslim than Muslim countries. Confirming the previous literature, Muslim countries have less educational gender equality than non-Muslim countries, and the difference is substantial. Non-Arab countries also seem to have less educational gender equality than Arab countries. Yet, controlling for extremist conservative Muslim countries indicates that the negative impact of religion on educational gender equality is not limited to the influence of conservative and moderately conservative Muslim countries only; Muslim countries in general have high educational gender inequality. When controlling for Muslim countries that are constitutionally committed to religion, the positive effect of liberalizing the constitution becomes insignificant, but the effect of urbanization remains positive and significant. The different levels of commitment to religion matter, and the relationship between gender equality in education and the different levels of commitment to religion in Muslim and non-Muslim countries is positive but not linear. Less religious countries in general have significantly higher female-to-male total school enrollment than countries that have higher levels of commitment to religion, but with a slight decrease for secular countries.

These results provide evidence that both a less religious constitution and high urbanization positively contribute to reducing gender inequality. The results also provide evidence that it is not only conservative Muslim countries that discriminate against women's education, all Muslim countries do. To demonstrate these results clearly, I run the same tests on Muslim countries alone and study the association between gender equality in total education in religiously extremist Muslim countries and less religiously extremist Muslim countries. Then I follow with another, similar test for non-Muslim countries.

EMPIRICAL TESTING AND ANALYSIS FOR MUSLIM COUNTRIES

Since Models 4, 5, and 6 show that Muslim countries are negatively associated with educational gender inequality more than non-Muslim countries, in this section I study Muslim countries separately from non-Muslim countries, to determine whether the variation of educational gender inequality in Muslim countries is due to their level of religious commitment and/or modernization. It is necessary to know whether the less religious Muslim countries are catching up with non-Muslim countries. I also examine the difference between Arab and non-Arab states in educational gender equality. Based on the religious and modernization theories, Muslim countries, regardless of whether they are Arab or non-Arab, are still considered religious in comparison to most non-Muslim countries; however, the level of conservativeness varies within Muslim countries (see Table 4.2). So, it is likely that religion has a stronger influence on these traditional societies than the same level of religious conservatism would on more modernized societies. The religious theory would expect religion to have a very strong negative influence on gender equality in education, while the modernization theory would expect a positive effect of urbanization. The decrease in the fertility rate should have a positive impact on educational gender equality. The increase in time also should have a positive impact on female-to-male total school enrollment, because it is difficult to capture all the cultural and economic changes for all the 29 Muslim countries in the study over 50 years by the few variables I have in the models. Model 3 in Table 4.1 will be used throughout this book, since the previous section, "Empirical Testing and Analysis for Muslim and Non-Muslim Countries," confirms that both Constitution and Urbanization variables are critical for explaining the gender gap in total school enrollment.

In the previous section, particularly in Model 4, I showed that there is a great difference between Muslim and non-Muslim countries in educational gender equality. Also, Model 6 indicates that it is not just the conservative Muslim countries that have an educational gender gap in comparison to non-Muslim countries, it is all Muslim countries. Thus, it becomes important to study Muslim countries separately from non-Muslim countries. The separation is important to determine the strength of the effect of religion and modernization variables on female-to-male total school enrollment in Muslim countries. So far, I have established that both liberalizing the constitution and increasing urbanization matter for both Muslim and non-Muslim countries. However, their effect on educational gender equality varies depending on whether the country is Muslim or not. For example, liberalizing the constitution seems to have a stronger effect on Muslim countries than on non-Muslim countries. In contrast, urbanization has a stronger effect on non-Muslim countries than on Muslim countries. Still, both Constitution and Urbanization seem to have only a modest positive effect in the combined models.

In this section, I separate Muslim countries from non-Muslim countries to examine the influence of religion and modernization variables on female-to-male total school enrollment in Muslim countries. The religious theory would expect religion to have a very strong negative influence on gender equality in education. The modernization theory would expect a positive effect of urbanization. The results in this section confirm those in the previous section and indicate that although having a less religious constitution has a slightly higher positive effect than the effect of urbanization on educational gender equality in Muslim countries, both variables have a modest effect. However, the decrease in the fertility rate seems to have the highest significant positive effect on educational gender equality. The increase in time has a positive impact on female-to-male total school enrollment, but the substitutive effect is also small. The effect of the variation in the level of religiosity within Muslim countries and liberalizing the constitution is generally positive, but not linear.

Like Model 3 in Table 4.1, Model 11 in Table 4.5 indicates that the greater the increase in urbanization and the less religiously extreme the country, the higher the gender equality in total education. However, the statistical and substantively significant effect of moving from having a very religious Muslim constitution to a less religious Muslim constitution is modest; decreasing the fertility rate, on the other hand, again seems to play a major positive role in educational gender equality. Time also has a statistical and positive association with education gender equality, but its coefficient is small, so the substantiveness of the positive impact is not significant. Model 10 answers the research question regarding whether Constitution and Urbanization matter to educational gender equality in Muslim states. It indicates that these two variables are positively associated with gender equality in education, but that their magnitude is small.

However, R^2 is much lower in Model 11 for Muslim countries alone than that in Model 3 for both Muslim and non-Muslim countries. This indicates that Model 11 explains only 21 percent of the variation of female-to-male total school enrollment in Muslim countries. This could be due to

Table 4.5 Only Muslim countries with the combined model and the model with different levels of religious conservativeness

DV: F/M total school enrollment	Model 11 Coef (SE)	Model 12 Coef (SE)	Model 13 Coef (SE)
Urbanization	0.174*** (0.048)	0.25*** (0.05)	0.050 (0.036)
Constitution	0.187** (0.092)	0.14 (0.10)	
Fertility	−6.483*** (0.435)	−6.19*** (0.43)	−7.301*** (0.394)
Time	0.066*** (0.026)	0.06*** (0.03)	0.090*** (0.026)
Arab		−8.30*** (1.60)	
MCON			−0.742 (0.541)
MLIB			0.992*** (0.586)
LIB			0.838 (0.740)
Secular			1.966*** (0.833)
_cons	77.212*** (3.877)	76.96*** (3.72)	86.726*** (3.418)
R^2	0.205	0.207	0.326
Wald Chi^2	389.79	446.56	615.99
N	1426	1426	1426

Coef coefficient, *DV* dependent variable, *F/M* female/male, *LIB* liberal, *MCON* moderately conservative, *MLIB* moderately liberal, *SE* standard error

***$p < 0.01$, **$p < 0.05$, *$p < 0.1$

having an omitted variable problem. In order to determine what might be causing the difference between Model 3 and Model 11, I test several other variables that could explain the variation in the dependent variables, such as oil production, GDP per capita, government budget balance, colonization, war, female representation in parliament, and the Convention on the Elimination of All Forms of Discrimination against Women (CEDAW), but the variables are not statistically significant and do not add value to the model (See Table 4.6 for more details).[6]

However, since the Arab variable was significant, I added it to Model 12. Model 12 shows that there is a significant difference between Arab and

Table 4.6 Variables used in the models, but subsequently deleted

Variable	Expectation	Results	Problems
GDP per capita	Positive and significant	Not stable	The sign kept changing because of the correlation with urbanization
Oil	Positive and significant, although Ross (2008) expected oil to have next effect on education	Positive but statistically insignificant	The data were available only from 1980
Oil/GDP per capita	Positive	Positive but not statistically insignificant	The data were available only from 1980
Balance of budget	Positive and significant	Sign not stable and not significant	
Immigration	Expected to be positive and significant	Negative and not significant	
Education aid	Positive and significant	Negative	This was available only from the 1970s and there were lots of missing data
RPE	Positive and significant	Negative or positive, but not statistically significant	The data for several countries were not available
RPR	Positive and significant	Negative or positive, but not statistically significant	The data for several countries were not available
Female in parliamentary lower house	Positive and significant	Just positive	
UN treaty (CEDAW)	Positive and significant	Negative or positive, but not statistically significant	Most of the empirical studies found no significant result because implementation of these treaties is very limited

RPE Relative Political Extraction, *RPR* Relative Political Reach non-Arab Muslim countries. For Arab countries, the predicted female-to-male total school enrollment would be 8.30 points lower than for non-Arab countries, holding all other variables constant. This indicates that educational gender equality in Arab countries is not merely lower than educational gender equality in non-Muslim countries, it is lower even than that in non-Arab Muslim countries. The negative effect of religion could be stronger in Arab countries because Islam originally started from there. Since Islam was exported to non-Arab Muslim countries, the Islamic heritage might not be as strongly embedded in society as is the case in Arab Muslim countries. Also, the difference could be because non-Arab countries, such as Malaysia, Indonesia, Turkey, and Iran, have their own historical heritage that is very different from the Arab heritage, so when Islam spread to those countries it became mixed with the country's original heritage. This may lower the intensity of the spread of some of the negative aspects of the Islamic Arab heritage. Controlling for Arab countries weakens the strength of the marginal effect of Constitution and its statistical significance. The marginal effect of Urbanization increases and remains significant at a 99 percent confidence level. This means that once Arab countries are controlled for, Urbanization seems to have a stronger effect on non-Arab Muslim countries. Fertility rate and Time remain about the same as in Model 11. R^2 is nearly the same as in Model 11, but Wald Chi^2 is smaller than in Model 11, which indicates that adding the Arab variable did not improve the fit of the overall model.

To answer whether there is a difference between religiously extremist Muslim countries and religiously moderate Muslim countries, I ran a regression model with the different religious categories that I explained in the previous section. Using CON as a reference group, Model 13 shows that the association between the different levels of Muslim religious conservativeness and gender equality in female-to-male total school enrollment is not linear. In comparison to CON, MCON has a negative coefficient, although not statistically significant. MLIB has a higher value than both CON and MCON, and it is positive and statistically significant at a 90 percent confidence level. The coefficient for LIB is still positive, but slightly smaller than MLIB and statistically not significant. This means that moderately liberal and liberal Muslim countries also have higher educational gender equality compared to conservative Muslim countries, but that the increase is modest since the coefficients are not significant or are significant at a 90 percent confidence level. Secular Muslim countries' predicted female-to-male total school enrollment would be 1.97 points higher than that for conservative Muslim countries, holding all other variables constant. This means that secularism is positively associated with educational gender equality, with a 95 percent confidence level.

The results show that the relationship between female-to-male total school enrollment and Constitution is positive, but not linear. Moving from being a very conservative or a very moderately conservative Muslim country makes the negative sign disappear, but the significant increase is shown only in moderately liberal and secular Muslim countries. The negative coefficient for moderately conservative countries could be linked to the negative effect of conservative Muslim countries that was shown in Model 6, Table 4.1; still, the coefficients for the three different religious levels are trivial. The positive sign for the Urbanization variable and for MLIB, LIB, and Secular Muslim countries indicates that increasing urbanization and having a less religious constitution help increase female total school enrollment, but decreasing the fertility rate has the strongest influence on the ratio of female-to-male school enrollment in Muslim countries than all other variables. This indicates that the decline in the fertility rate is a significant indicator for measuring modernization, especially for Muslim countries. Time is also positive and statistically significant, but the magnitude is small.

Regarding the association between female-to-male total school enrollment and the interaction term of Urbanization, the regression tests show that the association was negative and statistically significant in MCON, but positive and statistically significant for MLIB Muslim countries. It was also negative but insignificant for LIB Muslim countries; the results of the religious categories were positive but statistically insignificant. These results indicate that urbanization has different effects at the different levels of religion.[7] Urbanization seems to have the highest effect on educational gender equality in MLIB Muslim countries. The effect of urbanization on conservative countries is either modest, as is the case in CON, or negative, as in MCON. These results are not completely against Lerner's (1958) modernization theory, which states that urbanization is capable of defeating the negative influence of religion. In fact, they provide evidence that supports the modernization theory, although with an exception for extremist religiously conservative Muslim countries. Looking at the marginal effect for the different levels of religious conservativeness in Muslim countries, Urbanization seems to have a positive increase in linearity at all levels, except in CON and MCON countries. The graphs in Fig. 4.2 indicate that the effect of having a less religious constitution increases as

EMPIRICAL TESTING AND ANALYSIS OF DATA 109

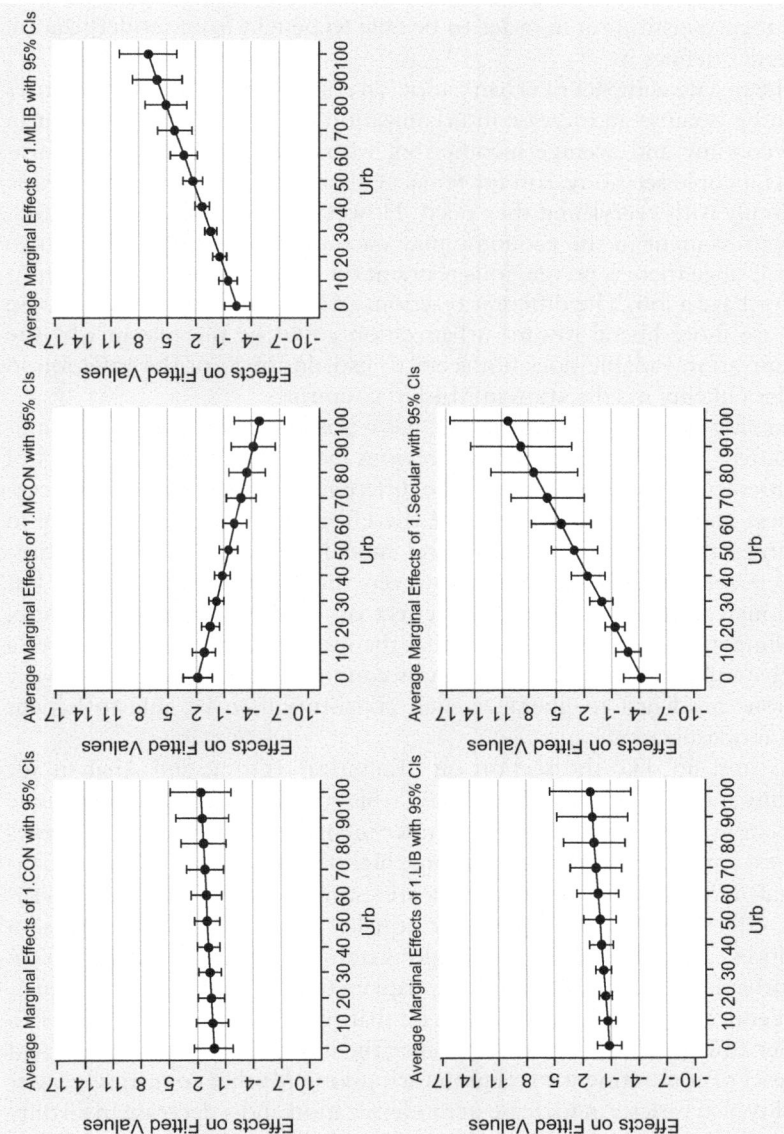

Fig. 4.2 The marginal effect of the different levels of religious constitutions in Muslim countries

urbanization increases. This indicates that Muslim countries need to liberalize their constitution in order to be able to benefit from modernization as Lerner defines it.

The negative impact of urbanization on conservative[8] Muslim countries could be because an increase in urbanization is a sign of improvement in the economy and average income. So, with extremist religious governments, people see no reason for female education if the male can provide his family with everything they need. However, in less religious societies, an improvement in the economy may encourage more females to go to school, since there is no religious restraint on their freedom to gain education or have a job. The different reactions of Muslim extremists and those who are more liberal toward urbanization could be the reason why the Urbanization variable does not seem to explain much of the variation in gender equality in education in Muslim countries.

Fertility rate, on the other hand, has a positive and statistically significant effect, as is the case in all the previous models. The marginal effect of the interaction variables between the different levels of religious conservativeness and Fertility indicates that the effect of having high fertility in countries that have conservative and moderately conservative constitutions is zero or close to zero. However, the increase in fertility in less religious countries has a negative effect on total female-to-male school enrollment.[9] Again, this indicates that the modernization variables have a positive influence only in less religious countries. Countries that are very religious need first to liberalize their constitution to be able to benefit from modernization.

To sum up, like the section on "Empirical Testing and Analysis for Muslim and Non-Muslim Countries," this section confirms the negative association between educational gender inequality and Muslim countries with extremely religious constitutions, high fertility rates, and low urbanization. Extremist Muslim countries are estimated to have a lower coefficient effect on educational gender equality than less religious Muslim countries. The influence of the religious status of a country's constitution and urbanization appear to modestly explain the variation in gender equality in education. These results indicate that religion makes a difference to gender equality in education, but, since the interpretation of religion and the level of commitment to religion vary among Muslim countries, gender equality also varies. An increase in modernization and a decrease in fertility do not seem to help conservative and moderately conservative Muslim countries; they have a positive effect only in less religious countries. This indicates that modernization can help increase educational gender equality in Muslim countries, but not in extremist Muslim countries. Time has a positive and statistical effect, but the substantive effect is also modest. However, fertility seems to provide the strongest explanation for the gender gap in education, since the coefficient remains large and significant for all models and the marginal effect is strong and significant in less religious Muslim countries.

Since Muslim countries differ from non-Muslim countries by having no conservative countries and a few countries that are moderately conservative, studying non-Muslim countries separately from Muslim countries is important. If the majority of non-Muslim countries are already liberal, does the constitution still make any difference? If not, then why do some non-Muslim countries continue to have lower female school enrollment than male? These questions are answered in the next section.

Empirical Testing and Analysis for Non-Muslim Countries

The first section, "Empirical Testing and Analysis for Muslim and Non-Muslim Countries," confirms that, in both Muslim and non-Muslim countries, less religious countries have higher gender equality than more religiously conservative countries. However, since non-Muslim countries have zero extremely conservative observations and only 78 observations in the moderately conservative religious category, I was concerned that my results were affected by the high number of Muslim-country observations in the first three religious categories: CON, MCON, and MLIB. So, I applied the same regression tests I performed in the previous two sections to the non-Muslim countries—though here the base category is MCON.

Like in the previous two sections, in Model 13 Urbanization, Fertility rate, and Time are associated with gender equality in education; however, unlike in the previous two sections, Constitution here is not statistically associated with educational gender equality (*ceteris paribus*). This is expected, since the majority of the non-Muslim countries in my sample fell into the liberal category. So, non-Muslim countries generally are less religious than Muslim countries, and most of them are modernized and have more girls than boys in school. Model 14 confirms the insignificant relationship between Constitution and gender equality in education, since neither MLIB, LIB, nor Secular is statistically significant in reference to

MCON countries. However, both MLIB and LIB have a positive coefficient in comparison to MCON non-Muslim countries. The coefficient for Secular countries is negative, but that is because it has an outlier, Benin; if that is dropped the coefficient becomes positive. However, even though all the coefficient values of the different levels of conservativeness would be positive if Benin were dropped from the sample, the model would still be non-linear.

In non-Muslim countries, Urbanization has a stronger positive effect on educational gender equality than in Muslim countries. Unlike in Muslim countries, the association between Urbanization and the ratio of total female-to-male school enrollment is positive in Models 13 and 14, and statistically significant at the 99 percent confidence level. This indicates that the difference in the level of educational gender equality in non-Muslim countries can be explained by the level of modernization. This can be confirmed by the results found in the association between female-to-male total school enrollment and the interaction term between Urbanization and the different religious categories. As in the section on "Empirical Testing and Analysis for Muslim Countries," the regression tests show that the association between Urbanization and non-Muslim moderately conservative countries is negative and statistically significant in comparison to non-Muslim, less religious countries. It is also negative, but statistically insignificant, for secular non-Muslim countries. The rest of the religious categories are positive but statistically insignificant.[10] This indicates that urbanization also has a stronger positive effect on non-Muslim less religious countries than on non-Muslim religious countries. The marginal effect of the influence of urbanization on the different levels of religious conservativeness is not as large as is the case in Muslim countries. This is because the influence of religion on educational gender equality in non-Muslim countries is weak. The graphs for the marginal effect indicate that, unlike in Muslim countries, the difference in the marginal effect of urbanization on the different levels of religious conservativeness in non-Muslim countries is limited.[11] This is expected, since the influence of religion in non-Muslim countries is not as strong as in Muslim countries. However, like Muslim countries, the lowest effect of urbanization, in comparison to other religious categories, is in conservative non-Muslim countries.

The increase in Fertility rate also has a negative effect on educational gender equality and is statistically significant at the 99 percent confidence level in both models, but the coefficients in both models are smaller than

Table 4.7 Only non-Muslim countries with the combined model and the model with different levels of conservativeness

DV: F/M total school enrollment	Model 13 Coef (SE)	Model 14 Coef (SE)
Urbanization	0.463***	0.389***
	(0.067)	(0.067)
Constitution	−0.165	
	(0.154)	
Fertility	−5.916***	−6.430***
	(0.448)	(0.474)
Time	0.123***	0.139***
	(0.045)	(0.047)
MLIB		0.436
		(0.538)
LIB		0.092
		(0.645)
Secular		−0.381
		(0.979)
_cons	86.595***	89.848***
	(6.570)	(6.453)
R^2	0.604	0.629
Wald Chi^2	1504.56	1396.37
N	1262	1262

Coef coefficient, *DV* dependent variable, *F/M* female/male, *LIB* liberal, *MLIB* moderately liberal, *SE* standard error

***$p < 0.01$, **$p < 0.05$, *$p < 0.1$

the coefficients in Models 11 and 13 in the section on "Empirical Testing and Analysis for Muslim Countries." However, Fertility rate in Table 4.7 is larger than in Model 12, where Arab countries are controlled for. In general, the results indicate that while increasing urbanization in non-Muslim countries has a better effect on educational gender equality than in Muslim countries, decreasing the fertility rate in Muslim countries contributes better to the increase in the ratio of total female-to-male school enrollment in Muslim countries. This means that although a decrease in the fertility rate has a strong positive impact in both Muslim and non-Muslim countries, its effect is stronger in traditional societies.

R^2 and Wald Chi^2 for the non-Muslim countries' models are much higher than in the Muslim countries' models. For example, for non-Muslim countries, R^2 in Model 12 is 60 percent and in Model 13 it is 63 percent. For Muslim countries, R^2 is 21 percent in Model 10 and in Model

11 it is 33 percent. This means that the regression models for non-Muslim countries explain the variation better than all the models for Muslim countries. As I mentioned before, unlike the regression models for non-Muslim countries, the models for Muslim countries suffer from major omitted variables. Traditional societies are very complex, and figuring out which factors may be associated with educational gender equality does not necessarily mean that measuring it would be possible. This is due to the lack of data and the expense of data collection.

To sum up this section, for non-Muslim countries, Fertility, Urbanization, and Time are significantly associated with gender equality in education. Constitution is not statistically significant, and that is to be expected, since most non-Muslim countries are not traditional societies. Nevertheless, like Muslim countries, moderately liberal and liberal non-Muslim countries have positive coefficients, which indicates that moving from being moderately conservative to moderately liberal or liberal has a positive effect on female education, although not a statistically significant one. The effect of urbanization on non-Muslim countries, although higher than its effect on Muslim countries, is modest, probably because the difference in the ratio of female-to-male school enrollment in non-Muslim countries is not significant. Most non-Muslim countries have high gender equality in education, with the ratio close to or equal to one and sometimes exceeding one, such as in Switzerland, Australia, South Korea, and Uruguay. I call this reverse gender discrimination. This problem is widespread among non-Muslim countries, and a few Muslim countries have started to have it in elementary and tertiary education, but not in secondary school enrollment.

Analysis of the Results

This chapter examines the association between religiously conservative and less conservative constitutions and gender equality in education. Several countries, such as Yemen, Tunisia, Egypt, Thailand, Libya, and Malaysia, still debate the proper role of religion in the constitution. The continuing debates over the appropriate official status of religion in these countries' constitutions indicate that it is highly expected, from the debaters' perspective, that the place of religion in the constitution has either a positive or a negative impact on these nations. This study focuses on the impact of religious constitutions on educational gender equality. In this chapter, I use the religious and modernization theories to examine the influence of religiously conservative constitutions and modernization on educational gender equality. The chapter studies the association between religiously conservative and less conservative constitutions and educational gender equality in both Muslim and non-Muslim countries. It also studies the association between educational gender equality and several modernization factors, such as urbanization and fertility. The purpose of this study is to examine whether religions have a negative association with educational gender equality, and if modernization can lessen that effect. It aims to inspect whether Muslim societies have less educational gender equality than non-Muslim societies, and whether Muslim societies are resistant to modernization. The chapter answers the four main questions that I presented in Chap. 3:

1. Does religion have a negative association with educational gender equality?
2. Do Muslim countries have higher gender inequality in education than non-Muslim countries, holding constant other related factors?
3. Is the variation of gender inequality in education due to the countries' levels of religious conservativeness?
4. Does modernization, as reflected by urbanization, reduce the impact of religion?

In response to the first question, the section on "Empirical Testing and Analysis for Muslim and Non-Muslim Countries" confirms the current literature that associates low gender equality in education with religion. The statistical models in this section confirm the statistically significant role of religion in increasing and decreasing educational gender equality, and the association between gender equality in education and the status of religion in a constitution, although the magnitude is small. The data also confirm that Muslim countries have higher gender inequality in education than non-Muslim countries. However, Model 3 shows that both Constitution and Urbanization play a significant role in increasing gender equality in education, but that modernization theory seems to maintain its positive statistically significant level in all models. This indicates that modernization theory explains the variation in gender equality in education better than religious theory.

The data analysis also suggests that countries' levels of religious conservativeness is associated with the variation of gender inequality in education in both Muslim and non-Muslim countries, but is more significant in

Muslim countries. However, controlling for conservative Muslim countries and Arab Muslim countries, instead of *all* Muslim countries, shows that the Arab Muslim countries and most conservative Muslim countries are highly associated with educational gender inequality compared to the rest of the countries in the sample. However, other Muslim—non-Arab and less conservative Muslim—countries still have higher educational gender equality compared to non-Muslim countries. Separating out the Arab and very conservative Muslim variable instead of the (all) Muslim variable suggests that it is the homogenous Muslim variable that explains the variation in gender equality in education; it is not only the Arab or conservative Muslim countries that provide most of the explanation for the educational gender gap. However, the disappearance of the statistical significance of Constitution after holding Arab and Muslim conservative and moderately conservative countries constant, while the modernization variables—Urbanization and Fertility—remain significant, indicates that the gap between non-Arab and less conservative Muslim countries and non-Muslim countries can be explained by modernization. This means that if conservative Muslim countries became less conservative and modernized, they could catch up with non-Muslim countries. These results confirm the first and second hypotheses in the alternative hypotheses that were built based on the current literature. They also confirm Inglehart's results that demonstrated a negative association between Muslim countries and gender equality and the effect of the cultural legacy. The stronger the Islamic cultural legacy, as is the case in the Arab countries, the higher the gender inequality. The weaker the Islamic cultural legacy, such as in non-Arab Muslim countries, the smaller the gender inequality.

The section on "Empirical Testing and Analysis for Muslim Countries" also confirms the results in the section on "Empirical Testing and Analysis for Muslim and Non-Muslim Countries," and answers the third research question regarding the impact of the different levels of religious conservativeness on female education. Conservative and moderately conservative Muslim countries seem to have lower female-to-male school enrollment than less conservative Muslim countries. Less religious Muslim countries have less gender inequality in education than moderately liberal, liberal, and secular Muslim countries, but the magnitude and the statistical significance level are modest. Although the increase is, to some extent, not linear and only some levels of religious conservativeness have statistical significance, this result leans toward supporting the second hypothesis, which suggests that there is a statistically positive effect of moving from a religious Muslim constitution to a less religious Muslim constitution. It also confirms the difference between Arab and non-Arab Muslim countries and the higher negative association between Arab countries and educational gender equality in comparison to non-Arab Muslim countries.

This section also indicates that what type of constitution a country has matters for both Muslim and non-Muslim countries, but it matters more for Muslim countries. Having a less religious Muslim constitution helps increase educational gender equality, and the increase is significant for secular Muslim countries in comparison to conservative Muslim countries. What makes the difference between secular and non-secular Muslim countries significant is the fact that the lowest ratio of total female-to-male school enrollment in secular Muslim countries is higher than the lowest ratio for each religious conservativeness category in Muslim countries. For example, the lowest ratio for total female-to-male school enrollment in a secular Muslim country is in Mali, which is 62 percent, while the lowest ratio in a conservative Muslim country is 34 percent. The situation is different with non-Muslim countries because the lowest ratio of female-to-male school enrollment in secular non-Muslim countries is 53.5 percent in Benin; however, unlike the situation in Muslim countries, Benin seems to be an outlier. If I drop Benin from the non-Muslim countries' sample, moderately liberal, liberal, and secular countries would have a higher ratio of female-to-male school enrollment compared to moderately conservative non-Muslim countries, but the increase is still non-linear. This section thus confirms the literature that argues in favor of secularism to reduce the negative impact of religions. However, the significant positive impact of secularism seems to be limited to traditional societies.

Based on the section on "Empirical Testing and Analysis for Non-Muslim Countries," the positive impact of having a less religious constitution can also be found in non-Muslim countries; however, the association is insignificant, because religion in most of the non-Muslim countries does not play a significant official role and the influence of religious scholars over individuals' choices is limited. Also many non-Muslim countries already have reverse gender discrimination, where more females than males are enrolled in school. This reverse discrimination also starts to appear in a very few Muslim countries, such as Malaysia, Algeria, and Albania, which are liberal and moderately liberal. Figure 4.3 shows the reverse discrimination in total female-to-male school enrollment in both Muslim and non-Muslim countries based on their level of religious conservativeness. It shows that several Muslim countries are catching up with

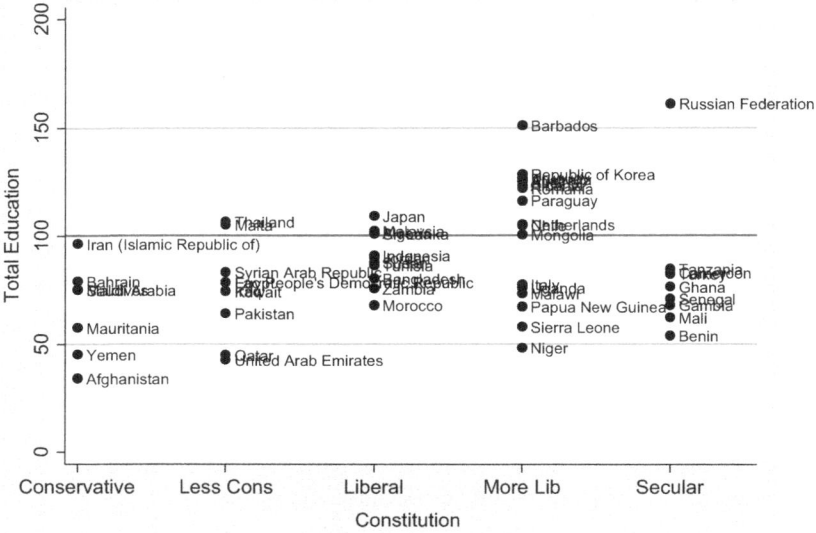

Fig. 4.3 Total female-to-male school enrollment for Muslim and non-Muslim countries (2010)

non-Muslim countries in educating as many girls as boys; however, many non-Muslim countries currently are educating more girls than boys. Reverse educational discrimination could cause a major problem in the future for both Muslim and non-Muslim countries, but the problem will be bigger in Muslim countries, since the majority of educated girls do not join the labor force.

Regarding the last research question, whether modernization factors reduce the negative impact of religion, as Lerner (1958) predicts, the available evidence says that modernization has a positive impact in less religious countries, but not in conservative countries. All urbanization models were stronger than religion models, and Urbanization was positive and statistically significant at a 99 percent confidence level in all models except Model 12, which was positive but not statistically significant. The coefficient was not large, but larger than Constitution in most models. This indicates that the association between modernization and total female-to-male school enrollment is positive and statistically significant. Increasing urbanization is positively associated with an increase in educational gender equality. Reducing the fertility rate, which seems to be a good indicator of modernization, is positively associated with an increase in total female-to-male school enrollment. The coefficient is significantly large in all models, which ensures a positive association between modernization and educational gender equality. The positive impact of reducing the fertility rate on educational gender equality is strong in both Muslim and non-Muslim countries, but it is much stronger in Muslim countries. This indicates that reducing the fertility rate could be a useful approach to increasing women's education even in traditional societies. The impact of the interaction variables between Muslim countries and the increase of urbanization, liberalizing the constitution, and decreasing the fertility rate on educational gender equality is positive, but stronger for the decrease in the fertility rate. Figure 4.4 shows that the marginal effect of the decline in the fertility rate in Muslim countries has the strongest impact on reducing educational gender inequality. This finding supports the modernization theory.

Although this chapter confirms the previous literature on the negative association between Muslim countries and educational gender equality, modernization could be a solution in all cases expect for conservative Muslim countries. However, not all conservative Muslim countries are associated with educational gender inequality. For example, although both Iran and Turkey are non-Arab Muslim countries, Iran, which is a conservative Muslim country, educates more girls than boys at all educational levels. It has a higher female-to-male total school enrollment than Turkey, which is a secular Muslim country. In the next chapter, I will discuss educational gender equality in Iran and Turkey, and analyze the reasons behind Iran's success in this issue.

Conclusion

This chapter provides detailed analytical tests of the association between the ratio of female-to-male total school enrollment and several religious and modernization factors in order to determine which theory has stronger support: religious or modernization theory. It shows that the positive influence of modernization on improving educational gender equality is robust for both Muslim and non-Muslim countries; however, its positive impact is higher in less religious conservative countries. Muslim countries have higher educational gender inequality compared to non-Muslim countries, but most of the negative effect comes from the most religiously

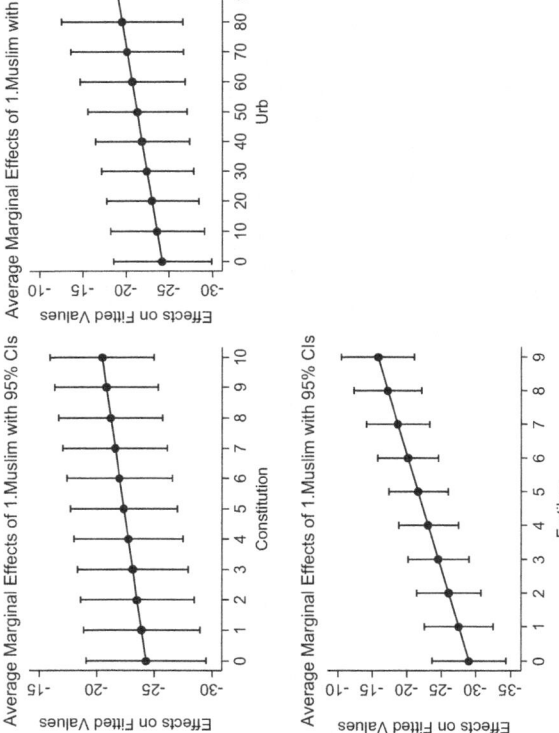

Fig. 4.4 Marginal effect for the interactive terms between Muslim countries and Constitution, Urbanization, and Fertility rate

conservative countries, such as Arab countries that hold an intense Islamic heritage compared to non-Arab Muslim countries. Liberating the constitution has a positive association with increasing educational gender equality, but the positive association is more significant in Muslim counties. Reducing the fertility rate also has a significant association with educational gender equality in both Muslim and non-Muslim countries, but its positive impact is higher in Muslim countries. This chapter confirms that conservative countries must become less conservative in order to benefit from modernization. In the next chapter, I provide a case study that analyzes educational gender equality in two Muslim countries with distinctive characteristics—Iran and Turkey—to be used as a model for other countries that would like to maintain their religious culture, and for those countries that tend to choose secularism.

Notes

1. Muslim countries are controlled by creating a Muslim dummy variable coded 0/1 (0 = non-Muslim, 1 = Muslim).
2. Very conservative and moderately conservative Muslim countries are controlled by creating a Conservative Muslim variable.
3. If I combine conservative and moderately conservative Muslim and non-Muslim countries, the decrease is positive and statistically significant, but it remains significant at a 95 percent confidence level. Everything else remains nearly the same.
4. See Appendix A, Table A.6.
5. For more details on the marginal effect, see Appendix A, Tables A.3 and A.4.
6. To add those variables I had to drop several countries and sometimes several years, because of the unavailability of all the data for all my countries and years. See Appendix A, Table A.5.
7. See Appendix A, Table A.3.
8. If Iran is dropped from the sample, very conservative Muslim countries will have a negative coefficient in the interaction term between CON and Urbanization. However, I cannot drop it because the literature supports the high ratio of female-to-male total school enrollment in Iran, due to the different way of interpreting women's right to education in Islam after the Islamic revolution in 1979 (see Hoodfar 2009).
9. See Appendix A, Fig. A.4.
10. See the regression table in Appendix A, Table A.4.
11. See the marginal effect in Appendix A, Fig. A.1.

REFERENCES

Hoodfar, H. (2009). Afghan Refugee Women in Iran. In K. M. Cuno & M. Desai (Eds.), *Family, Gender, and Law in a Globalizing Middle East and South Asia, Gender and Globalization* (p. 241). London: Syracuse University Press.

Lerner, D. (1958). *The Passing of Traditional Society: Modernizing the Middle East.* Glencoe, IL: The Free Press.

Rizzo, H., Abdel-Latif, A.-H., & Meyer, K. (2007). The Relationship Between Gender Equality and Democracy: A Comparison of Arab Versus Non-Arab Muslim Societies. *Sociology, 41*(6), 1151–1170.

Ross, M. L. (2008). Oil, Islam, and Women. *American Political Science Review, 102*(1), 107–123.

CHAPTER 5

Case Study

Iran and Turkey are the two major non-Arab players in the Muslim world, particularly in the Middle East and North Africa (MENA) region. These two countries are well known for their prominent involvement in MENA political and religious conflicts. Even when Turkey decided to abandon the Muslim world and become secular, that action had an impact on the MENA. Iran and Turkey differ from other MENA countries in their economic and political institutions, which are more advanced than those in the rest of the MENA. Such a situation made the international community consider Turkey and Iran as benchmarks that MENA countries should strive to match. For instance, from the 1920s to the 1950s, several MENA countries tried to follow in Turkey's religious ideological steps and move away from religion toward secularism. Examples of these attempted moves are Egypt, Iraq, Iran, and Tunisia. However, the liberal regimes in these countries failed, except in Tunisia, where it has managed to survive up to today.

After the 1950s, Turkey lost its popularity due to its economic struggle and Iran managed to take its place. Yet, after the Iranian revolution and Turkey's great economic and political progress, which started in 2003, Turkey became a more favorable example to the international community of a country that MENA countries should attempt to emulate. The ability of the Justice and Development Party (AKP), a political party with a partially religious background, to take advantage of the major social and economic failure of the secular parties and present Islam as the solution to these problems moved Turkey from being a secular country to a less secular one. The political and economic success of the AKP's leader, Recep Tayyip Erdoğan, the previous prime minister and current president of Turkey, revived Turkish popularity in the MENA and made the Turkish political system a good example to follow again. Turkey once more became a good model for the MENA countries, since the political system managed to be civil and tolerant with Islamists, who present themselves as modernists and who do not intend to establish an Islamic state based on Sharia.[1] The international favoritism for Turkey comes from the idea that secular governments are better at enhancing gender equality than religious governments. The relative success of the AKP's governments in promoting some elements of Islam brought the hope of being able to maintain the secular culture and democracy. Iran, on the other hand, used to be liberal und a strong ally of Western countries, particularly the United States, until 1979. At that time Iran was making some economic and political progress and it was considered one of the region's very powerful countries. However, Iran's influence on the MENA was limited, since the majority of the countries in the region are Sunnis and they consider themselves in competition with Iran, which is seen as the leader of the Shia nations. However, the international community treated Iran as the dominant country in the region. After the revolution, Iran became internationally isolated and its political and economic experiences—even though sometimes admired—were unwelcome. Regardless of the political and economic conflicts, today many people consider Iran a very conservative Muslim country, where the gender gap is high and women are heavily oppressed, while Turkey is a secular country where women have more rights and a smaller gender gap.

Studying the gender gap in Turkey and Iran is important, especially in recent years, because several countries in the MENA are trying to establish a new political system that is best for their nations. Until 2016, Turkey was becoming the country that both the international communities as well as new governments were using as a benchmark; regardless of the current political crisis, it is important to know whether Turkey is a good benchmark for these new governments, or if gender equality in Turkey's ideal model is just an illusion. It is also important to know if being a Muslim conservative country necessarily means low gender equality, or if that is also a misconception. As I mentioned before, testing the level of gender equality and women's rights is a difficult task, because gender equality involves many aspects and the definitions of women's rights differ from one society to another and are hard to measure. Thus, in this study, I am limiting my test to whether the gender gap in education and labor-force participation is better in secular countries, such as Turkey, or in conservative countries, such as Iran. The reason the hypotheses in this chapter include the gender gap in the labor force, while it was not mentioned in the previous chapters, is because the data for the labor force were not available for all the countries in my sample. Studying the level of female participation in the work force is important, because this is the most direct method of testing the impact of education on the economy. Also, working empowers women and helps increase gender equality.

H_O The gender gap in education and labor-force participation is greater in Iran than in Turkey.

H_a The gender gap in education and labor-force participation is lower in Iran than in Turkey.

I begin this chapter with a brief summary of the religious history of Turkey and Iran in the twentieth century and explain why nowadays Turkey is considered a liberal country, while Iran is a conservative country. I also provide a brief literature review about women's current educational and labor status in Iran and Turkey. Then, I describe the data and introduce the results. Finally, I analyze the data, offer conclusions, and provide policy options.

Turkey's Religious History

When we talk about the religious history of Turkey, we immediately think of the Ottoman Empire, which ruled Turkey for 600 years,[2] and of the modern Turkey that was established in 1923 by Mustafa Kemal Atatürk. The Ottoman Empire was an Islamic empire with multi-ethnic and multi-religious nations. In the sixteenth century, the Ottoman Empire was one of the great powers in the world; its authority expanded to reach many lands in Asia, Africa, and even Europe. However, it gradually lost its military superiority and lagged behind European countries in science and technology. In the mid-nineteenth century, it tried to make major reforms in administration, education, and law; however, these changes were not enough to maintain the integration of the empire. By the beginning of the twentieth century, the Ottoman Empire was considered to be the "sick man of Europe" and finally collapsed at the end of World War I. This led to the establishment of the Turkish Republic in 1923.[3]

Since Islam was the Ottoman Empire's official religion, the empire emphasized the subordination of women and considered that a religious duty. A *mullah*, a member of the Islamic clergy, from a village in northeastern Turkey named Iğdır once said, "A woman will never go to hell if she obeys the four principles of our Holy *Qur'an*, she must not go out without her husband's permission. Second, she must not give things away without her husband's permission. Third, she must pray and fast in Ramadan. Finally, she must not listen to voice of strangers except her immediate relatives … when a husband is away; the devil is present in a woman, tempting her to overthrow her virtue."[4] This quote summarizes the level of men's domination over women in the Ottoman Empire, and the definition of the "ideal household" at that period. However, the situation started to change roughly from 1908 to 1923, when several Turkish writers began advocating for reform. For example, Ziya Gokalp, a scholar and political activist, advocated for women's social, political, and economic rights. The Young Turk movement helped create dozens of philanthropic women's associations, which advocated for women's rights and changing the education and legal systems. In 1914, this movement led to allowing females, for the first time, to join Istanbul University. Some women started to abandon the face veil and, due to the long period of armed conflict during World War I and Turkey's war of independence, women were forced to start working outside the home and to join the labor force in urban areas. In addition, the family code of 1917 recognized women's right to divorce if the husband committed adultery or married another wife without the permission of the first wife.[5] These reforms were made to help the Ottoman Empire take steps toward modernization and rescue it from collapse. However, they failed to meet their purpose.

The establishers of the Turkish Republic were divided into two camps, Islamists and Westernists, who disagreed about the route to be followed to catch up with the West. The first camp, the Islamists, were against reforming females' status and argued that the reason for the decline of the Ottoman Empire was the Western reforms that started in the midnineteenth century. They argued that the empire built a great Islamic civilization that did not need major reform, so it made a mistake when it imitated Western institutions and culture. They claimed that the reform was supposed to be limited to the appreciation of Western industry and technology, not to change people's religious and cultural beliefs. The Westernists, on the other hand, were strongly in favor of reforming females' status, and argued that reforming institutional structures and culture was a must in order to change the country's science, industry, and technology. The empire needed a comprehensive program of modernization and one could not simply take institutions and leave the culture. The Westernist camp was strong enough to win the debate and to build the Turkish Republic based on Western secular views. For this group, "modernization meant Westernization." However, the debate did not end with the establishment of the Republic, it picked up later in 1946 due to the advancement of democracy. This debate gained further momentum in the 1980s and 1990s, and to the present public opinion is still divided into "Islamist" versus "Westernist" camps.[6]

For Atatürk, the founder of the Turkish Republic in 1923 and its first president, "the role of Islam in Ottoman society and politics was responsible for the failure to modernize."[7] He and his associates believed that "Islamic teaching and codes of behavior had kept Muslim women outside the public sphere, and the *ulema* (learned men of religion) had played a key role in the opposition to all forms of reform and progress in the empire."[8] Therefore, Atatürk launched a modernization project that aimed to end the religious function in education, law, and public administration. He radically revised the Ottoman reforms by eliminating religious courts, ending Islam as the state religion, and severely reducing religious education. He delegitimized religious education and established a rationalist secular modern educational system. He replaced the Arabic script by the Latin script in 1928, and tried to purify the Turkish language of Persian and Arabic influences: "The Turkish language became compulsory in national education, and the use of 'foreign' languages, other than Western ones, was forbidden. The change of script from Arabic to Latin contributed to the consolidation of secularism as well. It accomplished this by cutting the ties of the Turks to the language and the script of the Holy *Qur'an*, and to the Arabic and Muslim world in general."[9] Thus, the language reforms were considered a radical cultural shift toward the Western world. Atatürk also emancipated women and brought radical changes to their status. He promoted major reforms in women's status by increasing gender egalitarianism and women's role in public and the work force. The Civil Code of 1926 broke away from Sharia rule and ended some discriminatory practices such as polygamy and unequal inheritance rights.[10] It also "granted women equal rights in matters of divorce and child custody.

Turkish women were also granted suffrage rights, first in local elections in 1930, then in national elections in 1934," and they have been exercising these rights for the last 90 years.[11] Atatürk saw women's participation in developing Turkish society as central to modernization, nationalism, and a way to weaken religious institutions. These reforms were unique in the Muslim world and no other secular state in the Middle East had made such reforms. Atatürk and his associates did not openly challenge Islam; they claimed they were fighting clericalism, fanaticism, and superstitions.[12] He was not burdened, like in other Muslim countries, by colonial history, and was not accused of imitating colonizers, since Turkey was not colonized by any Western power.

Although Atatürk was supportive of women's rights, he did not allow women's independent mobilization.[13] For example, until 1990, the former Civil Code, Article 154, stated that "[T]he marriage is legally represented by the husband, assigning the man as the head of household…. Article 159, required men's permission for women to work."[14] These articles gave men power over women and limited females' opportunities. In addition, the beneficiaries of Atatürk's reforms were mostly urban bourgeois women. Many of the changes in gender laws were not enforced in the rural interior in the eastern region, especially legislation related to marriage. Following Atatürk's death in 1938, his policies started to be challenged, especially after World War II. Turkey moved from having one single party to a multi-party political system. This change gave the opposition parties power to make some changes. For example, under pressure from the Democratic Party, the Republican People's Party (RPP) allowed religious instruction in public schools and made it compulsory, unless parents requested in writing that their children should not receive such classes. The party also permitted the opening of some religious places, and the establishment of a theological department in Ankara to train imams. In 1950, the Democrats expanded religious education to secondary schools and increased the number of institutions for training imams. The law that prohibited the use of Arabic in mosques was revoked and several mosques were built by government funds.[15] However, the military coup in 1960 and the constitutional reform in 1961 slowed down the Islamist movement.

In 1980, the liberal feminists' movement highlighted the shortcoming of Atatürk's reforms and demanded more reforms to a different kind of inequality experienced by women, such as domestic violence, sexual harassment, and virginity examinations. They demanded a stronger implementation of government policies regarding early marriage and honor crimes,[16] especially in rural areas, such as the southeast of Turkey. The international community's contribution to improving gender equality in Turkey was limited until Turkey started to ask to join the EU. On April 14, 1987, the Turkish government under Prime Minister Turgut Özal formally applied for EU membership, but on December 20, 1989 the European Commission gave its negative opinion on the Turkish application and recommended improvements in many areas, including women's rights.[17] Domestic and international pressure led to a constitutional amendment in 1990, which favored the rights of women and minorities. Therefore, from the 1990s onward, gender equality issues have been more in the spotlight in the Turkish political arena, and that increased after 1999 when Turkey officially became a candidate for EU membership.[18] Before Turkey requested to join the EU, most of the international community focused only on what Turkish women have already gained under the secular state and less on what they still had to gain. This could be due to Turkish women's Westernized appearance, which gives the impression that women in Turkey have more freedom and more equal rights to men than the majority of women in the MENA countries.

However, up to today, Turkey continues to score poorly in international statistics on gender equality and empowerment compared to Western countries. The state still recognizes "men as providers and decision makers and define[s] women's primary and proper place as being in home,"[19] and Article 159 still includes the statement that "the harmony and welfare of the marriage union should be borne in mind when choosing and performing a job or profession."[20] This emphasizes the power of men over women and the restraints placed on women's autonomy. Women's participation in the work force is still less than 25 percent, and women's political participation remains low, such as their representation in parliament, which is less than 5 percent. Women's opportunities to get top administrative positions are still very rare; and women remain the victims of domestic violence, honor killings, and sexual harassment in the work place.[21]

Iran's Religious History

Like Turkey, when we talk about the history of Iran in the twenty-first century, we are talking about three eras. The first and the second eras were a monarchic political system under the Pahlavi family dynasty. The first monarchic era was led by Reza Khan (later Reza Shah Pahlavi) from 1925 to 1941, while the second monarchic era was under his son Mohammad Reza Pahlavi, from 1941 to 1979. The third and current era is the Islamic political system after the 1979 revolution. Women's rights under Reza Khan changed significantly after his visit to Turkey in 1934. In the early Reza Khan period, there was no significant improvement in women's rights. His major contribution was in expanding public education for both genders, and encouraging women to contribute to building Iran by working in appropriate jobs that suited mothers, such as teaching. Because he was a tough and brutal soldier to his opponents, he spent his early period building his army and putting down several political and tribal movements. He focused on ending Western privileges and building a modern nation-state. He encouraged industry and education, but with Iranian nationalist ideology. He tried to weaken the power of the religious scholars, but his break with religious leaders was not as sharp as was the case with Atatürk. Reza Khan's visit to Turkey was a turning point for women's rights. He was impressed by women's roles in the country and Atatürk's modernizing reforms. So he formed a Ladies Center under the leadership of his daughter, Ashraf Pahlavi, to prepare the ground for unveiling and enabling a public role for women. In 1936, women in Iran were forbidden from wearing the hijab.[22] He arrested several *mullas* because they prevented the queen and some of her companions from attending an important shrine unveiled. He established a minimum age for marriage and required all marriages, divorces, births, and deaths to be registered with the state. However, his era ended in 1941, when Britain and Russia insisted on removing him because of his lenient attitude to the Nazi ideology, and preferred to replace him as Shah with his son Mohammad.

Iran from 1941 to 1953 was ruled by a parliamentary monarchy political system. During this period, women became politically active and established several political magazines, organizations, and associations. They demanded political and social rights as well as protections and equal pay. However, women did not accomplish much until the 1953 coup, which led to the overthrew of Mohammad Mosaddeq, the prime minister of an elected government, and the outlawing of the National Front, Tudeh, and Islamist extremist Feda'yan-e Islam parties. In 1956, women had access to political positions and participated in many social programs that were supported by the government. In 1963, the Shah granted women the right to vote. In 1967, the Family Protection Act, which permitted women to file for a divorce and forbade polygamy without the first wife's consent, was enacted.[23] Women were encouraged to study and were able to become judges. However, like in Turkey, women's mobility was still restricted by her guardian or husband's permission and honor killings were not punished.[24]

In 1979, Iran experienced a revolution, which was a mix of religious motives and a liberal backlash for social justice. The Shah was criticized for his strong affiliation with the West and his tough economic plan that brought economic inflation. He was accused of being an oppressor, corrupt and extravagant.[25] During the revolution, women stood beside the men and were promised equal rights afterward. After the revolution, women's rights to a better education, health, and work-force participation did increase, but their right to wear whatever they wanted was limited, and family law clauses became more favorable for men.[26] For example, women were prevented from filing for divorce, and the legal age of marriage was lowered to 9 for girls and 15 for boys. Women were also forbidden from becoming judges, and the women who were judges before the revolution were required to leave their jobs.[27] In addition, pre-university schools became gender segregated and women were not allowed to study many subjects such as mining, agriculture, and oil engineering.[28] Such actions disappointed the middle- and upper-class women who supported the revolution, but did not seem to stop them from continuing to ask for their rights. The domestic pressure and the change in the political and economic situation led to relaxation or phasing out of many of those restrictions. For example, because of the Iran–Iraq war, the new rulers were supportive of women's education and participation in public health programs. Girls' education was encouraged and promoted even in rural and tribal areas. Women's education was not limited to teaching; it included medicine, and even the arts. The high level of literacy among women led to more female political activists, who managed to restore some of women's marriage rights, such as limiting a husband's right to prevent his wife from taking a job. In 1995, women were again allowed to become consulting judges, the prohibition on birth control was reversed, and free contraceptives were distributed by the government. The spread of education seemed to empower Iranian women and strengthen their fight against the conservative political regime.[29]

Currently, females in Iran enjoy more rights than many of their counterparts in other, more liberal and conservative Islamic nations. For example, female enrollment rates at all levels of education are higher than in many Muslim countries. In 2010, there was 100 percent female enrollment at primary school level, and "[d]uring the 1999–2000 academic year, 53 per cent of the students accepted at state universities were women."[30] The educational gender gap has been reduced at all educational levels. In 2010, female-to-male primary enrollment was 112 percent in favor of females, 87 percent in secondary school, and 87 percent in tertiary education. There has also been an increase in the number of girls at secondary school who study "masculine" fields such as math, physics, and experimental sciences. At the university level, "more and more women are studying 'male oriented' disciplines such as agriculture, veterinary science, and engineering. 58 per cent of all university students in the medical school are women."[31] In addition, "in 2005, women occupied 4.1 per cent of the seats in *majlis* or parliament, as compared to 4.4 per cent representation of women at the Turkish parliament, and they accounted for 6.7 per cent of ministerial and government jobs, as compared to women occupying 4.3 per cent of similar positions in Turkey. In the same year, women accounted for 13 per cent of senior officials, legislators, and managers in Iran, as compared to 6 per cent of such positions in Turkey."[32] Furthermore, women currently can "file for divorce on the grounds of abuse, drug addiction to the extent that it prevents the husband from performing his duties, second marriage of husband without the wife's permission, husband's prolonged absence and inability to financially support his family."[33]

However, despite these changes, gender equality still needs major improvement. For example, although the Iranian constitution does not prohibit women from becoming president, female presidential candidates are dismissed, because they are considered to be disqualified through their lack of experience and of sufficient knowledge of Islam. Like many other religions, women still cannot be a religious leader; and single women are not eligible for government scholarships to study abroad. In addition, it is still much easier for a man to divorce than for a woman, and when divorce does occur, "the custody of children above the age of five automatically goes to the husband."[34]

In summary, Iran and Turkey have much in common. Besides being non-Arab Muslim countries, both have experienced significant political and economic changes. Those changes are unique to the region and made them, at different stages of history, good models for the MENA countries to follow. In comparison to most countries in the Muslim world, both Iran and Turkey are considered modern, and women have gained more political, social, and economic rights. For example, currently females in both countries have a high standard of education compared to other women in the region. Women have the right to participate in elections as voters and candidates. Women political activists have more freedom than other women in the region. Magazines and organizations that advocate for women's rights are available. However, Iran and Turkey differ in many important aspects. The first is the role of religion in the constitution. Iran's current constitution states that Iran is an Islamic country and that Sharia is the only source of legislation. In Turkey, however, it was only recently that Islamists started to become politically active. Turkey has been a secular country for nearly 100 years and it seems set to remain secular for the near future. In addition, Turkish law gives females more rights than Iran's law. The law in Turkey does not restrict women from becoming a judge or even president, and there is no strict dress code, as is the case in Iran. Women's mobility in Iran is more restricted than women's mobility in Turkey.

Based on three dimensions, the country's constitution, women's social mobility, and women's ability to be a judge, I classify the current status of Turkey as a liberal country and Iran as a conservative country. Turkey was declared a secular country in 1928. Its constitution, part one article two, states that "The Republic of Turkey is a democratic, secular and social state governed by the rule of law; bearing in mind the concepts of public peace, national solidarity and justice; respecting human rights; loyal to the nationalism of Atatürk, and based on the fundamental tenets set forth in the Preamble."[35] Women in Turkey can be judges. In addition, women do not need to have permission to leave the country or get a job.[36] On the other hand, Iran "establishes Shi'a Islam of the Twelver (Jaafari) sect as Iran's official religion in December 1979."[37] Before that, Islam was the state religion, although Sharia was not strictly enforced. Currently, Iranian women cannot be judges and need permission from a male relative to work or leave the country (Table 5.1).

Table 5.1 The differences between Iran and Turkey in different religious aspects related to women's rights

	Turkey	Iran
Constitution	A secular constitution	An Islamic country
Work opportunities	Women can be judges	Women cannot be judges
Freedom of mobility	Women do not need permission to work or leave the country	Women need permission to work or leave the country
Personal freedom	Females do not need to cover their hair	Females have to cover their hair

Females' Education and Labor Force Participation

Although measuring women's rights and gender equality should not be limited solely to the gender gap in education and women's participation in the labor force, these two factors can give us a good idea of where gender equality is heading. In Chap. 1, I explained why education is critical for improving social life and economic growth. I mentioned that the literature already confirms that education contributes positively to people's attitudes toward gender equality and more egalitarian societies. Education also improves the economy by increasing women's productivity inside and outside the home. It decreases the fertility rate and improves family health, child survival, and the investment in human capital. Education also improves employees' skills, and increases their learning capacity and speed. It not only helps individuals to be more productive and aware of their rights, but also contributes to countries' overall economic growth. For example, Stephan Klasen and Francesca Lamanna in *The Impact of Gender Inequality in Education and Employment on Economic Growth* find that "the combined 'costs' of education and employment gaps in the Middle East and North Africa, and South Asia amount respectively to 0.9–1.7 and 0.1–1.6 percentage point differences in growth compared to East Asia."[38] In fact, as Barro and Lee (1993) find, increasing women's education without increasing women's participation in the work force could have a negative effect on economic growth, since many governments subsidize education as a way to invest in human capital. When women do not enter the labor market, it can be said that the government—if we do not consider the indirect economic benefits of females' education—has lost its investment. With education and joining the labor force, individuals can help themselves and others to obtain a better standard of living. This indicates that the gender gap in education and the labor force does not merely increase awareness of human rights, but also contributes to economic growth and the country's prosperity. Therefore, before examining other measurements to understand the gender gap, we need to start with education and labor-force participation, since these two factors are key to solving many other gender inequality problems. In this chapter, I try to compare the level of female education and of labor-force participation in Turkey and Iran to determine which country has invested better in its female assets, and how that investment is going to better prepare women to change their futures.

Females' Education in Turkey

Although Turkey opened its first girls' school in 1858 and women got access to university in 1911,[39] the country is still struggling with closing the gap between girls' and boys' access to educational services. Up to the present, the participation of the female population in education has been much lower than the participation of their male counterparts. The fact that Turkey has been a secular country since 1929 and was built based on the concept of gender equality did not help close the gender gap in education. Turkey's enforcement of laws related to women's rights was not strong enough to achieve the country's educational millennium goals. Such weakness is due to the failure of the Turkish government to provide enough schools and teachers. In addition, the historical religious roots of the Ottoman Empire are still deep in Turkish society, especially in rural areas. Changing the regulations and imposing new ones is not difficult when there is political will and when the government is autocratic; however, enforcing those laws is the challenge. Since the country became secular, families have found themselves forced to send their girls to mixed schools (boys and girls) and their girls are made to take off their headscarves. In addition, there were few schools in rural areas and public transportation was not available. Even after the economic improvements, schools and universities are still limited in rural areas and rural people are not willing to use school buses or boarding schools.[40] Those problems were summarized by the Ministry of National Education (MoNE) 2003 in the "Quantitative Data on National Education 2002–2003" report:

> (1) shortage of schools and classrooms especially in many parts of the southeast; (2) schools are often located far from home and many parents do not want their children, especially girls, to travel far; (3) parents do not want to send their children to schools which are in a poor physical state with no latrines or running water; (4) many families suffer from economic hardships; (5) the traditional gender bias stemming from cultural and patriarchal family structure favors the needs of men and boys over those of women and girls; (6) the harsh necessity for scraping a living forces many families to coopt their children as additional labor resources in order to augment their income; (7) many families do not view girls' education as being very important because their early marriage is more of a priority and thus many are kept at home to help with household chores; (8) the absence of female role models means that there is little to stir the aspirations of the girls in villages.[41]

The government, with the support of local and international organizations, tried to address some of these issues by launching several programs. For example, since many small villages had only a five-grade primary school, the MoNE decided to close down the primary schools in these small villages and provide free buses to move students to bigger villages or towns.[42] However, this attempt failed to attract girls, since parents were unwilling to let their daughters get on shuttles unchaperoned. Another popular program called "Come on girls, let's go to school," which was initiated by the MoNE with the support of the UN Children's Fund and the World Bank, was launched in 2003. It aimed at increasing girls' enrollment and attendance rates in rural areas and southeast regions of Turkey. This program depends on a vast network of volunteers who go door to door lobbying parents on the value of education. A study by Bedrettin Yazan (2014) showed that the program has contributed modestly to the improvement in female school enrollment in some provinces, but Turkey has not yet met the standard of equal education.[43]

Females' Education in Iran

In comparison to Turkey, female access to education in Iran was delayed for 49 years. As I mentioned before, the first girls' school opened in Tehran in 1907, and women were allowed to enter university only in 1936. Iran managed to catch up with Turkey and surpass the Turkish accomplishments, nevertheless. Both Iran and Turkey already have more girls than boys in elementary school; however, Iran attained gender equality in 1990, while Turkey achieved it only in 2000. In regard to secondary and tertiary education, the World Bank data indicate that Iran also has more girls than boys at both levels, but Barro and Lee's (2013) dataset shows that both Iran and Turkey still have more boys than girls in secondary and tertiary education, yet Iran is closer to equality than Turkey. How Iran managed to overcome the negative impact of religion and increase female education is the question that will be answered in this chapter.

Reza Shah and his son Mohammad gave females access to schools and universities, and encouraged female participation in the public sphere. However, total female-to-male school enrollment was only 55.5 percent in 1979. That percentage increased dramatically after the Islamic revolution and females' education became the focus of the new political government. This government aimed to use education to create the ideal Islamic woman, and attempted to create a new generation of women who understood their "appropriate" Islamic political and social role in post-revolutionary Iran. Ayatollah Khomeini believed that "if women change, the society changes."[44] The ideal Islamic woman, from the perspective of the new political regime, was supposed to be formed on the model of Fatima, the daughter of Prophet Mohammed, the wife of the first Shi'i Imam Ali, and the mother of Imam Hossein.[45] So, Iranian women are expected to play a dual role as a devoted mother and wife and a fighter against tyranny and injustice. They should adopt Fatima's female virtues and modesty, as well as her active participation in the social and political affairs of her time.

To achieve that goal, coeducation was banned only three months after the Islamic authorities took power. Since then, all schools, except universities and a few schools in some rural areas, are segregated by gender. Language schools and universities contain both men and women, but women usually occupy the back seats in the classrooms or some kind of partition is put up to separate men and women. Single women are allowed to study higher education abroad and married women can receive a government scholarship. Women are encouraged to become teachers, since teaching girls is preferably done by females. Men teach boys and are allowed to teach girls if there is a shortage of female teachers. If necessary, female teachers can teach boys, but only at the first and second elementary levels. At the university level, both male and female university professors teach at coeducational as well as women's universities.[46] Those restrictions are not limited to female students in Iran. Several Muslim and MENA countries, such as Yemen and several in the Arabian Gulf, apply the same rules. However, while those restrictions are considered obstacles in these countries, in Iran they were not a problem. In fact, unlike those countries, female school enrollment at all educational levels has increased significantly in Iran in the last 35 years, even with all those restrictions. Therefore, in the next section I provide more details about female school enrollment at different educational levels in both Iran and Turkey. I apply the same test I used in the previous chapter to test whether religion and modernization have a significant positive effect on educational gender equality. I try to answer why Iran after the Islamic revolution managed to make great progress in closing the educational gender gap, while other religious and less religious countries such as Turkey still lag behind on this issue.

Data Description

For education, I use the Barro and Lee (1993) dataset that I have employed throughout this book. However, instead of using only total female-to-male school enrollment, I also use female-to-male school enrollment at all three levels: elementary, secondary, and tertiary. For the labor force, I utilize two different datasets. The first data are on the ratio of female-to-male labor-force participation (as a percentage) from 1990 to 2010. These data were obtained from World Development Indicators. The second type of data are those for the labor force based on educational level, which were only available for four years, 1997, 2005, 2007, and 2008. These data were obtained from the International Labour Organization (ILO). For the education statistical test I employ the same method, the panel-corrected standard error (PCSE), which estimates linear cross-sectional time-series models without bias. This test is very suitable for this analysis because my N is smaller than my T: I have two countries, Iran and Turkey, over a 50-year period.

Empirical Testing

As I mentioned before, Iran is an outlier in my sample, because even though it is considered a religiously conservative Muslim country, female-to-male total school enrollment is higher than in most other, less religious Muslim countries. I chose Turkey as the best example to compare with Iran, not only because Turkey has been considered by many people as a good political model to follow, but also because it represents one of the most extremist secular Muslim countries. It is the only Middle Eastern country that, up to now, still declares its secularism in its constitution. It also shares a great deal of historical and cultural background with most of the MENA countries, thus the result has the potential to be generalized and applied to other less religious Muslim countries. Comparing Iran to Turkey provides strong evidence of the positive impact of modernization on educational gender equality. More importantly, it shows how religion can be used positively to increase educational gender equality if the political will is available.

Results for Education Enrollment

In this section, I provide a description of several graphs that illustrate the status of female-to-male school enrollment in different educational grades in both Iran and Turkey. Figure 5.1 presents the mean of the ratio of

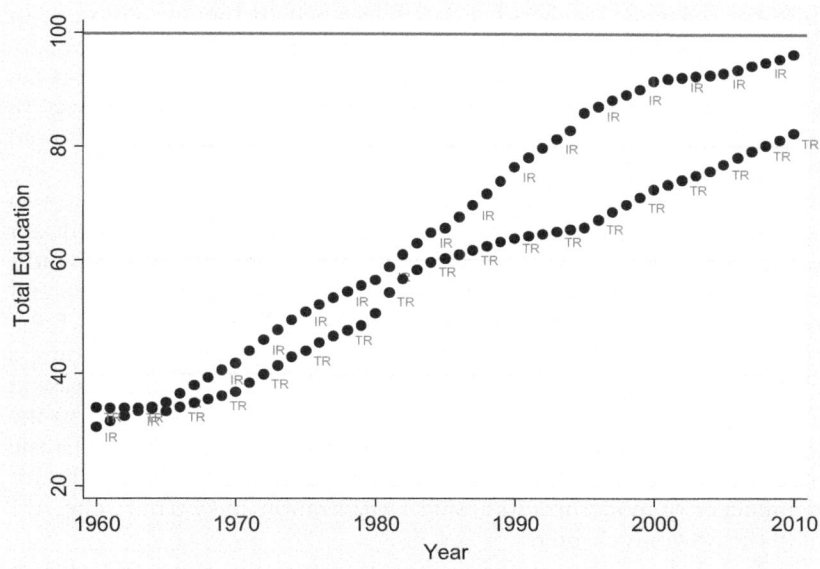

Fig. 5.1 Female-to-male total school enrollment in Iran and Turkey (1960–2010)

female-to-male total school enrollment from 1960 to 2010. The red line is the required level for gender equality in education, which is 100 percent. What this means is that if we have a 100 percent ratio of females to males in the different stages of education, that would mean we have 50 percent females and 50 percent males at each stage. In other words, 100 percent indicates that for every one boy there is one girl; less than 100 percent indicates that there are more boys than girls, and more than 100 percent indicates that there are more boys than girls. Figure 5.1 shows that in 1960, Turkey was educating more girls than Iran. Around 1964, the ratio of female-to-male total school enrollment in Iran caught up with Turkey, and female school enrollment in Iran continued to increase until it exceeded female school enrollment in Turkey. The gap between Iran and Turkey in female-to-male total school enrollment increased significantly after the Islamic revolution. In 2010, Iran's ratio of female-to-male total school enrollment was 96.32 percent, while in Turkey it was 82.32 percent. These percentages indicate that female total school enrollment in Iran is closer to male total school enrolment. They show that Turkey, which has remained secular since 1929, lags behind Iran, which is one of the most religiously conservative countries in the world.

How Iran achieved this significant progress in women's education can be attributed to two reasons: modernization, and the different way of interpreting females' roles in Islam. In the previous chapters, I showed how conservative Muslim countries are resistant to change even when they are considered modern. I provided evidence that associates religion with less educational gender equality. The negative association was significant in Muslim countries because of the way Islam has been interpreted in most conservative Muslim countries. The past and even the current interpretations of Islam do not encourage parents to send their daughters to school. Iran succeeded in increasing educational gender equality by providing a better alternative way of interpreting Islam. However, the total increase in female-to-male school enrollment cannot be regarded as due only to the different interpretation of Islam, since Iran surpassed Turkey's female school enrollment even before the Islamic revolution. Therefore, I test for the influence of modernization using Urbanization and Fertility rate, as I did in the previous chapter.

Table 5.2 shows that modernization is statistically associated with an increase in female-to-male total school enrollment. This result contradicts the previous results in Chap. 4, which indicate that modernization does not contribute to increasing female school enrollment in conservative Muslim countries. The statistical test shows that both Urbanization and Fertility rate have a high coefficient and are statistically significant at 99 percent confidence level. An increase in urbanization and a decrease in the fertility rate are statistically associated with an increase in total female-to-male school enrollment. For 1 percentage point increase in urbanization, there is a positive, 1.18 percentage point increase in female-to-male total school enrollment. Also, the coefficient for Fertility shows that for 1 percentage point increase in the fertility rate there is a negative 2.36 percentage point increase in female-to-male total school enrollment. The change in the constitution's level of religious conservativeness is negative, but statistically not significant. This is expected, since Iran is a unique, religiously conservative Muslim country that has shown a significant improvement in women's education. Also, the variable that measures the change over time due to some unmeasurable omitted variable shows a positive association between time and female-to-male total school enrollment, but is not statistically significant. This is also expected, since the improvement in females' education in Iran accelerated the regular improvement that is

Table 5.2 Iran and Turkey regression models with religious and modernization variables

DV: F/M total school enrollment	Model 6 Coef (SE)
Urbanization	1.18***
	(0.112)
Constitution	−0.913
	(0.150)
Fertility	−2.360***
	(0.719)
Time	0.037
	(0.332)
_cons	14.733***
	(8.667)
R^2	0.887
Wald Chi^2	2337.21
N	102

Coef coefficient, *DV* dependent variable, *F/M* female/male, *SE* standard error

***$p < 0.01$, **$p < 0.05$, *$p < 0.1$

expected over time. R^2 is 0.88, which means that 88 percent of the variation in female-to-male total school enrollment is explained by the model. The high Wald Chi^2 confirms that the model is well fitted.

In the previous chapter, I showed how modernization would not have a positive influence on women's education if the country is religiously very conservative. In this section, I have shown how modernization, with a different way of interpreting religion, could contribute significantly to improving educational gender equality. However, the previous graph and statistical test give us only the general picture of the situation of women's education, they do not offer the detail about females' education at different educational levels. Studying the status of female-to-male school enrollment at each of the three main educational levels—elementary, secondary, and tertiary—provides confirmation of my findings.

Looking at Fig. 5.2, female-to-male elementary school enrollment shows that both Iran and Turkey have met the millennium educational goal of improving females' education at primary level. Looking back at 1960, we see that there were more girls at Turkish elementary schools than in Iran; however, Iran caught up with Turkey in 1964. Nevertheless, after 16 years of progress, female-to-male elementary enrollment started decreasing during the Iran–Iraq war, to become similar to female-to-male elementary enrollment in Turkey. After the war, female enrollment in Iran

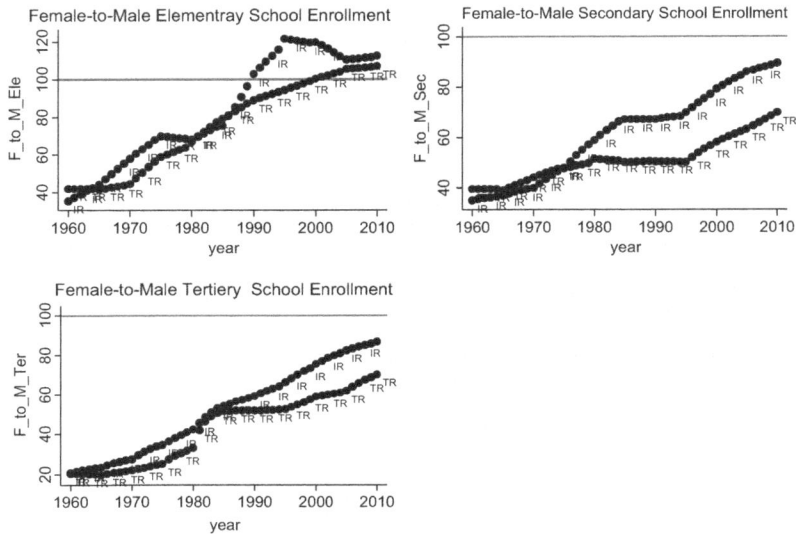

Fig. 5.2 Female-to-male educational school enrollment, 1960–2010

increased until it exceeded 100 percent. Turkey lagged behind Iran, but also managed to follow it and exceed the 100 percent marker. In addition, for a few years there was reverse educational gender discrimination in Iran: more girls than boys were enrolled in elementary school. This increase is not necessarily positive, because it could mean that there are more females than males in Iran's society, which would lead to having more females than males at elementary school, or that there are more adult females going to school, or that far fewer males are going to school.

However, based on the *CIA Fact Book*, there are 1.02 males for every female in Iran,[47] which means that the increase in the ratio of female-to-male enrollment is not due to having more female children than male. Also, the ratio of males to females seems to be high at all ages. This tells us that the sex birth rate cannot be the reason behind the increase in the ratio of female-to-male enrollment at primary school. The second reason cannot be valid, because the increase in the ratio of female-to-male enrollment is very substantial, and that increase is unlikely to be only due to the increase in adult female students. The third assumption also cannot be realistic, especially since the reverse discrimination is at the elementary educational level. If the increase was at the tertiary level, we could assume that maybe there are more women than men because men choose to work or study abroad. However, there is no reason to assume that parents prefer to send their daughters to school more than their sons. In any case, the reverse discrimination decreased and in 2010 reached a reasonable level.

The second graph in Fig. 5.2 shows female-to-male secondary school enrollment. It is obvious that up to 2010, neither Iran nor Turkey had achieved educational gender equality; however, Iran was closer to reaching that target than Turkey. From 1960 to 1979, the difference between female-to-male secondary enrollment in Iran and Turkey was not significant, although Turkey had more girls at secondary school than Iran. The situation changed after the Islamic revolution and females' secondary school enrollment improved dramatically, which led to the increase in the gap between Iran and Turkey's female secondary school enrollment. Women's secondary enrollment in Turkey seems far from the internationally required level, and achieving the millennium target in a few years does not seem possible based on this trend.

Tertiary education differs from the other education levels in the fact that Iran has had higher female-to-male tertiary enrollment than Turkey since 1960. During the 1980s, the extent of female tertiary education in Turkey increased to meet that in Iran. However, the gap increased again after 1990 and Iran exceeded Turkey in women's tertiary education. Neither Iran nor Turkey has met educational gender equality at this educational level, but Iran is closer than Turkey to doing so Figure 5.2 indicates that although both Iran and Turkey have not yet achieved educational gender equality in secondary and tertiary education, Iran is doing much better in improving women's educational status. When it comes to elementary education, both countries have already met the required educational standard. These graphs confirm that the negative effect of religion does not apply to this case study.

The statistical tests for the three levels of education confirm the result in Table 5.2.[48] They show that modernization is associated with Iran's progress in female education; however, we know from the previous chapter that modernization alone does not have a positive effect on females' education. A country needs to liberalize its constitution to be able to benefit from modernization. However, as I explained before, Iran is a unique case. In the case of Iran and Turkey, modernization variables have a positive statistical association with women's education at all three levels, and liberalizing the constitution does not have a positive effect on female-to-male enrollment in elementary, secondary, and tertiary education. In fact, it has a negative statistical effect. R^2 is also above 50 percent in all tests. Basically, the results for the statistical tests for the three educational levels confirm the results in the statistical test in Table 5.2. I used the World Bank data to test for robustness, and the results also confirm those in this section. However, as I mentioned before, the World Bank data are inflated, so reverse discrimination appeared at all three educational levels in Iran; still, reverse educational gender inequity was more significant for the elementary level, as is the case in this study.

Results for Labor-Force Participation

Barro and Lee (1993) find that educating females is less rewarding to the economy than educating males, since educated females do not usually participate in the labor force. This is the case in nearly all countries in the world, but is more persistent in traditional societies due to cultural and religious barriers. Both Iran and Turkey are still considered traditional societies. However, Turkey's updated law due to its long history of secularism and the Turkish government's willingness to join the EU, which added pressure to improve its economic, political, and humanitarian international status, make Turkey appear as if it is more modern than Iran. Thus, the expectation would be that there would be more women in the Turkish labor force than in the Iranian work force. Looking at Fig. 5.3, the ratio of female-to-male labor-force participation seems higher in Turkey than in Iran. The gap was enormous during the 1990s, but it became very small in 2005, because of the increase in the ratio of female-to-male labor-force participation in Iran and the decrease of the ratio in Turkey. The gap increased again, because of the increase of the ratio of females to males in Turkey, and the decrease of the ratio in Iran. The first impression one gets from this graph is that Turkey has more women in the work force than Iran. However, since I have already shown that Iran has more urban areas than Turkey, the increase in the female labor force in Turkey could be due to females' participation in low-skilled jobs, such as working in agriculture. Turkey has been well known for having more females in the agricultural sector. Such jobs do not require education, are unpaid, and do not contribute to improving females' status in society. The increase in the ratio of female-to-male labor-force participation in 2005 in Turkey could be due to the significant improvement in the Turkish econ-

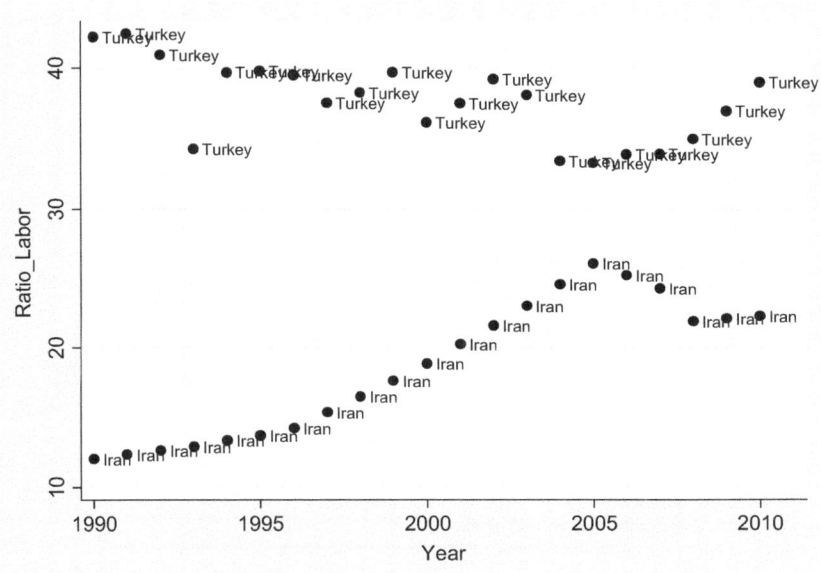

Fig. 5.3 Ratio of female-to-male labor-force participation (%), 1990–2010

omy. So 2005 might have been a transfer period from low-skilled jobs to jobs that require more sophisticated skills. Therefore, it is important to determine which country has a more educated female labor force—Iran or Turkey—in order to know which country services females' equal gender rights.

While Fig. 5.3 shows that the number of females participating in labor force in Turkey is higher than females participating in the labor force in Iran, Fig. 5.4 indicates that Turkey has more males than females with elementary education participating in the work force than in Iran. The gap between females and males with an elementary degree in the labor force in Turkey is much smaller than the gap between the genders in Iran. This confirms that the small ratio of female-to-male labor-force participation is only due to females' high participation in low-skilled jobs. However, in Iran there are more educated females with secondary and tertiary education than in Turkey, and there are also more educated men with secondary and tertiary education in Iran than in Turkey. The results indicate that Turkey has fewer educated men and women participating in the labor

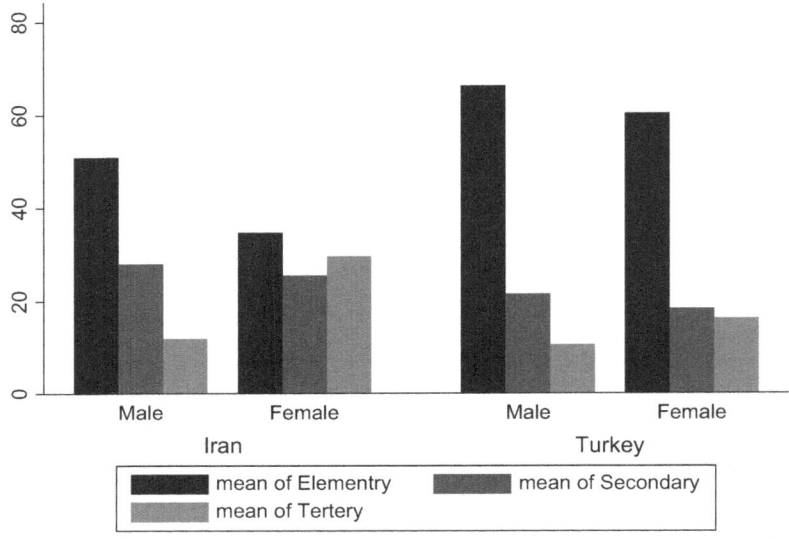

Fig. 5.4 Labor force by level of educational attainment (distribution; by sex and country)

force than Iran, which means that Iran is more dependent on skilled workers than Turkey. Furthermore, the percentage of females with secondary and tertiary education in the work force in Iran is higher than the percentage of males with secondary and tertiary education. Moreover, in both Iran and Turkey, the percentage of females participating in the labor force with tertiary education is higher than the percentage of males participating in the labor force with tertiary education. This indicates that both countries economically benefit more from educated females than from males, since there are more high-skilled females participating in the labor force than males. However, Iran takes more advantage of its educated females, since Iran has more educated females participating in the labor force than Turkey. If these results also apply to other countries, then Barro and Lee's conclusion about the negative association between females' education and economic growth needs to be reconsidered.

It is ironic to see more educated females than males in the labor force in both Iran and Turkey. One possible explanation could refer to the

Islamic cultural heritage, which puts more of a financial burden on males than females. A male in a Muslim country is expected to be fully responsible for taking care of his family, so finding a good job that pays well and helps establish his family is more important than education. Therefore, men find themselves forced to drop university and join the military or find any good job available. Unlike men, women are not in a rush to find a job, since they do not have the same financial responsibilities. Women have more time to pursue their education and get a job later if the cultural barriers are not high.

However, if religion is the reason, then Turkey should not have more females than males in the labor force, since Turkey is technically a secular country that believes in gender equality. This situation makes Iran a more distinct case, because it does not only have high female-to-male school enrollment at all three educational levels, it also has more educated females in the labor force than Turkey. Several factors could be behind Turkey's lag in having a high percentage of educated females participating in the labor force. For example, the oil revolution in Iran and some other Muslim countries, such as Kuwait, the United Arab Emirates, Qatar, and Saudi Arabia, made jobs easily available for local citizens. Males seem to choose to start their career early to establish themselves faster, since good jobs are available without having to have an education. Females usually cannot take advantage of the available jobs because of job-market barriers for women. Typically, high job-market barriers have a cultural and legal basis. In addition, unlike men, women without an education are more likely to have much less of a chance of getting a low-skilled job than uneducated men in religiously conservative countries, such as Iran. Rewarding jobs that do not require education, such as jobs with the military, are culturally and sometimes even legally not allowed. For example, joining the military is often the first option for people with no education who are looking for a high-paid job, since most Arab countries, especially the small Arabian Gulf countries, provide attractive financial packages. However, for many years those countries have not allowed females to join the military. Nevertheless, since the terrorist attack on the World Trade Center in New York on September 11, 2001, some of those countries have started to recruit women to join the military, although the percentage is still very low and the tasks remain limited. Other jobs that also require physical strength or freedom of mobility, such as civil engineering, are culturally not preferred for females and are highly discouraged unless the role would be limited to working in the office. These barriers and more create a working environment that forces females to have a high educational qualification to be able to compete with males in the work force. In addition, due to the limitation on the type of jobs that are accessible to women, females have to compete aggressively not only with other females, but also with males. These women who have a higher education have a better chance of getting the job than men and women who do not.

Analysis of the Data

In Chap. 4, I proved that modernization by itself could not improve women's education in religiously conservative countries, because the current way of interpreting some religions, such as Islam, hinders the improvement in gender equality. In this chapter, I have presented a case where religion has been used in a positive way that helped significantly increase women's education. The results in this chapter indicate that even though Iran is a religiously conservative country, it managed to improve females' education better than Turkey, a secular country. In addition, Turkey has failed to reach the millennium educational goal and lags behind Iran, because it is not enough to change legislation, the lack of modernization and the conflict between the changes and people's values slow down the improvement. The reason for the ratio of female-to-male enrollment and educated female labor-force participation being higher in Iran, a conservative country, than in Turkey, a secular country, can be explained by the increase in modernization and the different interpretations of religion.

In 1920, "Mustafa Kemal and his followers lunched a modernization project that involved the westernization and secularization of society, thereby ending religion's function as a source of law."[49] Atatürk saw religion as a problem and the reason behind the backwardness of Turkey. He apparently embraced many things that came from the West and tried to abandon everything identified as Islamic. He saw the solution as empowering women by abandoning religion and embracing Western laws and lifestyle. So he adopted the Western style, even though the "European legal codes and cultural norms that informed the Turkish modernization project were themselves patriarchal."[50] For example, the Turkish civil code that was meant to enhance women's position in Turkey was adopted from Swiss and Italian laws. The 1926 civil code of Turkey was taken from Swiss law, which "placed men as first among equals … identified the husband as the head of the union of marriage … assigned the right and responsibility of deciding the place of residence … in case of argument guardianship was granted to the father."[51] In addition, as I mentioned before, women's legal representation was limited to matters that were related to providing the needs of the house, and women needed explicit or implicit permission to work.[52] Furthermore, the family code in Turkey that was adopted from Italy included gender biases and restrictions on women in the areas of adultery and abortion.[53] For example, women could be charged with adultery because of just one incident of sexual intercourse, but a husband could not be charged with adultery if he had a sexual relationship with married woman.[54] The labor law of 1972 "banned women from working at night and in certain places, such as under-ground or -water, or involvement in physically demanding, dangerous or poisonous activities."[55] Based on these laws, we notice that women's roles and responsibilities in modern Turkey do not differ much in principle from women's roles and responsibilities under popular interpretations of Islam. The secular system in Turkey attempted to make the Turkish people abandon their cultural identity and forced them to adopt others' principles, and that apparently created resistance in Turkish society. However, during all the previous years, the Turkish people persevered to maintain their Islamic identity and traditions, even more than nations that were ruled by Islamic governments. Atatürk chose that path with low expectations of the high resistance of Turkish society, and whether such action would be the best approach to modernizing Turkey.

On the other hand, Iran, before and after the revolution, dealt with women's inequality differently than Turkey. After 1928, the monarchic system showed its tendency toward Western culture, but the system did not despise religion or fight religious beliefs the way Atatürk and his fellows did in Turkey. Before the revolution, Iranian women were encouraged to follow the steps of Western women. Women were forbidden to wear scarves, and polygamy was banned; however, Reza Khan and his son did not detach themselves from being Muslims.[56] The fight between people who believed in secularism and those who wanted to maintain their traditional beliefs was less severe in Iran than in Turkey, and that could be the reason why people in Iran were less resistant to change than those in Turkey. In addition, after the revolution, the Islamic Republic launched "a campaign—framed as a Jihad—to eradicate illiteracy and encourage girls' education. Huge city billboards, radio and television programs, and broadcast sermons proclaimed literacy essential to being a 'good Muslim.'"[57] Looking at female enrollment and the level of educated female labor-force participation in Iran after the revolution, we can tell that Iran's uncommon interpretation of religion helped the country to close the gender gap in education and increase the percentage of the female labor force. It seems that the different interpretations of religion and identity could work much better than trying to diminish them totally.

The different interpretation of religion helped Iran to increase the percentage of educated females, which led to an increase in women's awareness of their rights and responsibilities. Ebadi said that women in Iran "continue to make important strides into the educational, cultural, and employment domains, thereby increasing the awareness of women's rights and issues at social level."[58] Women in Iran after the revolution were deprived of some of their rights; however, because of education, they are fighting aggressively to gain back those rights and more. On the other hand, in Turkey there was a significant improvement in women's legal rights, especially in the last 20 years, but the enforcement of these rights is still weak. Part of the problem could be due to the fact that most of the demand for improving women's status and respecting their rights comes from outside rather than inside the country.[59]

Both Turkey and Iran receive plenty of criticism regarding women's rights; Iran does not seem to care about the opinion of the international community on women's rights, although Turkey does. Turkey is trying to join the EU, which seems to focus very much on human rights.[60] The importance of joining the EU helped improve legislation, but did not necessarily help to change culture. Changing culture, as I mentioned above, needs to come from inside through education and spreading awareness. Without the education that gives women the desire to fight for their rights, as for example the concept of "jihad" or the slogan of "True Muslim" in Iran, women in Turkey will not be able to take advantage of the international pressure on Turkey.

Conclusion

As I mentioned in the first chapter, the Arab Spring created a debate over which political system is better for the MENA. The international community views a secular Muslim country more favorably than a conservative Muslim country, especially when it concerns women's rights and gender inequality in the MENA. This study examines the gender gap in education and labor-force participation in a secular Muslim country, Turkey, and a conservative Muslim country, Iran. Based on the results, female enrollment in elementary, secondary, and tertiary education in Iran is higher than female enrollment in elementary, secondary, and tertiary education in Turkey. In addition, more educated women work in Iran than in Turkey.

Based on this result, I accept the alternative hypothesis that the gender gaps in education and labor-force participation are smaller in Iran than in Turkey. Unlike the general perception, the gender gap in education in Iran is smaller than in Turkey, and the percentage of educated women who participate in the labor force is higher in Iran than in Turkey. In fact, there are many more females than males who go to school in Iran and more educated women who participate in the labor force than educated males. The reason women in Iran go to school more than women in Turkey is associated with modernization and the different methods that both governments are using to increase the percentage of female enrollment. In this case, maintaining identity and improving the interpretation of Islam seem to be more rewarding than declaring a war against people's identity and religious beliefs. International pressure can help improve legislation, but it cannot guarantee that people will take advantage of these legislated opportunities. Even with government enforcement, people tend to be reluctant to change if they are not convinced to change. This research is not meant to defend some of Iran's unfair treatment of women and their rights, nor is it intended to ignore Turkey's efforts to improve gender equality and women's rights. The purpose of this analysis is to show that having a secular political system does not necessarily mean a higher percentage of females going to school or joining the labor force, and that having a conservative political system does not always have to be associated with having a high percentage of women who are deprived of their rights to be educated or join the labor force. Therefore, if females' education and labor-force participation are one of the main concerns for the new governments in the MENA, as well as the international community, both need to stop arguing over which is better, a secular country or a religious country, and rather focus on what type of secular country or religious country provides the best policies for society.

Notes

1. Dede (2011: 27).
2. Cuno and Desai (2009: 79).
3. Toprak (2005: 28).
4. Khomeini (2001: 580).
5. Keddie (2007: 82).

6. Toprak (2005: 28–30).
7. Toprak (2005: 30).
8. Ibid.
9. Göle (1997: 51).
10. Cuno and Desai (2009: 82).
11. Turkish Culture Foundation (2011).
12. Daver (1967: 64).
13. Keddie (2007: 119).
14. Dedeoglu (2012: 176).
15. Daver (1967: 59).
16. Acts of violence, usually murder, committed by male family members against female family members who are perceived to have brought dishonor upon the family by being suspected of committing adultery.
17. Fraczek et al. (2016: 172).
18. Dedeoglu (2012: 270).
19. Cuno and Desai (2009: 85).
20. Dedeoglu (2012: 276).
21. Toprak (2005: 31).
22. Keddie (2007: 87).
23. Mohadjer (2007).
24. Ghorbani and Tung (2007: 383).
25. Mir-Hosseini and Tapper (2006).
26. Hoodfar (2009: 241).
27. Ebadi (2009).
28. Ghorbani and Tung (2007: 383–384).
29. Ghorbani and Tung (2007: 384).
30. Mehran (2003: 70).
31. Ibid.
32. Ghorbani and Tung (2007: 384).
33. Ibid.
34. Ibid.
35. *Constitutional Court of the Republic of Turkey* (2011).
36. *Enjoy turkey.com* (2010).
37. *U.S. Department of State* (2011a, b).
38. Klasen and Lamanna (2009, 91–132).
39. Keddie (2007: 84).
40. Yazan (2014: 844).
41. MoNE (2003: 1–2).
42. Yazan (2014: 844).
43. Yazan (2014: 854).
44. Ministry of Education (1984).
45. Khomeini (1984).

46. Mehran (1991: 2).
47. Central Intelligence Agency (2011).
48. See Appendix A, Table A.7.
49. Cuno and Desai (2009: 82).
50. Cuno and Desai (2009: 82).
51. Cuno and Desai (2009: 83).
52. Ibid.
53. Ibid.
54. Ibid.
55. Cuno and Desai (2009: 84).
56. Nasr (2007: 123).
57. Hoodfar (2009: 241).
58. Ellen Lust (2011: 428).
59. Cuno and Desai (2009: 91).
60. Cuno and Desai (2009: 91).

References

Barro, R. J., & Lee, J. W. (1993). International Comparisons of Educational Attainment. *Journal of Monetary Economics, 32*(3), 363–394.

Barro, R. J., & Lee, J. W. (2013). Data Set on Lont-term Educational Attainment by Country. Retrieved from http://barrolee.com/data/oup_download_b.htm

Central Intelligence Agency. (2011). Iran. Retrieved from https://www.cia.gov/library/publications/the-world-factbook/geos/ir.html

Constitutional Court of the Republic of Turkey. (2011). The Constitution of the Republic of Turkey 1982. Retrieved from http://www.anayasa.gov.tr/index.php?l=template&id=210&lang=1&c=1

Cuno, K. M., & Desai, M. (2009). Institutions and Women's Rights. In K. M. Cuno (Ed.), *Family, Gender, and Law in a Globalizing Middle East and South Asia.* Syracuse, NY: Syracuse University Press.

Daver, B. (1967). Secularizm in Turkey. *Ankara Üniversitesi SBF Dergisi, 22*(01).

Dede, A. Y. (2011). The Arab Uprisings: Debating the "Turkish Model". *Insight Turkey, 13*(2), 23.

Dedeoglu, S. (2012). Equality, Protection or Discrimination: Gender Equality Policies in Turkey. *Social Politics, 19*(2), 269–290.

Ebadi, S. (2009). Women's Rights Under Iran's Revolution. *CNN.* Retrieved from http://news.bbc.co.uk/2/hi/7879797.stm

Fraczek, S., Huszka, B., & Körtvélyesi, Z. (2016). The Role of Human Rights in the EU's External Action in the Western Balkans and Turkey. *FRAME.*

Ghorbani, M., & Tung, R. L. (2007). Behind the Veil: An Exploratory Study of the Myths and Realities of Women in the Iranian Workforce. *Human Resource Management Journal, 17*(4), 376–392.

Göle, N. (1997). Secularism and Islamism in Turkey: The Making of Elites and Counter-Elites. *The Middle East Journal, 51,* 46–58.

Hoodfar, H. (2009). Afghan Refugee Women in Iran. In K. M. Cuno & M. Desai (Eds.), *Family, Gender, and Law in a Globalizing Middle East and South Asia, Gender and Globalization* (p. 241). London: Syracuse University Press.

Keddie, N. R. (2007). *Women in the Middle East: Past and Present.* Princeton, NJ: Princeton University Press.

Khomeini, A. R. (1984). *Dar Jostoju-ye Rah az Kalam-e Imam: Zan (In Search of the Path from the Words of Imam: Woman).* Tehran: Amir Kabir.

Khomeini, R. (2001). *The Position of Women from the Viewpoint of Imam Khomeini.* The Institute for Compilation and Publication of Imam Khomeini's Works, Alhoda UK.

Klasen, S., & Lamanna, F. (2009). The Impact of Gender Inequality in Education and Employment on Economic Growth: New Evidence for a Panel of Countries. *Feminist Economics, 15*(3), 91–132.

Lust, E. (Ed.). (2011). Iran. In *The Middle East* (12th ed.). Yale University Press.

Mehran, G. (1991). The Creation of the New Muslim Woman: Female Education in the Islamic Republic of Iran. *Convergence, 24*(4), 42. Page 2.

Mehran, G. (2003). Does the Future for Central Asian Women Lie in the Past? An Overview of Current Gender Trends in the Region. In A. Bertone & H. Esfandiari (Eds.), *Middle Eastern Women on the Move.* Washington, DC: Woodrow Wilson International Center for Scholars.

Ministry of Education. (1984). *Educational System of the Islamic Republic of Iran.* Tehran: Ministry of Education.

Mir-Hosseini, Z., & Tapper, R. (2006). *Islam and Democracy in Iran: Eshkevari and the Quest for Reform.* IB Tauris.

Mohadjer, N. (2007). *Why Iranian Women Should not Be Denied the Right to Seek Divorce?* Iran Chamber Society. Retrieved from http://www.iranchamber.com/society/articles/divorce_social_suicide.pdf

MoNE. 2003. "Milli Egitim Sayısal Veriler 2002–2003." [Quantitative Data on National Education 2002–2003.] Ankara: MEB, Aras̩tırma, Planlama ve Koordinasyon Kurulu Bas̩kanlıǧı.

Nasr, V. (2007). "Khomeini's Moment." The Shia Revival. *Military Review, 87*(3), 9.

Toprak, B. (2005). Secularism and Islam: The Building of Modern Turkey. *Macalester International, 15*(9). Retrieved from http://digitalcommons.macalester.edu/macintl/vol15/iss1/9

Turkish Culture Foundation. (2011). Women in Turkey: Education Is a Precept for All Muslims, Women and Men. Retrieved from http://www.turkishculture.org/lifestyles/turkish-culture-portal/the-women/women-in-turkey-201.htm?type=1

U.S. Department of State. (2011a). Background Note: Iran. Retrieved from http://www.state.gov/r/pa/ei/bgn/5314.htm

U.S. Department of State. (2011b). Country Specific Information. Retrieved from http://travel.state.gov/travel/cis_pa_tw/cis/cis_1142.html

Yazan, B. (2014). 'Come on Girls, Let's Go to School': An Effort Towards Gender Educational Equity in Turkey. *International Journal of Inclusive Education, 18*(8), 836–856. Page 844.

CHAPTER 6

Conclusion and Policy Implications

This book contributes to the existing literature by providing a new approach to studying the influence of religions on educational gender equality. It provides the Al-Kohlani Constitution Religiousness Index to differentiate between religiously conservative and less religiously conservative societies. This new approach provides more valuable results and helps improve the current debate on the impact of religion and modernization on educational gender equality. The book answers several questions that have been the subject of debate. It starts by contributing to the argument regarding the association between religion and educational gender equality. The current literature still disputes whether religion has a negative influence on gender equality, in particular gender equality in education, and whether Islam is the cause of the high gender inequality in education in most of the Muslim world. Some scholars argue that religions do indeed have a strong negative influence on gender equality as well as educational gender equality; however, the level of discrimination varies depending on the type of religion. Most of these scholars agree that Muslim countries appear to have the highest inequality in education. The second group, led by Lerner (1958), argues that although religion does have a negative impact on educational gender equality, modernization is capable of eliminating this negative influence. The third group is less optimistic and claims that modernization has the ability to change the culture of any society, except for a few religious societies such as Muslim societies.

© The Author(s) 2018
S. A. Al-Kohlani, *Improving Educational Gender Equality in Religious Societies*, https://doi.org/10.1007/978-3-319-70536-1_6

The results in this book provide evidence that supports parts of the three previous claims. They show that religions do indeed have a negative association with educational gender equality. The lower the level of the state's religiosity, the higher the educational gender equality, but the increase is not linear. This result applies to both Muslim and non-Muslim countries, but it is stronger and more significant in Muslim countries. This is to be expected, since most Muslim countries are still more religiously conservative than the majority of the countries in the world with different religions. In addition, modernization does have a positive association with educational gender equality and, as Lerner (1958) found, has a positive effect even in Muslim countries. However, the positive impact of modernization is limited in less religious Muslim countries. Conservative Muslim countries are resistant to change. This result indicates that, unlike Inglehart's conclusion that Muslim culture has a legacy that resists change, modernization can reduce educational gender equality in Muslim countries as well, yet that, like Inglehart's conclusion, conservative Muslim countries that maintain a strong religious legacy are unlikely to benefit from modernization. The idea here is that not all Muslim countries are the same, and that since the deep roots of the Islamic culture vary, so does the impact of religion on educational gender equality. Hence, in regard to the first question, this book confirms the findings in the previous literature and indicates that despite the negative effect of religions, modernization can reduce that effect, but only in less religious countries. This result includes less conservative Muslim countries as well.

The second question that is still in dispute is whether Muslim countries in particular have high educational gender inequality compared to the rest of the world. The results in this book confirm that Muslim countries, in comparison to non-Muslim countries, do indeed have high educational gender inequality. They also confirm Inglehart's claim regarding the negative impact of some cultural legacies, since I found that Arab Muslim countries do have a higher educational gender gap than non-Arab Muslim countries. However, non-Arab Muslim countries still have higher gender inequality in education compared to non-Muslim countries. In addition, if conservative Muslim countries are controlled for, the negative influence of religion in the remaining Muslim countries becomes weak.

The third question under discussion is whether the variation in educational gender equality can be associated with a variation in the countries' level of religiosity. The results indicate that there is an association between the countries' level of religiosity and educational gender equality. This result applies to both Muslim and non-Muslim countries; however, the results are stronger in Muslim countries. Dividing countries into conservative, moderately conservative, moderately liberal, liberal, and secular confirms that moving from being a very religiously conservative country to a less religious country has a positive association with educational gender equality, even though the increase is not linear due to a few outliers. The positive effect of moving from religiously conservative to liberal is stronger in Muslim countries, since moving from being a very conservative Muslim country to a secular country has a strong significant association with educational gender equality. The result is different in non-Muslim countries, as, despite the difference between conservative non-Muslim countries and less religious non-Muslim countries, secular non-Muslim countries seem to have a negative association with educational gender equality. This weak association between the different levels of religious conservativeness and educational gender equality in non-Muslim countries indicates that Muslim and non-Muslim countries are living in different phases. Muslim countries are still struggling with religion to various degrees, whereas most non-Muslim countries seem to have already passed that struggle. Moving from a religious to a less religious constitution still has a positive effect on non-Muslim countries, but it is not major. Moving to the very extreme—that is, being a secular country—seems to have a positive impact on educational gender equality in Muslim countries, but it has a negative impact in non-Muslim countries. Muslim countries may need a strong religious shock and strict secular rules to overcome the traditional culture and reduce the Islamic legacy; however, the roots of religions in non-Muslim countries are already weak, so going to the extreme could actually create a backlash.

The fourth controversial question concerns the impact of modernization on educational gender equality. The result confirms the positive robustness of the association between modernization and educational gender equality. However, the positive association between urbanization and gender equality is stronger in non-Muslim countries. Urbanization also has a positive effect in Muslim countries, but not all Muslim countries benefit from urbanization. Urbanization does not seem to have a positive effect on educational gender equality in conservative Muslim countries, because urbanization does not mean modernization. Urbanization is just one important indicator of modernization, meaning that urbanization always leads to modernization, but it is not always the best measurement of modernization. Many countries, such as those that grew rich due to high exports of natural resources, have managed to expand their urban areas by building an advanced infrastructure, but economic change did not follow intellectual change. So females' roles in such societies are likely to remain traditional. Urbanization is supposed to provide people with job opportunities, and with different tools and methods to improve their skills in order to be able to compete in the job market and the sophisticated modern society. However, in conservative religious societies such competition is likely to be limited to males. As the previous literature confirms, in comparison to females, it takes males more time to change their attitudes toward more gender equality. Females in these societies are not empowered, so even if their attitudes toward their expected role have changed due to education or other external factors, their actual status may not change. This does not mean that religious countries with a high degree of economic development will never change, it only means that it would take them longer than other societies to change. Luckily, there are very few religiously conservative countries remaining in the world. Most countries—Muslim and non-Muslim—have already moved from being very religious to less religious. Over time it is probable that all conservative countries will find themselves forced to change and become less religious.

Besides urbanization, several other factors could contribute to changes in conservative countries. First, a change could occur due to a decrease in the fertility rate. Traditional families used to have lots of children because children meant wealth. Boys grow up helping their father on the farm, and girls help their mother at home. When people live in urban areas, the need to have many children decreases, because the economic reward of having a large family reduces and parents' responsibility increases. So the results indicate that reducing the fertility rate could help significantly in increasing educational gender equality in all societies; however, Muslim societies can benefit more from reducing fertility than non-Muslim countries. The results also indicate that time has a positive, significant effect in increasing educational gender equality. Over time, people's perceptions of the importance of education improve and it becomes an essential part of parents' duties to educate their children. Although time has a positive effect in all societies, it seems stronger in non-Muslim countries.

The bottom line is this: Muslim countries do indeed have a higher educational gender gap than non-Muslim countries. Modernization, represented by urbanization and the decrease of the fertility rate, can contribute positively and significantly to improving women's education in non-Muslim countries. As for Muslim countries, they must first move from being very conservative to less conservative to be able to benefit from modernization. Modernization would not solve educational gender equality in Muslim countries if the countries remained conservative. If Muslim states cannot or do not have the will to move from being very conservative to less conservative, then changing the religious culture, such as is the case in Iran, is another approach to improving educational gender equality.

This study also highlights the significant role governments play in adopting and enforcing policies that help achieve their goals. It also shows the importance of governments' willingness to mobilize society in order to apply the policies that have been approved. Without governments' incentive to overcome these problems, international and even domestic pressure will not be able to solve these obstacles. Governments, regardless of whether they are democratic or autocratic, can arrive at their goals if they are committed to them. Committed governments can achieve the change they aim at peacefully or by force; however, the peaceful approach is much better, since society would accept it willingly and the change would be strongly embedded in the culture. This conclusion also supports Inglehart and Norris (2003) in their emphasis on the critical role of government in improving gender equality.

Policy Recommendations

One of the main aims of this book is to provide a better understanding of the influence of religions on educational gender equality, to assist the public, political activists, feminist activists, and policy decision-makers in their efforts to improve women's domestic and societal status. The study investigated two main ideas: the impact of the level of religious conservatism on female-to-male school enrollment; and whether an increase in urbanization can mitigate the negative impact of religion. This study confirms the negative impact of religious conservativeness on females' education, and indicates that the more religiously liberal a country's constitution is, the smaller the gender gap in total school education. However, changing policy is a difficult process, which involves high cost and effort. Therefore, policy advocates and decision-makers need to be convinced that the benefit from advocating or implementing a certain policy would exceed the cost. In this case, advocating for less religious constitutions does not seem very rewarding, except in one case where Muslim countries move to being secular. Arguing over whether the constitution should be the only source of legislation or one source of legislation would not make a major difference to educational gender equality. However, it could be considered a step forward.

Women's rights advocates and policy-makers in both Muslim and non-Muslim countries have several ways to approach the problem of educational gender inequality. As I mentioned above, reducing the level of the influence of constitutional religion has the potential to increase educational gender equality, especially for conservative Muslim countries. The other approach is to increase urbanization and reduce fertility. Although reducing fertility could also lead to a clash between religious scholars and strong believers on the one hand, and the advocates of such an approach on the other, the reward is high. Therefore, states that cannot change their constitution to become less religious due to societal, political, and religious opposition could start by adopting programs to make reducing fertility appealing to citizens.

If that approach is also still challenging, then the best alternative is to advocate for a different way of interpreting females' rights in religion. Religions have always been open to different interpretations, so sticking with the most extremist version would lead to maintaining traditional gender roles. In fact, this approach can succeed very well if implemented in conservative societies, since people in these societies are more responsive to religious instruction. However, the negative side of this approach is increasing the tangled relationship between religion and politics, which could be dangerous if applied to other topics.

The results in this book should encourage international decision-makers and local liberal decision-makers, in particular in the Arab Spring conservative countries, to push for more religiously liberal constitutions. The results indicate that if Egypt, Tunisia, Libya, and Syria moved from being moderately liberal to conservative, their chance of maintaining or reducing gender inequality in education would decrease and their chance of benefiting from urbanization would also decrease. Also, if countries such as Yemen stay conservative, the gender gap in education may remain as bad as it currently is, or may even get worse. The other critical step those countries need to take is to introduce programs to reduce the fertility rate. Except for Yemen, they have the potential to benefit from modernization and lower the educational gender gap. Yemen, however, would need a mixed approach, of increasing urbanization, reducing fertility, and changing the religious interpretation of gender roles in Islam.

The modernization argument that suggests that an increase in urbanization can change the negative impact of religion is not strongly supported. Urbanization can help improve gender equality in education, but the magnitude of the positive impact of urbanization on highly religiously conservative countries seems blunted. An increase in urbanization appears to help female education in less religious countries, but does less to help female education in extremely religious countries. This could be the case because high urbanization is a sign of improvement in the economy, so females' education and participation in the work force may seem unnecessary, since males can provide a decent standard of living without female support. Therefore, if a country such as Yemen somehow experienced an increase in urbanization, it is unlikely that women's status would change unless there was a break from religion or a different way of interpreting women's role in Islam.

The evidence presented here suggests that policy-makers should be aware of the various options they can choose to improve gender equality, particularly in education. Although for conservative Muslim countries the first thing that must be done is adopting a less religious constitution or providing a different interpretation of religion, for other countries modernization could gradually solve the problem. Although such a claim needs further investigation, the primary results suggest that when the society is religiously very conservative, an increase in the standard of living, either due to improvement in the economy or to foreign aid, may lead to a negative impact on female education and women joining the labor force. For scholars who are interested in education, the results suggest that for less religious countries—Muslim and non-Muslim alike—female education can be increased by increasing different elements of modernization, but for conservative countries, liberalization of the constitution and/or providing a different interpretation of religion come first. Studying the impact of religion by using only religious affiliation is not enough. Differentiating between the different levels of religious conservativeness is very useful for more accurate results and for understanding the complex interactions between religiousness and modernization.

Future Studies

In this book, I used the ratio of female-to-male total educational enrollment to study the association between the religious and modernization theories and educational gender equality. Although total education was a good start for studying this complicated subject, in the future the same study should be applied to primary, secondary, and tertiary education separately. I anticipate that female enrollment rates at these three education levels would vary significantly depending on religious conservativeness and modernization. Doing this would reveal some important information about the difference between conservative and secular countries. Also, several countries, including Muslim countries, seem to have more females than males at the different levels of education, particularly tertiary education. The reasons for and the consequences behind such reverse discrimination need to be studied.

In addition, the book shows that the status of religion in countries' constitutions affects gender equality in education. The second step is to use this independent variable to study the association between religion and female participation in the labor force. It would also be useful to study the relationship with other gender equality issues, such as female marriage and family rights. There is also a need for more studies on other measures, besides the constitution, that could capture the different levels of conservativeness within major religions in constitutionally liberal countries, as well as more measures that contribute to modernization.

References

Lerner, D. (1958). *The Passing of Traditional Society: Modernizing the Middle East.* New York: Free Press.

Inglehart, R., & Norris, P. (2003). *Rising Tide: Gender Equality and Cultural Change Around the World.* Cambridge University Press.

Appendix A

1. There were 48 Muslim countries that had a Muslim population above 45 percent in 1990 (which is the earliest for open-access data that give the percentage of population of each major religion), but I had to drop 14 countries: Azerbaijan, Burkina Faso, Chad, Comoros, Djibouti, Kosovo, Lebanon, Mayotte, Nigeria, Oman, Palestinian territories, Somalia, Uzbekistan, and Western Sahara, because the Barro and Lee education database (2013) does not cover them. After matching, I had to drop another five Muslim countries and seven non-Muslim countries because by 1980 they were still not independent or because data on the constitution were not available. Comparing the data, for example female political representatives, which was one of my main independent variables, before and after some countries gained their independence from Russia shows that the difference is huge, which indicates that those countries were ruled by a constitution that does not reflect their culture and beliefs.
2. If Barro and Lee (1993) and Klasen and Lamanna (2009) are correct in their results and justifications, this would mean that the reason why females' education does not have a direct significant effect on economic growth is not the ineffectiveness of female education, but the barriers that do not allow educated females to participate in the labor force. In addition, these scholars found that gender inequality in education and/or the labor force damages economic

growth, but they did not examine why some developing nations have gender inequality in education and the labor force while other countries do not. So, we should move from asking whether gender inequality in education has a positive impact on economic growth to asking why some countries have high gender inequality in education and the labor force while other countries do not. Finding the barriers to female education and labor-force participation is important, especially for policy-makers. In this book, I focus only on the reasons behind gender inequality in education.
3. There is a big difference between "the" and "a." The first indicates that religion is the only source of legislation, but the second means that religion is one of the sources of legislation; for example, other sources such as international law could be considered a source of legislation. In addition, I believe my coding is more reliable than Johnathan Fox's coding because for several Muslim states he could not find data that indicate whether Islam is the source or a source of legislation, but I did find data.
4. I tested for nearly all the variables that were used in the previous literature and expected to have a positive statistical significance in educational gender equality, such as female political representative, Convention on the Elimination of All Forms of Discrimination against Women (CEDAW), urbanization, GDP per capita, colonization, immigration, oil, government budget balance, relative political extraction (RPE), relative political reach (RPR), and international financial aid for education. As I expected, out of all the potential religious or patriarchal variables, only the constitutional variable was statistically significant. Also from the modernization variables only urbanization and GDP per capita were statistically significant. Out of all the control variables, only fertility and (in some models) oil were statistically significant.

Table A.1 Marginal effect for Muslim × Constitution

1.Muslim_at	dy/dx	Std. err.	z	$p > z$	[95% conf. interval]	
1	−24.2741	2.656462	−9.14	0	−29.48068	−19.06754
2	−23.5021	2.522212	−9.32	0	−28.44558	−18.55869
3	−22.7302	2.41674	−9.41	0	−27.46689	−17.99344
4	−21.9582	2.343933	−9.37	0	−26.55221	−17.36416
5	−21.1862	2.306887	−9.18	0	−25.70763	−16.6648
6	−20.4142	2.307324	−8.85	0	−24.93651	−15.89197

Table A.2 Marginal effect for Muslim × Urbanization

1.Muslim_at	dy/dx	Std. err.	z	p > z	[95% conf. interval]	
1	−24.2129	2.90504	−8.33	0	−29.90671	−18.51917
2	−23.6289	2.78718	−8.48	0	−29.09164	−18.1661
3	−23.0448	2.729068	−8.44	0	−28.39367	−17.69592
4	−22.4607	2.734515	−8.21	0	−27.82028	−17.10118
5	−21.8767	2.80315	−7.8	0	−27.37073	−16.38258
6	−21.2926	2.930537	−7.27	0	−27.03633	−15.54884
7	−20.7085	3.109464	−6.66	0	−26.80295	−14.61408
8	−20.1244	3.331637	−6.04	0	−26.65433	−13.59455
9	−19.5404	3.589034	−5.44	0	−26.57475	−12.50599
10	−18.9563	3.874641	−4.89	0	−26.55046	−11.36214
11	−18.3722	4.182684	−4.39	0	−26.57014	−10.17432

Table A.3 Interaction terms between the different levels of Muslim conservativeness with Urbanization

DV: F/M total school enrollment	CONCoef (SE)	MCONCoef (SE)	MLIBCoef (SE)	LIBCoef (SE)	SecularCoef (SE)
Urbanization	0.185***	0.105**	0.176***	0.167***	0.171***
	(0.048)	(0.044)	(0.046)	(0.047)	(0.048)
Constitution	0.246**	0.073	0.069	0.201**	0.148
	(0.107)	(0.093)	(0.094)	(0.091)	(0.114)
Fertility	−6.410***	−6.823***	−6.575***	−6.525***	−6.484***
	(0.436)	(0.425)	(0.429)	(0.434)	(0.435)
Time	0.064**	0.075***	0.067***	0.067***	0.066**
	(0.026)	(0.026)	(0.026)	(0.026)	(0.026)
CON × Urb	0.015				
	(0.014)				
MCON × Urb		−0.039***			
		(0.011)			
MLIB × Urb			0.041***		
			(0.011)		
LIB × Urb				−0.006	
				(0.015)	
Secular × Urb					0.019
					(0.022)
_cons	75.965***	81.776***	78.811***	77.650***	77.465***
	(3.881)	(3.716)	(3.778)	(3.862)	(3.902)
R^2	0.197	0.253	0.224	0.211	0.206
Wald Chi^2	383.050	459.630	422.940	399.460	399.080

Coef coefficient, *CON* conservative, *DV* dependent variable, *F/M* female/male, *LIB* liberal, *MCON* moderately conservative, *MLIB* moderately liberal, *SE* standard error

***$p < 0.01$, **$p < 0.05$, *$p < 0.1$

Table A.4 The interaction terms between the different levels of non-Muslim conservativeness with urbanization

DV: F/M total school enrollment	FirstCoef (SE)	SecondCoef (SE)	ThirdCoef (SE)	FourthCoef (SE)
Constitution	−0.374**	−0.138	−0.176	−0.157
	(0.189)	(0.168)	(0.164)	(0.172)
Urbanization	0.425***	0.454***	0.460***	0.463***
	(0.067)	(0.067)	(0.067)	(0.067)
Fertility	−6.215***	−5.975***	−5.912***	−5.916***
	(0.479)	(0.452)	(0.449)	(0.448)
Time	0.135***	0.125***	0.123***	0.123***
	(0.048)	(0.046)	(0.046)	(0.045)
MCON × Urb	−0.105***			
	(0.030)			
MLIB × Urb		0.002		
		(0.008)		
LIB × Urb			0.004	
			(0.010)	
Secular × Urb				−0.001
				(0.017)
_cons	90.983***	86.919***	86.702***	86.536***
	(6.715)	(6.618)	(6.598)	(6.513)
R^2	0.623	0.607	0.604	0.604
Wald Chi^2	1295.4	1,484.920	1,511.960	1,508

Coef coefficient, *DV* dependent variable, *F/M* female/male, *LIB* liberal, *MCON* moderately conservative, *MLIB* moderately liberal, *SE* standard error

***$p < 0.01$, ** $p < 0.05$, *$p < 0.1$

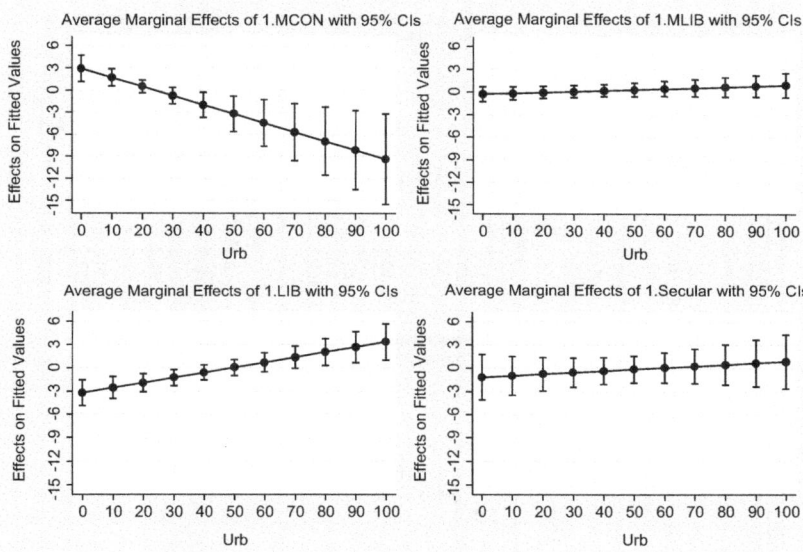

Fig. A.1 Marginal effect of the different levels of religious constitutions in non-Muslim countries

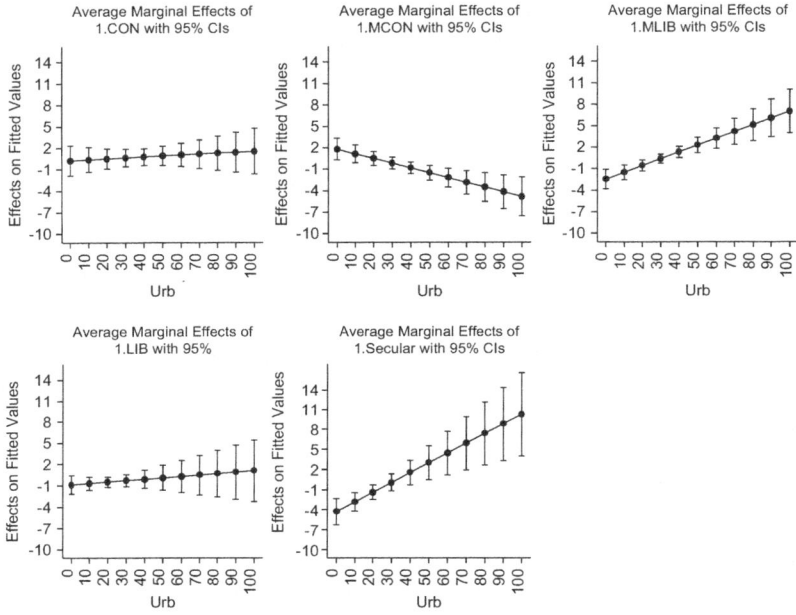

Fig. A.2 Marginal effect of the different levels of religious constitutions in Muslim and non-Muslim countries

Table A.5 Muslim/non-Muslim basic regression models

DV: F/M total school enrollment	Model 1 Coef (SE)	Model 2 Coef (SE)	Model 3 Coef (SE)	Model 4 Coef (SE)
Urbanization	0.061	0.127***	0.135***	0.195***
	(0.046)	(0.042)	(0.042)	(0.046)
Constitution	0.766***	0.137	−0.284	0.128
	(0.148)	(0.114)	(0.188)	(0.115)
Fertility	−7.209***	−4.650***	−4.584***	−4.719***
	(0.682)	(0.505)	(0.500)	(0.500)
Lag_oilgdp	1.597	2.077	2.072	2.163
	(1.315)	(1.318)	(1.323)	(1.340)
Time	0.317***	0.455***	0.459***	0.456***
	(0.058)	(0.053)	(0.052)	(0.052)

(*continued*)

Table A.5 (continued)

DV: F/M total school enrollment	Model 1 Coef (SE)	Model 2 Coef (SE)	Model 3 Coef (SE)	Model 4 Coef (SE)
Muslim		−30.967***	−36.467***	−23.691***
		(1.247)	(2.133)	(1.897)
Muslim × Constitution			0.806***	
			(0.221)	
Muslim × Urb				−0.143***
				(0.039)
_cons	94.126***	98.202***	100.790***	95.052***
	(5.036)	(4.002)	(4.097)	(3.948)
R^2	0.592	0.632	0.634	0.639

Coef coefficient, *DV* dependent variable, *F/M* female/male, *SE* standard error

***$p < 0.01$, **$p < 0.05$, *$p < 0.1$

Table A.6 Muslim/non-Muslim regression models with Muslim and religiously conservative countries

DV: F/M total school enrollment	Model 7 Coef (SE)
Urbanization	0.24***
	(0.0397)
Constitution	−0.0191
	(0.105)
Fertility	−7.09***
	(0.322)
Time	0.0959
	(0.0356)
Muslim	−21.2***
	(2.18)
Conservative_Muslim	−1.65***
	(0.523)
_cons	99.7***
	(5.23)
R^2	0.517
Wald Test	1980.95
N	2688

Coef coefficient, *DV* dependent variable, *F/M* female/male, *SE* standard error

***$p < 0.01$, **$p < 0.05$, *$p < 0.1$

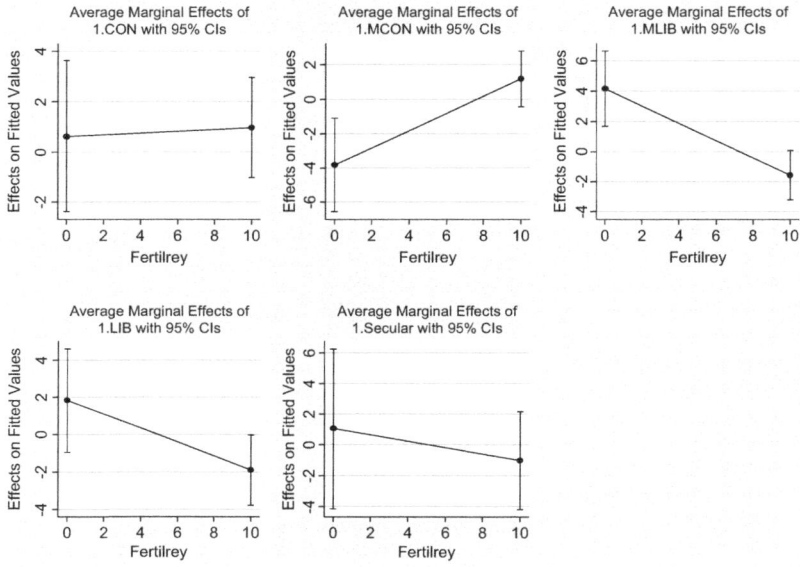

Fig. A.3 Marginal effect of the different levels of religious constitutions in Muslim and non-Muslim countries with fertility

Table A.7 Iran and Turkey regression models for the three educational levels

DV: F/M total school enrollment	ElementaryCoef (SE)	SecondaryCoef (SE)	TertiaryCoef (SE)
Constitution	−0.192	−1.67***	−1.30***
	(0.243)	(0.171)	(0.147)
Urbanization	0.851***	0.577***	1.24***
	(0.229)	(0.142)	(0.127)
Fertility	−8.50***	−1.42***	−2.0***
	(1.77)	(0.712)	(0.571)
Time	0.0124	0.197**	0.050***
	(0.066)	(0.021)	(0.076)
_cons	70.9***	38.5***	−0.95
	(18.5)	(9.25)	(8.0)
R^2	0.523	0.83	0.91
Wald Chi^2	390.17	627.57	1433
N	102	102	102

Coef coefficient, *DV* dependent variable, *F/M* female/male, *SE* standard error

***$p < 0.01$, **$p < 0.05$, *$p < 0.1$

REFERENCES

Barro, R. J., & Lee, J. W. (1993). International Comparisons of Educational Attainment. *Journal of Monetary Economics, 32*(3), 363–394.

Klasen, S., & Lamanna, F. (2009). The Impact of Gender Inequality in Education and Employment on Economic Growth: New Evidence for a Panel of Countries. *Feminist Economics, 15*(3), 91–132.

Appendix B

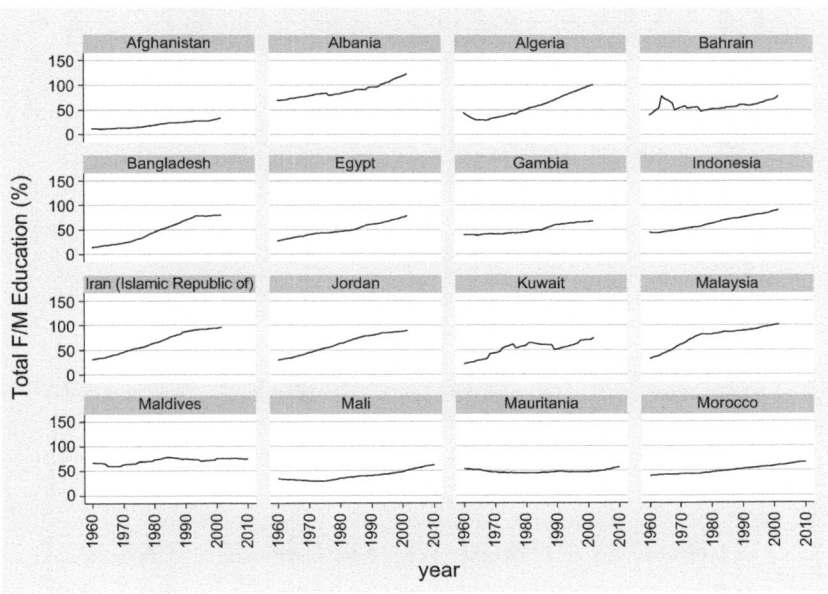

Fig. B.1 Female-to-male total school enrollment for the first 16 countries over 50 years

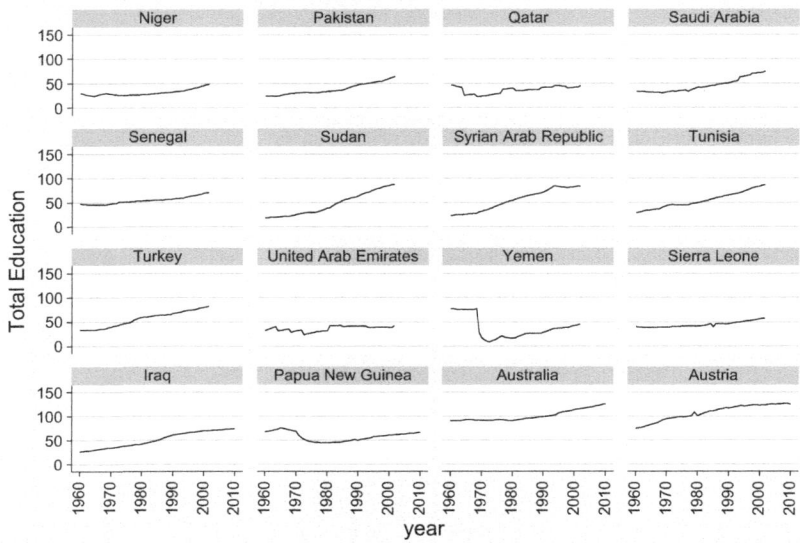

Fig. B.2 Female-to-male total school enrollment for the second 16 countries over 50 years

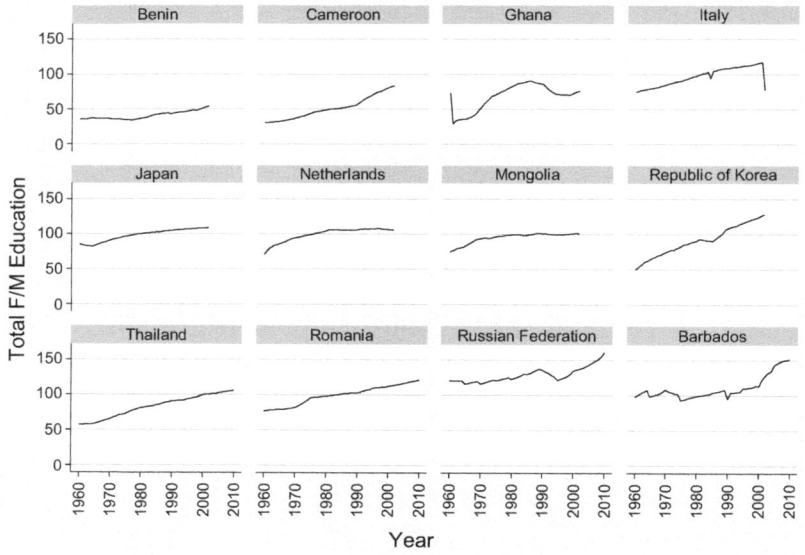

Fig. B.3 Female-to-male total school enrollment for 12 countries over 50 years

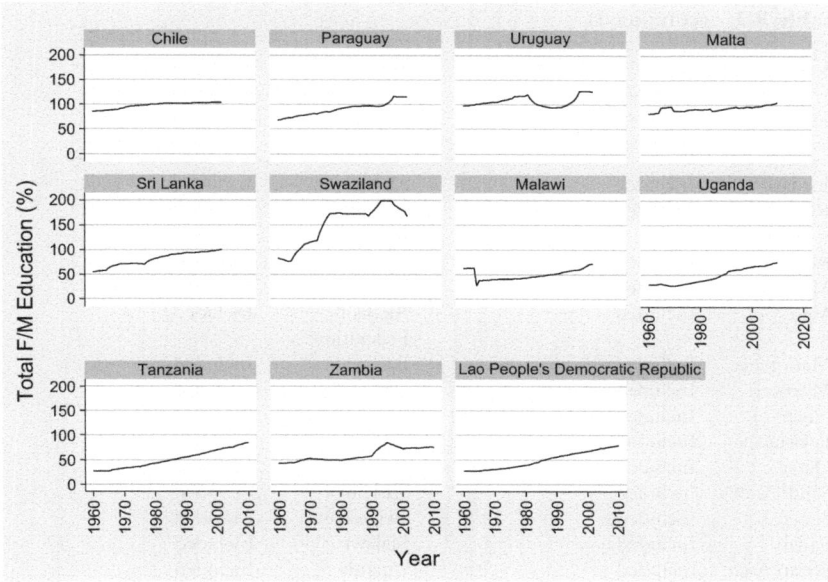

Fig. B.4 Female-to-male total school enrollment for the last 11 countries over 50 years

Table B.1 Detailed information on inclusion and exclusion of countries

Country	Inclusion or exclusion of Muslim countries	Reason if excluded	Inclusion or exclusion of non-Muslim countries	Reason if excluded
Afghanistan	Included		Australia	Included
Albania	Included		Austria	Included
Algeria	Included		Benin	Included
Bahrain	Included		Cameroon	Included
Bangladesh	Included		Ghana	Included
Egypt	Included		Italy	Included
Gambia	Included		Japan	Included
Indonesia	Included		Netherlands	Included
Iran (Islamic Republic of)	Included		Lao People's Democratic Republic	Included

(*continued*)

Table B.1 (continued)

Country	Inclusion or exclusion of Muslim countries	Reason if excluded	Inclusion or exclusion of non-Muslim countries	Reason if excluded
Jordan	Included		Mongolia[1]	Included
Kuwait	Included		Republic of Korea	Included
Malaysia	Included		Thailand	Included
Maldives	Included		Romania	Included
Mali	Included		Russian Federation	Included
Mauritania	Included		Barbados	Included
Morocco	Included		Chile	Included
Niger	Included		Paraguay	Included
Pakistan	Included		Uruguay	Included
Qatar	Included		Malta	Included
Saudi Arabia	Included		Sri Lanka	Included
Senegal	Included		Switzerland	Included
Sudan	Included		Malawi	Included
Syrian Arab Republic	Included		Uganda	Included
Tunisia	Included		Tanzania	Included
Turkey	Included		Zambia	Included
United Arab Emirates	Included		Papua New Guinea	Included
Yemen	Included		Macao	Excluded	Not independent from China
Sierra Leone	Included		Gabon[a]	Excluded	Excessive outlier
Iraq	Included		Lesotho[a]	Excluded	Excessive outlier
Azerbaijan	Excluded	Education data not available	Armenia	Excluded	Not independent from Russia
Burkina Faso	Excluded	Education data not available	Estonia	Excluded	Not independent from Russia
Chad	Excluded	Education data not available	Botswana[a]	Excluded	Excessive outlier
Comoros	Excluded	Education data not available			

(*continued*)

Table B.1 (continued)

Country	Inclusion or exclusion of Muslim countries	Reason if excluded	Inclusion or exclusion of non-Muslim countries	Reason if excluded
Djibouti	Excluded	Education data not available		
Kosovo	Excluded	Education data not available		
Lebanon	Excluded	Education data not available		
Mayotte	Excluded	Education data not available		
Nigeria	Excluded	Education data not available		
Oman	Excluded	Education data not available		
Palestinian territories	Excluded	Education data not available		
Somalia	Excluded	Education data not available		
Uzbekistan	Excluded	Education data not available		
Western Sahara	Excluded	Education data were not available		
Libya	Excluded	Outlier because no legitimate constitution		
Kazakhstan	Excluded	Not independent from Russia		
Tajikistan	Excluded	Not independent from Russia		
Kyrgyzstan[2]	Excluded	Not independent from Russia		
Brunei Darussalam	Excluded	Constitution data not available		

Note: I dropped Gabon, Lesotho, and Botswana after I examined my data because the education data did not seem to be accurate. They had three females for each male, which does not make sense since that ratio is higher than in any developed country

[1] In Mongolia 53% of the population is Buddhist

[2] This is considered a Muslim country because 86.3% of the population is Muslim

Index[1]

A
Abortion, 7, 13, 149
Abu Hurairah, 27
Academic scholars, 3
Accomplishment, 10, 12, 136
Acts of violence, 152n16
Administration, 125, 127
Adult illiterates, 8
Aegis, 13
Affiliation, 70, 131, 161
Age, 6, 7, 9, 13, 29, 59, 90, 130–132
Agnostic, 17
Agrarian societies, 44
Agricultural, 7, 9, 58, 131, 132, 144
Agriculture sector, 9
Aisha bint Abu Bakr, 26
Alcohol abuse, 23
Ali, Imam, 137
Al-Islah political party, 24
Al-Kohlani's Constitution, 76, 82, 86, 155
Allah, 77
Al Nahda political party, 2
Al Najaf, 24

Alternative hypotheses, 72, 73, 116, 151
Ancient Israel, 50
Ancient world, 50
Anticolonial movements, 22, 23
Arabian Gulf oil-producing countries, 6
Arabic influences, 127
Arabic script, 127
Arab Muslim countries, 107, 116, 117, 156
Arab Spring, vii, viii, 1, 2, 7–10, 150, 160
Arab states, 9, 94
Aristocratic families, 28
Article 154, 128
Article 159, 128, 129
Ataturk, Mustafa Kemal, 3, 125, 127, 128, 130, 133, 148, 149
Atheists, 17, 50
Attending school, 9
Attitude toward gender roles, 31
Austerities, 17
Authorities, 1, 9, 17, 18, 55, 125, 137
Autocratic regimes, 52
Awra, 27, 28

[1] Note: Page numbers followed by 'n' refer to notes.

B

Backlash, 44, 131, 157
Backlash against modernization, 44
Backward extrapolation, 74
Balance of Budget, 81, 106
Beauty myth, 14
Beijing Fourth World Conference on Women (1995), 12
Benchmarks, 123, 124
Biased standard errors, 85
Bible, 49, 77
Biologically weak, 13
Birth control, 21, 131
Birth rate, 6, 142
Bishops, 49
Blacks, 14
Body surgery, 14
Bourgeois women, 128
Brahmanical religion, 17
Brahmin monks, 17
Breadwinner, 32, 59
British colonial history, 45
Brotherhood
  associations, 23
  female activists, 23
  feminist, 23
  view, 23
Buddha, 17, 19
  teachings, 18
Buddhism, 17–20, 48, 49
Buddhist
  believers, 30
  culture, 19
  feminists, 18, 20, 30
  monasteries, 19
  societies, 18, 45
  teaching (dharma), 19
  tradition, 17
Businesswoman, 48

C

Cairo Program of Action, 12
Campaign for women's rights, 13
The Cairo International Conference on Population and Development (ICPD) (1994), 12
Capitalism, 13–16
Capitalist societies, 43
Capitalist system, 16
Career, 15, 24, 47, 147
  challenges, 58
  pressure, 47, 58
Catholic Church, 7
Catholicism, 49
Census/survey observations, 74
Challenge Islam, 128
Challenges of power, 14
Changes culture, 43, 56
Chaperoned, 29
Characteristics in common, 13
Cheaper education, 78
Childbirth, 8, 17
Childcare
  facilities, 10
  services, 10
Children, 2, 6, 7, 9, 12, 25, 26, 28, 31–33, 47, 58, 59, 81, 128, 132, 135, 142, 158
  custody, 127, 132
  daycare, 6
  survival, 33, 134
Christianity, 44, 48–50, 67
Church, 50
Church of England, 49
Citizen's culture, 5
Citizenship, 2, 13, 21
Civil Code of 1926, 127
Civilizational goals, 52
Civil societies, 3
Civil wars, 2
Clarke, Edward H. (1872), 15, 16
Class of oppressors, 13
Class struggle, 13, 14
Clement of Alexandria, 7
Coeducational, 15, 28, 29, 47, 137
Colonial history, 45, 128
Come on girls, let's go to school, 136

Commit adultery, 126, 152n16
Common characteristic, 68
Communal ties, 55
Communist, 4, 10, 52, 55
  model, 55
  regimes, 52
Comparative politics, viii
Competitive environment, 58
Conference, 11, 12
Conflict zones, 2
Consciousness raising, 13
Conservative
  countries, 53, 55, 70, 72, 73, 90, 97, 108, 111, 112, 116, 118, 119, 121, 125, 140, 147, 148, 158, 160, 161
  societies, 3, 70, 155, 160
Constitution
  extreme religious countries, 96, 104, 110, 161
  religious status, 52
  responsibilities, 53
  rules, 53
  variable, 76, 164
Constitutional amendment (1990), 129
Constitutional Amendments Committee, 2
Constitutional reform (1961), 128
Contemporary Western Feminist theories, 14
Contingencies, 14
Control variables, 60, 80–82, 85, 95, 164
Controversial issue, 16
Correlated across panels, 85
Correlation, 57, 60, 78, 81, 85
Cost, 7, 19, 58, 60, 78, 134, 159
Cost of living, 7, 58, 60, 78
Countries
  constitution, 53, 68, 75, 76, 91, 94, 114, 162

  identity, 68
Coup d'etat, 52
Crime of honor, 129
Cross-sectional study, 12, 45
Culture
  background, 138
  barriers, 147
  beliefs, 20, 44, 127
  factors, 5
  identity, 149
  legacy, 55, 116, 156
  mistrustful, 55
  movement, 12
  norms, 12
  restricts, 58
  shift, 31, 127
  of the society, 78
  values, 52

D

Data collection, 114
Death, 15, 26, 52, 128, 130
Debatable issue, 16
Decade for Human Rights Education, 12
Decision-making, 2, 8–10, 31
Decision roles, 31
Democracy, 43, 51, 124, 127
Democratic Party, 128
Democratic political processes, 2
Democratic regimes, 52
Demonstrations, 1, 2
Dependency, 14, 51
Dependent variable, 73–75, 86, 91, 98, 99, 105, 113, 141, 165, 166, 169, 170
Developed countries, 9, 59
Developing countries, 8, 32, 33, 59, 86n1
Dharmasästras, 17
Difficult task, 124

Discovery of vaccines, 7
Discrimination, 2, 10, 11, 15, 18, 20–22, 43, 48, 49, 70, 117, 118, 142–144, 155
Discriminatory labor practices, 16
Diversity, 13
Divine rules, 17
Divorce, 13, 126, 127, 130–132
    policies, 10
Doctor, 1, 47
Domestic
    duties, 27
    jobs, 9
    pressure, 129, 131, 159
    sphere, 26, 48
    violence, 128, 129
Domesticity, 13
Dress code/dressing code, vii, 21, 50, 133
Drug addiction, 132
Dual role, 137
Dual workload, 13
Dummy variable, 68, 75, 81, 82, 85, 89, 94–97, 121n1
Dutch
    colonial, 28
    occupation (1600s–1945), 28
    schools, 28
Duties, 25, 26, 46, 126, 132, 158

E
Early marriage, 129, 135
Eastern countries, 11
Economy
    activity, 45
    benefits, 146
    changes, 60, 103, 132, 158
    development, viii, 3, 5, 6, 33, 43, 158
    growth, 8, 33, 34, 54, 58, 134, 146, 163, 164
    interdependence, 58
    movement, 12
    prosperity, 34
    rights, 34, 126, 132
    violence, 8
Educated parents, 6
Education Aid, 81
Education database, 73, 74, 163
Education disparity, 8, 9, 20
Educational
    atmosphere, 29
    discrimination, 48, 118, 142
    gender equality, viii, 3–5, 7, 10, 11, 35, 44, 48, 52, 54, 60, 61, 70, 71, 86, 89–97, 100–104, 107, 108, 111–115, 117, 119, 121, 137, 138, 140, 141, 143, 155–161, 164
    gender inequality, 3, 4, 19, 34, 35, 46, 53, 94, 97, 103, 110, 116, 119, 156
    level, xviii, 119, 131, 137, 138, 141, 143, 144, 147
    literatures, viii
    millennium goals, 141, 148
    status, 143
    system, 13, 16, 127
Egalitarian
    attitudes, 32
    ethics, 21
    fashion, 21
    gender attitudes, 32
    society, 32, 134
    transition, 55
Elderly parent, 9
Elementary level, 9, 19, 137, 144
Elimination of All Forms of Discrimination Against Women, 11, 105, 164
Empathy, 57
Empirical
    analysis, 68

evidence, 6, 56
  tests, 67, 89–121, 138
Empowerment, 12, 49, 129
Enemy of modernization, 60
Engineer, 47
Entrepreneurial activities, 54
Environment, 4, 57, 58, 148
Equal
  citizenship, 2
  contract, 13
  creatures, 22
  education, 136
  employment payment, 10, 13
  gender rights, 10, 12, 22, 34, 145
  in humanity, 46
  human rights, 10
  opportunities, 10, 13
  property rights, 13
  rights, 10, 26, 50, 127, 129, 131
  to men, 26
  work opportunity, 10
  work payment, 10, 13
Equality, viii, 3, 16, 44, 70, 89, 124, 155
Erdogan, Recep Tyyip, 3, 124
Estimated magnitude, 94, 96
Ethnicity, 21
European Union (EU), 2, 10, 129, 144, 150
Exploitation, 3, 15
Extremists, 95, 96, 102, 107, 108, 110, 111, 130, 138, 160

F
Family code, 21, 126, 149
Family code of 1917, 126
Family decisions, 31
Family health, 33, 134
Family Protection Act 1967, 130
Fanaticism, 128
Fashionable styles, 21

Fatima female virtues, 137
Fatima's model, 137
Female
  education, 6, 18, 25, 29, 30, 32, 33, 44, 45, 51, 53, 56, 61, 68, 83, 89, 110, 114, 116, 134–137, 140, 141, 143, 146, 148, 151, 159, 161, 163, 164
  enrollment rates, 131, 162
  labor force participation, 33, 45, 148, 149
  political activists, 131
  rights, 12, 13, 15, 20, 24, 35, 160
  school enrollment, 7, 29, 67, 72, 96, 111, 136, 137, 139, 140
  schooling, 33
Female-to-male, 67, 72–75, 82–84, 89, 90, 92–94, 96–98, 100, 102–104, 107, 108, 110, 112–114, 116–119, 121n8, 132, 136, 138–145, 147, 161
Feminism history, 12, 14
Feminism studies, 10
Feminists
  goals, 11
  literature, 17
  movements, 10, 12–14, 20–23, 30, 34
  scholars, 17, 18, 21–24, 26, 28
  three wave, 12
Fertility rate, 5–7, 54, 59–61, 81, 83, 85, 89, 92–94, 96, 97, 103, 104, 107, 108, 110–113, 119, 121, 134, 140, 158, 160
Financial
  burden, 147
  independent, 34
  packages, 147
  responsibilities, 147
  status, 81
Fiqh, 22
First generation, 58

First-wave feminism, 13, 15
Fitnah, 27
Fixed power relations, 14
Fixed-effect method, 85
Fixed-effects model, 81
Forced marriage, 3
Foreign
   aid, 161
   languages, 127
   males, 47
Forged *Hadiths*, 29
Fox's data, 68, 78
Fragile physique, 13
Free critical thinking, 19
Freedom, 2, 4, 11, 16, 27, 50, 110, 129, 133, 147
Freedom of choice, 4
Freedom of movement, 11, 27
Freedom of religion, 50, 51
Free-thinking, 26
Fundamentalist sects in Muslim, 44
Future alliances, 20
Future career, 47, 48, 58

G
Gay's rights, 50
Gender
   balance in decision-making, 9
   discrimination, 18, 20, 21, 43, 48, 114, 117, 142
   disparities, 8, 9, 20
   egalitarianism, 48, 127
   equality, viii, 3–12, 16, 20, 29–32, 34, 35, 44, 46, 48, 52–55, 59–61, 70, 76, 81, 82, 84–86, 89–99, 101–104, 107, 108, 110–117, 119, 121, 124, 125, 129, 132, 134–140, 143, 147, 148, 155–160, 162, 164
   gap, 9, 10, 124, 158–160
   gap in education, 8, 33, 44, 45, 65, 103, 111, 116, 125, 132, 134, 135, 137, 150, 151, 156, 159, 160
   inequality, viii, 3, 4, 9, 15, 16, 19, 34, 35, 44–46, 53, 54, 59, 67, 72, 83, 84, 93, 94, 96, 97, 101–103, 110, 115, 116, 119, 134, 150, 155, 156, 160, 163, 164
   quotas, 52
Gendered division, 13
General Social Survey (GSS), 32
Generation of migrants, 58
Girls, vii, 3, 6, 9, 15, 19, 26, 28–31, 45, 47, 49, 59, 67, 70, 72, 74, 90, 111, 118, 119, 131, 132, 135–137, 139, 141–143, 149, 158
Globalization, 14
Globally, 11
Goals of agency, 14
God, 22, 26–28, 46
Goddess, 13
Government
   commitment, 29
   constitutions, 52, 53, 78
   cooperation, 29
   funds, 128
   institutions, 50, 60
   officials, 53, 76
   pressure, 23
   scholarships, 132, 137
   strategy, 23
   subsidize, 134
   vision, 23
Grandson, 7
Great powers, 125
Gross Domestic Product (GDP), 5, 6, 33, 44, 54, 70, 81, 105, 164
Group right, 13
Guru, 49

H

Habitual experience, 57
Hadiths, 21, 25, 27, 29, 46, 47
   literature, 22
Hafsa bint Umar, 26
Halakhic, 49
Head of household, 128
Head scarves, 135, 149
Heads of Government, 9
Heads of State, 9, 11
Health
   awareness, 6
   benefits, 15
   facilities, 7
   sector, 7
Heaven, 7
Hepburn, Katherine (1942), 12
Heteroscedastic, 85
Heteroscedastic across panels, 85
Hierarchy, 22
Higher education, 45, 94, 97, 107, 116, 119, 137, 148, 156, 158
Hijab, vii, 21, 28, 130
Hinduism, 7, 17, 44
Hindu religion, 49
Historical events, 56
Historical sequences, 56
HIV-positive adults, 8
Holy Qur'an, 7, 21, 22, 25, 27–29, 46, 47, 126, 127
Home, 2, 6, 9, 12, 13, 20, 24, 25, 28, 31–33, 46, 47, 58, 59, 126, 129, 134, 135, 158
Homosexuals, 14
Hossein, Imam, 137
House of Representative, 2
Householder, 17
Household tasks, 32
Housewives, 13
Housework, 9, 21
Howe, Julia Ward (1874), 15
Human
   capital, 33, 43, 134
   development, 55
   lives, 32
   rights, viii, 10–12, 21, 24, 26, 30, 34, 35, 133, 134, 150
   rights activist, 24
Humanitarian international status, 144
Husband, 8, 12, 17, 25–27, 31, 47, 49, 59, 81, 126, 128, 131, 132, 148, 149
   permission, 25, 126, 131
   rights, 131

I

Ibn Abd al-Wahhab, Muhammad, 25
Ideal household, 126
Ideological differences, 14
Ijtehad, 20, 21
Illiterate women, 8
Imams, 128
Immigration, 81, 164
Immortality, 7
Imperialism, 13
Imputation data, 74
Income, viii, 6, 31, 33, 59, 81, 110, 135
Independent mobilization, 128
Independent reasoning, 20
Independent variables, 60, 75–81, 162
Indicator, 5, 31, 45, 60, 61, 73–75, 78, 81, 108, 119, 138, 157
Individual psyche, 16
Industry, 126, 127, 130
Infertility, 15
Influence of religion, 8, 11, 34, 43, 50, 60, 76, 84, 101, 104, 108, 112, 155, 156, 159
Infrastructure, 158
Inherited social status, 55
Injustice, 137
Insanity, 15

Institution, 7, 18, 43, 45, 50–52, 55, 60, 123, 126–128
Institutional development, 18
Institutional structure, 55, 127
Institutions of societies, 43
Intellectual capacities, 49
Interaction variables, 82, 83, 110, 119
Interdisciplinary study, viii
Interest groups, 53
International
    commitment, 29
    community, 8, 11, 123, 124, 129, 150, 151
    decision makers, 160
    organizations, 3, 29, 136
    statistics, 129
    system, 16
The International Labour Organization (ILO), 138
Interpretation of Qur'an, 46
Interpretation of secularism, 50
Interpreting Islam, 140
Interpreting religion, 141
Intrastate wars, 2
Iran Awakening: A Memoir of Revolution and Hope, 24
Iranian revolution, 24, 123
Iran–Iraq war, 131, 141
Islam
    authorities, 137
    clergy, 126
    doctrine, 23
    feminism, 20–30
    heritage, 55, 107, 121
    identity, 149
    law, 20, 28, 29, 48
    revolution, 136, 137, 139, 140, 143, 147
    sacred text, 21
    sects, 30
    is the solution, vii, 3
    state, 21, 124
    terrorist groups, 51
    virtues, 23
Islamic Arab heritage, 107
Islamic Constitutional Movement (ICM), 24
Islamist extremist Feda'yan, 130
Islamists, 3, 124, 126–128, 130, 133
Islamists movement, 128

J
Jewish culture, 48
Jewish kindergartens, 49
Jihad, 149, 150
Job market, 147, 158
Judaism, 44, 48, 49
Judge, 24, 47, 48, 131, 133
Justice, 13, 30, 131, 133
Justice and Development party (AKP), 123, 124

K
Karma, 7
Kemalist reforms, 125
Khomeini, Ayatollah, 137
Kindergartens, 6, 49
Knesset, 49
Knowledge, 5, 16, 25, 26, 46, 48, 57, 132

L
Labor
    force, vii, 5, 9, 11, 31, 33, 45, 49, 81, 118, 125, 126, 134, 138, 144–151, 161, 162
    force participation, 9, 33, 45, 125, 134, 148, 149, 151
    market, 13, 134
    productivity, 33

Ladies Center under the leadership, 130
Latin script, 127
Laws, vii, 2, 4, 10, 17, 20–22, 28, 29, 47, 48, 50, 52, 76, 78, 125, 127, 128, 131, 133, 135, 144, 148, 149
Leadership, 49, 55
Leadership positions, 49
Leftist feminists, 20
Left-wing scholars, 20
Legacy of Communism, 55
Legal
  basis, 147
  norms, 21
  protection, 12
  restriction, 48
  rights, 150
  system, 126
Legislator, 9, 132
Less conservative countries, 53, 90
Less conservative society, 4, 155
Less developed countries, 9
Less liberal countries, 125
Less religious conservative countries, 119
Liberal
  countries, 162
  feminists, 21, 128
  rulers, 4
Liberal Feminist theory, 21
Liberalizing constitutions, 3
Life expectancy, 8
Lifestyle, 4, 7, 44, 56, 57, 148
Life-threatening, 8
Limited choices of educational, 19
Linear interpolation method, 74
Literacy, 12, 31, 56–58, 80, 84, 131, 149
Literacy rates, 84
Literature, viii, 3, 4, 8, 17, 22, 32, 33, 45, 67, 72, 91, 92, 97, 102, 115–117, 119, 125, 134, 155, 156, 158

Lobby, 136
Local elections (1930), 128
Longitudinal study, 31
Low skilled jobs, 58, 144, 145, 147
Luxury, 6, 59

M
Machine operators, 9
Madahib, 22
Magazines, 130, 133
Magazine *Zanan*, 20
Main source of legislation, 52, 53, 77
Majlis, 132
Male
  accompaniment, 47
  companion, 11, 29, 59
  labor force participation, 33
  oriented disciplines, 132
  relative, 47, 59, 133
Managers, 9, 132
Manhood, 14
Marginal effect, xv, xvii, 82, 94, 99–101, 107–109, 111, 112, 119, 120
Marital status, 31, 81
Marriage, 3, 7, 10, 11, 15, 58, 128–132, 135, 148, 162
Marriage policies, 129
Marriage union, 129, 148
Married women, 18, 59, 137, 149
Marxist feminism, 13
Masculine
  behavior, 13
  fields, 132
Masculinization, 15
Materialistic life, 7
Maternity, 13
Media
  exposure, 57
  participation, 56
Medical therapies, 7
Medicine, 7, 131

Mehitza, 49
Middle East and North Africa (MENA), 14, 33, 123, 124, 129, 132, 134, 137, 138, 150, 151
Migrant families, 58
Military coup, 128
Military superiority, 125
Ministry of National Education (MoNE), 135, 136
Misconception, 124
Misinterpretation, 29
Missing observations, 74
Moderate conservative countries, 79
Moderate liberal countries, 68, 79
Modernization, viii, 3–8, 11, 23, 31, 34, 35, 60, 68, 70–73, 78, 80, 81, 84, 86, 89, 90, 93, 95, 97, 101, 103, 104, 108, 110, 112, 115, 116, 118, 119, 121, 126–128, 137, 138, 140, 141, 143, 148, 151, 155–162, 164
Modernization life-style, 4, 7, 44, 56
Modernization project, 127, 148
Modernization theory, viii, 35, 54–60, 81, 84, 85, 89, 90, 92, 97, 101–104, 108, 115, 119, 161
Modern nation-state, 23, 130
Modern societies, 4, 6, 16, 31, 57, 61, 78, 89, 158
Monarchic political system, 129
Monarchy regime, 4
Monastic education, 19–20
Monastic order, 19
Money, 6, 23, 58
Monks' order, 19
Morsi, Mohamed government, 2
Mortality rate, 5, 34
Mosaddeq, Mohammad, 130
Mosques, 23, 128
Mother, 6, 13, 26, 28, 32, 59, 81, 130, 137, 158
Mullah, 126

Multicultural society, 78
Multi-ethnic nations, 125
Multi party political system, 128
Multi-religious nations, 125
Murder, 152n16
Muslim
 constitution, 84, 104, 117
 countries, xi, 3, 5, 7–9, 22, 23, 29, 35, 44–48, 51, 52, 54–56, 58–61, 67, 68, 70–73, 76, 78, 82, 86, 89, 103–119, 121n8, 124, 128, 131, 132, 138, 140, 147, 150, 155–163, 175–177
 feminist, 23, 30
 liberal, 5
 societies, 23, 27–29, 44, 45, 56, 60, 67, 70, 115, 155, 158

N
National education, 19, 127, 135
National elections (1934), 128
National Front parties, 130
Nationalist ideology, 130
Nationalist movements, 22, 23
National parliament's seats, 9
Natural resource, 5, 54, 158
Natural resource revolution, 54
Nazi ideology, 130
Network, 11
Network of volunteers, 136
New age, 13
New Feminism, 14
New generation, vii, 137
New paradise, 13
Nineteenth centuries, 12
Non-governmental organizations (NGOs), 12
Non-Muslim countries, viii, xv, 3, 5, 8, 9, 35, 68, 71–73, 75, 82, 84, 89–102, 111–119, 121n3, 156–158, 160, 175–177

INDEX   189

Non-Muslim societies, 115
Nuns, 19, 49
Nurseries, 6

O
Official
    order, 76
    religion, 19, 76, 77, 126, 133
    religious guideline, 24
Oil
    engineering, 131
    producers countries, 6
    revolution, 147
Old constitutions, viii, 164
Omitted variables, 81, 84, 85, 93, 100, 105, 114, 140
On-Arab Muslim countries, 91, 94, 97, 107, 116, 117, 119, 121, 132, 156
One source of legislation, 76, 78, 160
Opportunity for women, 11–13
Opposition parties, 128
Oppressed culture, 13
Oppression, 11, 13, 15, 16
Organizational capacities, 49
Orthodox Judaism, 49
Orthodox synagogues, 49
Ottoman Empire, 125, 126, 135
Özal, Turgut, 129

P
Pahlavi family dynasty, 129
Paid parental leave, 10
Panel-corrected standard error model (PCSE), 85, 91, 138
Panel-data analysis, 44
Parental rights, 10
Parents' education, 6, 32, 135, 136, 140, 143, 158
Parliament, 2, 5, 49, 52, 105, 129, 132

Parliamentary monarchy political system, 130
Parliamentary representation, 9, 10
The Passing of Traditional Society, 56
Path dependency, 51
Patriarchal societies, 21
Patriarchal values, 56
Patriarchy, 13, 17
Peace, 15, 50, 133
Persian influence, 127
Personal
    relationships, 18
    rights, 10
    status law, 21
Philosophers, 50
Philosophy, 50
Physical
    abuse, 8
    appearance, 27
    capability, 16
    mobility, 57
    vulnerability, 27
Policy makers, viii, 35, 160, 161, 164
Polis, 50
Political
    activists, 3, 7, 126, 131, 133, 159
    affairs, 137
    agenda, 24
    arena, 13, 48, 129
    campaigns, 23
    chaos, vii
    crisis, 124
    culture, 52
    gender equality, viii, 11
    identity, 14
    institutions, 50, 52, 123
    leaders, 53
    literature, viii, 164
    participation, 10, 11, 24, 57, 129
    party, 2, 24, 49, 123
    positions, 129, 130
    progress, 11, 123, 124
    regimes, 1, 12, 34, 52, 131, 137

Political (*cont.*)
  religion, viii, 35, 50, 52, 159
  revolutions, 1, 24, 136
  rights, 1, 10
  sphere, 31, 49
  will, 135, 138
Political-social conflict, 50
Politician, 47, 53
Polygamy, 127, 130, 149
Polytheism, 50
Poor
  families, 28
  girls, 19
  physical state, 135
Population and Housing Survey (PHS), 45
Population
  density, 58
  growth, 8
  size, 68, 73
Pornofication of the media, 14
Post-Communist, 10
Postindustrial societies, 55
Postmaterialism, 31
Post-revolutionary Iran, 137
Poverty gap, 10
Power, 8–10, 13, 14, 23, 51, 52, 125, 128–130, 137
Practical traditions, 22
Pregnancy, 8
President, 124, 127, 132, 133
Presidential candidates, 132
Pre-university schools, 131
Priest, 49
Primary
  education, 9
  enrollment, 9
  school, 9, 131, 136, 142
Productive labor, 14
Profession, 129
Professional development, 45
Prohibition of discrimination, 10
Prophet Mohamed, 22, 26, 27, 46, 47, 137
Prophet Mohamed's wives, 29
Protestantism, 43
Protester, 1, 2
Psychological violence, 8
Public
  activities, 13
  administration, 127
  arena, 48
  decision-making, 2
  education, 28, 130
  health programs, 131
  movement, 49
  opinion, 52, 127
  policy in education, viii
  role, 130
  school, 128
  service, 24
  spaces, 26, 29
  sphere, 49, 127, 136

Q
Qom, 24
Qualitative methods, viii
Quantitative Data on National Education (2002–2003), 135
Quantitative methods, viii

R
Rabbi, 49
Radical feminist theory, 14
Radical theorists, 16
Ramadan, 126
Random sample, 68
Ratio of female-to-male labor force participation rate, 144, 145
Regimes, vii, 1–4, 23, 24, 52, 57, 123
Regions, 4, 8, 9, 44, 123, 124, 128, 132, 133, 136
Regression tests, 108, 111, 112
Reinterpret Islamic law, 20
Relative political extraction (RPE), 81, 82, 106, 164

Relative political reach (RPR), 82, 106, 164
Religion-free politics, 50, 51
Religio-political movements, 51
Religious
  authorities, 55
  beliefs, 4, 20, 25, 50, 51, 54, 55, 149, 151
  boundaries, 24
  categories, 97, 107, 108, 111, 112
  commitment, 51, 67, 103
  conservative, 2, 4, 5, 8, 19, 46, 56, 68, 70–73, 91, 93, 96–98, 108, 114, 115, 119, 138, 140, 155–157
  conservative constitution, viii, 8, 114
  conservative countries, xviii, 53, 55, 72, 73, 89, 90, 111, 119–121, 140, 147, 148, 157, 158, 161, 169
  conservativeness, 3, 35, 53, 54, 61, 68, 71, 89, 92, 95–97, 105, 107, 108, 110, 112, 115–117, 140, 157, 159, 161, 162
  conservative societies, 3, 5, 70, 155
  constitutions, viii, xv, 84, 90, 94, 100–102, 104, 108–110, 114, 117, 157, 159, 161
  courts, 127
  feminism, 16, 17, 30
  frame, 10
  groups, 25, 30
  identity, 17, 51
  instructions, 51, 128, 160
  interpretation, 20, 160
  leaders, 130, 132
  lessons, 23, 26
  liberal, viii, 4, 53, 72, 83, 84, 93, 159, 160
  liberty, 4
  literature, 60
  misbeliefs, 22
  political system, vii, viii
  revival, 44
  schools, 19, 24, 26
  scripts, 20
  societies, 6, 7, 44, 51, 60, 110, 155, 158
  statements, 29
  status, 52, 110
  theory, viii, 35, 43–54, 84, 89, 92, 97, 101–104, 115
  traditions, 55
  values, 43, 46, 55
  views, 7, 17, 24
  Zionist school, 48
Renunciate community, 18
Reproductive control, 31
Republic People Party (RPP), 128
Research questions, 52, 71, 93, 96, 97, 99, 104, 116, 118
Reverse educational discrimination, 118
Rewards, 4, 7, 46, 53, 160
Reza Khan, Mohammad (1941–1979), 129
Right to abortion, 13
Right to vote, 13, 130
Rights of minorities, 129
Rising Tide: Gender Equality and Cultural Change around the World, 55
Ritual task, 49
Roman Catholicism, 49
Root of religions, 135, 157
R-square, 90–92, 97–99, 107, 108, 111, 112, 114, 141
Rural areas, 58, 78, 129, 135–137

S
Sabbath, 49
Salafists, 25
Sales workers, 9
Sample of study, 56

Saud, Muhammad bin, 25
Schools, 6, 7, 9, 16, 19, 20, 22, 24, 26, 28–31, 44, 67, 89, 128, 159
Science, 125, 127, 132
Seclusion, 21
Secondary
  female attainment, 44
  level, 9, 19, 44
  school, 9, 114, 128, 132, 143
Second generation, 58
Second-wave feminism, 13
Second World Conference on Women, Copenhagen (1980), 11
Secular
  constitution, 133
  countries, 4, 51, 53, 68, 70, 76, 102, 112, 117, 124, 125, 133, 135, 147, 148, 151, 157, 162
  feminism, 16, 30
  political system, vii, 5, 11, 151
  schools, 19
  system, 5, 149
Secularism, viii, 21, 50, 54, 108, 117, 121, 123, 127, 138, 144, 149
  is the solution, 3
Seek education, 46, 57
Segregated schools, 29, 30
Self-mutilation, 14
Senior officials, 9, 132
Serious erotic distraction, 49
Service sector, 58
Sexes, 9, 14, 15, 21, 28, 32, 46, 89, 142, 146
Sex in Education or a Fair Chance for Girls, 15
Sexist language, 14
Sex-role attitudes, 31
Sex roles, 14, 58
Sex segregation, 27, 29
Sexual
  harassment, 10, 128, 129
  intercourse, 149
  violence, 8

Shah, 130, 131
Shah of Iran, 4
Shared characteristics, 68
Sharia, 3, 21, 48, 124, 127, 133
Shia
  feminist, 24
  nations, 124
  religious rules, 24
Shrine, 130
Sick man of Europe, 126
Single political system, 128
Single women, 132, 137
Sisterhood, 14
Skill, 5, 34, 35, 57–59, 134, 145, 158
Slogans, 3, 14, 150
Small brain, 13
Social
  agenda, 24
  barriers, 17
  benefits, 15
  change, 21, 43, 56, 57
  class, 28, 59
  division, 16
  feminism, 15, 16
  feminist theory, 14
  mobility, 48, 57, 133
  movement, 13
  norms, 44
  order, 48
  pressure, 24, 47, 58
  rights, 10, 13, 25, 35, 130
  rule, 48
  safety net, 31
  sanctions, 55
  science, 34
  transformation, 23
Socialist feminism, 13
Societal circle, 17–21, 23
Societal modernization, 31, 55
Society
  advancement, 20
  quality of life, 34
  values, 52

Socioeconomics factors, viii, 4, 31
Soldier, 47, 130
Solidarity, 14, 133
Son, 7, 149
Spatial segregation, 29
Spiritual guidance, 19
Spiritual path, 17
Spot light, 129
Spreading awareness, 85, 150
Śramaṇa, 17
Sramanic movement, 17
Stable democracy, 43
Standard of living, 1, 2, 5, 10, 59, 134, 161
State
  constitutions, 76
  religiosity, 156
  role, 52
Statistical
  empirical, 6
  inference, 85
  method, 56
  models, 35, 61, 83, 84, 115
Status of women, 2, 8, 18
Stereotype barriers, 16
Stereotypically, 14
Structures, 14, 15, 17, 30, 44, 54, 82, 83, 135
Suffrage rights, 128
Sufis, 25
Sunnah, 22
Sunnis, 124
Superstitions, 128
Superstructure, 13
Supply-and-demand reciprocal, 57
Suppression, 14
Systematic variables, 81

T
Taboo, 27
Teacher, 29, 47, 135, 137
Technique of matching, 68

Technology, 125, 127
Tertiary
  education, 9, 19, 114, 132, 136, 143–146, 151, 162
  enrollment, 9, 74, 143
Theocratic state, 50
Theological department in Ankara, 128
Third-wave feminism, 14
Third World Conference on Women, Nairobi (1985), 11
Time period, 23, 33, 56, 61, 73
Time-series models, 85, 138
Time series study, 12
"Top-down" policy initiatives, 52
Torah learning, 49
Totalitarian Islam, 21
Total ratio of female-to-male school enrollment, 73, 75
Trade workers, 9
Traditional
  authority, 55
  beliefs, 149
  division of sex roles, 58
  feminine role, 49
  life, 35
  religious societies, 6
  social role, 53
  societies, 4, 6, 7, 17, 28, 31, 59, 67, 70, 78, 81, 99, 103, 113, 114, 117, 119, 144
  stereotype, 32
  world, 16
Trafficking, 3, 14
Training schools, 58
Transitional period, 2
Transportation, 6, 58, 78, 135
Tribal areas, 131
Tribal movements, 130
Tropical climates, 45
True Muslim, 150
True woman, 12
Tudeh party, 130

Turkish language, 127
Turkish Republic (1923), 126, 127
Twelver (Jaafari), 133
Twentieth centuries, 12
Tyranny, 137

U
Ulema, 127
Ultra-polluting, 17
Underrepresented, 9
Unequal inheritance rights, 127
United Nations (UN), 8, 74
United Nations Decade for Women (1975), 11
United Nations Educational, Scientific and Cultural Organization (UNESCO), 74
United Nations International Conference on Human Rights, 11
United Nations Literacy Decade: Education for All, 12
University professors, 137
Unpaid domestic jobs, 9
UN Treaty (CEDAW), 82
Upper middle-class white women, 14
Urban
 areas, 5, 7, 57–59, 78, 80, 126, 144, 158
 environment, 58
Urbanization, viii, 5, 6, 8, 45, 54, 56–61, 70, 72, 78, 80–85, 89, 90, 92–97, 99–104, 107, 108, 110–116, 118–120, 140, 157–161

V
Vaccines, 7
Values, 4, 5, 43, 44, 46, 52, 55, 56, 60, 72–74, 84, 93, 94, 96, 105, 107, 112, 136, 148

Variety of disciplines, 14
Veil, 21, 27–30, 47, 126
Vienna World Conference in 1993, 12
Vietnam War, 14
Violence, 8, 128, 129
 against women, 14
Virginity examinations, 128

W
Wages for housework, 21
Wahhabis, 25
Wald Chi2 score, 93, 94, 96
Wanderer, 17
Wat (temple), 19
Wealth, 6, 7, 17, 57, 158
Welfare, 129
Western
 countries, 10, 11, 30, 50, 51, 56, 124, 129
 culture, 22, 60, 149
 feminist, 12–17, 22, 30, 35
 model of society, 25
 occupiers, 28
 privileges, 130
 values, 44
 wars, 50
 world, 43, 57, 127
Westernists, 126, 127
Westernization, 23, 127, 148
Westphalia agreement (1648), 50
Wife, 2, 6, 26, 49, 126, 130–132, 137
 consent, 2, 130
Woman of the Year, 12
Woman
 activism, 23
 collective, 13
 economic role, 3
 education, 9, 19, 26, 28, 30, 32, 102, 131, 134, 140, 141, 143, 148, 158
 empowerment, 12, 49

health, 12
look, 13, 34, 149
mosque movement, 23
parliamentary lower house, 82
participation in labor force, 9, 33, 45, 134, 148, 149
political role, 1, 24
productivity, 33, 134
representation, 9, 49, 132, 149
social mobility, 133
social role, 53, 58
status, 2, 9, 22, 28, 30, 34, 126, 127, 138, 141, 144, 150, 161
struggle, 14
unity, 14
universities, 137
in workforce, 9, 16, 47, 48, 125, 127, 129, 131, 134, 144–146, 148, 161
Womanhood, 14
Working classes, 13, 14

World Bank dataset, 74, 75
World Development Indicators, 138
Worldly life, 7
World order, 13
World politics, 44
World Value Survey (WVS), 44
World War I, 126
World War II, 128
World's interest, 13
Worldwide, 7, 9, 11, 81

Y
Young-adult mortality, 45
Younger generation, 31
Youngest generation, 55

Z
Zaydi Shia, 24
Zaynab bint Ali, 26